TONY BENN
The Making of a Politician

'As for the best leaders, the people do not notice their
   existence.
The next best the people honour and praise.
The next the people fear, and the next the people hate.
But when the best leader's work is done the people say,
"We did it ourselves".'

(*quoted by Tony Benn from Lao Tzu*)

TONY BENN

The Making of a Politician

Alfred Browne

W. H. ALLEN · LONDON
A Howard & Wyndham Company
1983

Copyright © Alfred Browne 1983

Phototypeset by Input Typesetting Ltd, London
Printed and bound in Great Britain by
Biddles Ltd, Guildford & King's Lynn
for the Publishers, W. H. Allen & Co. Ltd
44 Hill Street, London W1X 8LB

ISBN 0 491 03020 7

Contents

THE BENNS

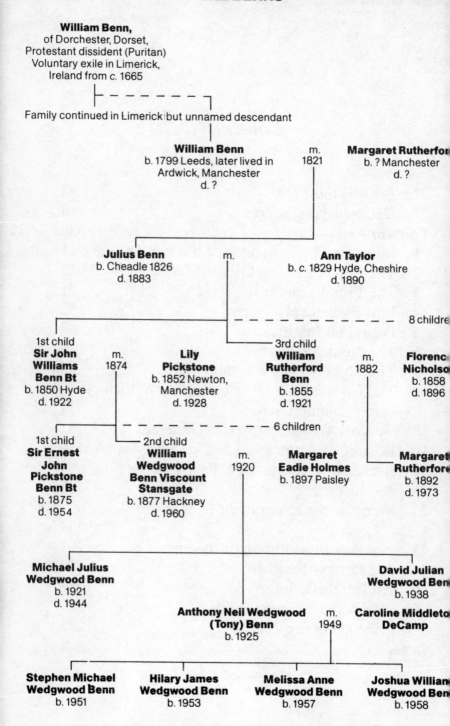

William Benn,
of Dorchester, Dorset,
Protestant dissident (Puritan)
Voluntary exile in Limerick,
Ireland from *c.* 1665

Family continued in Limerick but unnamed descendant

William Benn
b. 1799 Leeds, later lived in
Ardwick, Manchester
d. ?

m.
1821

Margaret Rutherfor
b. ? Manchester
d. ?

Julius Benn
b. Cheadle 1826
d. 1883

m.

Ann Taylor
b. *c.* 1829 Hyde, Cheshire
d. 1890

8 childre

1st child
**Sir John
Williams
Benn Bt**
b. 1850 Hyde
d. 1922

m.
1874

**Lily
Pickstone**
b. 1852 Newton,
Manchester
d. 1928

3rd child
**William
Rutherford
Benn**
b. 1855
d. 1921

m.
1882

**Florenc
Nicholso**
b. 1858
d. 1896

1st child
**Sir Ernest
John
Pickstone
Benn Bt**
b. 1875
d. 1954

6 children

2nd child
**William
Wedgwood
Benn Viscount
Stansgate**
b. 1877 Hackney
d. 1960

m.
1920

**Margaret
Eadie Holmes**
b. 1897 Paisley

**Margaret
Rutherfore**
b. 1892
d. 1973

**Michael Julius
Wedgwood Benn**
b. 1921
d. 1944

**David Julian
Wedgwood Ben**
b. 1938

**Anthony Neil Wedgwood
(Tony) Benn**
b. 1925

m.
1949

**Caroline Middleto
DeCamp**

**Stephen Michael
Wedgwood Benn**
b. 1951

**Hilary James
Wedgwood Benn**
b. 1953

**Melissa Anne
Wedgwood Benn**
b. 1957

**Joshua Willian
Wedgwood Ben**
b. 1958

Based on research by Hugh Peskett

THE DECAMPS

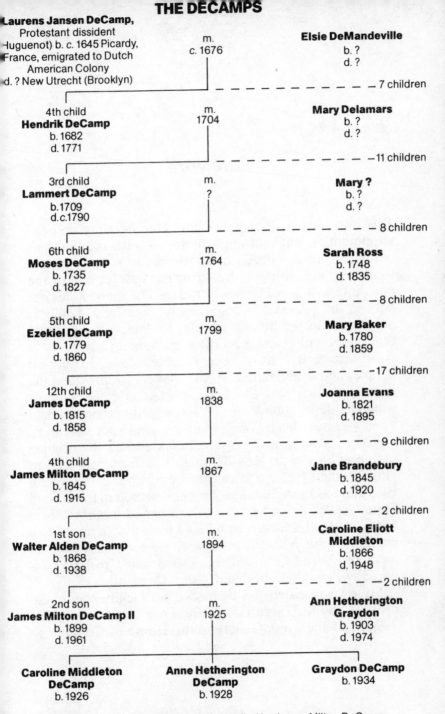

Laurens Jansen DeCamp,
Protestant dissident
(Huguenot) b. c. 1645 Picardy,
France, emigrated to Dutch
American Colony
d. ? New Utrecht (Brooklyn)

m.
c. 1676

Elsie DeMandeville
b. ?
d. ?

— 7 children

4th child
Hendrik DeCamp
b. 1682
d. 1771

m.
1704

Mary Delamars
b. ?
d. ?

— 11 children

3rd child
Lammert DeCamp
b.1709
d.c.1790

m.
?

Mary ?
b. ?
d. ?

— 8 children

6th child
Moses DeCamp
b. 1735
d. 1827

m.
1764

Sarah Ross
b. 1748
d. 1835

— 8 children

5th child
Ezekiel DeCamp
b. 1779
d. 1860

m.
1799

Mary Baker
b. 1780
d. 1859

— 17 children

12th child
James DeCamp
b. 1815
d. 1858

m.
1838

Joanna Evans
b. 1821
d. 1895

— 9 children

4th child
James Milton DeCamp
b. 1845
d. 1915

m.
1867

Jane Brandebury
b. 1845
d. 1920

— 2 children

1st son
Walter Alden DeCamp
b. 1868
d. 1938

m.
1894

**Caroline Eliott
Middleton**
b. 1866
d. 1948

— 2 children

2nd son
James Milton DeCamp II
b. 1899
d. 1961

m.
1925

**Ann Hetherington
Graydon**
b. 1903
d. 1974

**Caroline Middleton
DeCamp**
b. 1926

**Anne Hetherington
DeCamp**
b. 1928

Graydon DeCamp
b. 1934

Based on *The DeCamp Family,* first compiled by James Milton DeCamp,
Caroline's great-grandfather and published in 1896, extended in 1976 by
Graydon DeCamp and his boyhood friend and remote cousin, Crane DeCamp
(descended from Ezekiel DeCamp through another son, Joseph)

Foreword

This book is an attempt to show how heredity and environment, talent and opportunity — with the determination to use it — each plays its part in making people what they are, through the particular case of one of the most interesting politicians of today. The interest lies not only in the man but in his heredity. The Benn family is notable for its wealth of talent, for its demonstration, too, that talent and eccentricity often go hand in hand.

In writing it I have been indebted to a number of people, above all Harold Brooks-Baker. He provided the stimulus which saw the book started and the support which made its completion far less exacting than it would otherwise have been. Without him it would not have been written, for his was the original idea and he the original organiser of the project. Through him I am indebted to Hugh Peskett for his genealogical researches in the British Isles and to Dawn Simmons for her research in the United States as well as for her accounts of her adoptant mother, Margaret Rutherford. The books I have drawn upon have included *John Williams Benn and the Progressive Movement* by Alfred G. Gardiner, and Susan Crosland's biography of her late husband, Tony Crosland.

My own research has depended on facilities and help provided by the Librarians of the Press Association, *The Times* and the Press Gallery at the House of Commons.

CHAPTER ONE

Julius Benn — Founder of the Family

If the Labour Party has its roots in the Methodist social conscience of the nineteenth century, then Tony Benn can claim an impeccable ancestry.

Religious dissent comes with the first Benn of whom there is any trace, the Reverend William Benn, of Dorchester in Dorset, who was one of 2,000 Anglican clergymen to fall victim to the Five Mile Act of 1665. This followed on the Act of Uniformity of 1662, which had rejected the Puritanism of the Commonwealth in favour of High Church views, by forbidding any noncomforming clergyman to come within five miles of any town of which he had been a minister, or to act as tutor or schoolmaster. Virtually exiled for his Puritanism, William Benn went to Limerick, in Ireland, to begin what turned out to be a long Congregational tradition — a seventeenth-century engraving of the dissident clergyman was a treasured possession of the nineteenth-century Benns.

Certainly, the Benns have Irish connections, though the current head of the family might wish they had begun in some other way than they did, with the granting of a licence of land in Ireland by Oliver Cromwell to William Benn just ten years before his expulsion.

In Limerick William was among other Protestant refugees, from France, Alsace and Germany and evidence of intermarriage is suggested by the names of some of his descendants. Julius, with its German overtones, was a popular name among the Benns — a Julius Caesar Benn was baptized in Limerick in 1718 — and the Benn fond-

1

ness for preserving connections in second names, as witnessed by the appearance of 'Wedgwood' later, is presumably the reason why Julius Delmege Benn, baptized there in 1838, was given his French middle name.

The first direct ancestor of Tony Benn to have his life recorded in detail was his great-grandfather, Julius, a Congregational minister. He was born at Cheadle, near Manchester, in 1826, the son of a quilt maker who had returned to England from Limerick. His mother died when he was quite small, and when his father married again, stepmother and stepson failed to get on together. Julius, still not in his teens, decided to run away to sea.

He got as far as Liverpool, thirty miles away, where, family tradition has it, a Quaker, moved by a sudden urge to walk along a quayside, found the small boy, hungry, penniless, cold and miserable, on the point of suicide. In the fashion of nineteenth-century tracts the Quaker said to himself on seeing the boy, 'Surely this is one of the least of these, my brethren', touched Julius on the shoulder and spoke aloud, 'Friend, follow me'. Julius did, to a new home and education.

Whatever the truth of this account, based on a tale Julius later in life told his children, it seems the situation was resolved on a family basis. Young Julius went to live with an uncle, Francis Benn, who had a haberdasher's shop in Broad Street, Limerick.

While there he fell under the sway of one of the brilliant noncomformist ministers of the nineteenth century, John de Kewer Williams, who was to become a lifelong friend and influence. He outlived Julius and conducted the funeral service after Julius's tragic death.

The Hungry Forties were upon Ireland and Williams founded a society for helping the least fortunate people of that most unfortunate country. Under the unprepossessing title of 'The Eclectic Society', he pressed for educational and social reform. Whatever the society's effects in relieving distress it had a profound effect on its members, all of whom, except one, became Congregational ministers themselves. Its influence on Julius seems not to have fitted him for trade in the eyes of his employer. Employer and employee fell out about the correctness of the description of some goods which Julius was told to deliver to a customer and soon he was on his way back to Manchester.

He was then 22, described as tall, self-absorbed, with large grey eyes, black hair, pale face and mobile features. Any resemblance detected here to his illustrious great-grandson might be countered by a further description of him as 'very nervous and somewhat excitable'. Whatever the truth of that, he seems to have had in good measure the Benn trait of being able to make his way in the world, whether in terms of reputation or material prosperity or both. All the Benns seem to have had the ability to lift themselves by their own bootlaces and generally chose wives from similarly able families.

Julius, as probably the most unworldly of the Benns, may have been a little less typically Benn-like in his marriage. Back in Manchester he travelled around hunting, not very successfully, for a job as a teacher. One evening, alone in a strange town, he went into a chapel and lost his loneliness for ever. His eldest son, John, used to say he grew out of a hymnbook and it was Julius's lack of hymnbook which brought him his bride. Ann Taylor, daughter of a joiner and shuttle maker, passed him hers and immediately he fell in love. Poor Ann was to know little prosperity, suffer much hardship, become an invalid and be widowed in the most unhappy way that can happen to a loving wife and mother. Despite all this, however, her son John Williams Benn (named after the Limerick minister) described her as vivacious, with a 'genius for happiness'. She was tiny, 'so diminutive,' he once wrote, 'you could have stowed her, without overcrowding, into a long bottom drawer'.

Married, Julius had to work and so he started his own

school, in the chapel where he had met his bride. She helped with sewing lessons for the girls. But even before the children started to arrive it was hard to make ends meet. Then in 1851 came the opportunity for the Benn reforming spirit to find its true outlet. Julius was invited by the London City Mission to become a city missionary, probably at the behest of de Kewer Williams, anxious that the talents of his brightest pupil should not be lost.

Benn moved to Stepney, in East London, where, for the rest of his life, except for a short break, he was to labour among the poor, probably as poor himself as most of those he tried to help. His special interest was in the street arabs, the boys who ran wild in the streets, and he was asked by a group of philanthropists to run a 'Ragged School', one of the first institutions for reforming criminal boys. Grandiloquently named 'Star in the East' it was set in a disused warehouse. Among other social reformers who came to inspect and admire was Charles Dickens, who wrote of Julius, 'One could see by the expression of this man's eye and by his kindly face that Love ruled rather than Fear and Love was triumphant.'

Success in the East End brought Julius to the notice of the Government which, under pressure from the Earl of Shaftesbury, had belatedly become conscious of the appalling deprivations of child life (as portrayed in the Dickensian world of Bill Sykes and the Artful Dodger) and had decided to set up child reformatories. Julius was appointed governor of the first of the new institutions, at Tiffield in Northamptonshire, in 1856. The rapidly growing Benn family, now with a secure income and, probably for the first time, not in dire want, exchanged the streets of Stepney for the countryside but, alas, not for long. It had seemed that Julius had found his life's calling. He was successful and well liked in his job, his income was adequate for his and Ann's needs, but beneath it all there still lurked the dangers of religious dissent — in those

4

days more damning, if anything, than political dissent today.

It was the Congregationalist tradition, dating back to that first Benn, and the Catechism which first brought trouble. Julius had arranged with the rector that young John Williams Benn need not answer certain questions. Inevitably the other boys noticed, the awful secret came out and, in the manner of orthodox boys everywhere and at all times, they followed John Williams with their taunts. In this case it was 'Bennie, who gave you your name?', for it was that Catechismal question which, apparently, was the crux of the matter. Benns have never been ones not to fight back. John did, on the village green and, after Ann had lovingly wiped the blood from his nose, he found himself sent supperless to bed by Julius. In fighting to uphold one principle, he learned, he had only gone against another.

But that was only a minor skirmish. Soon there was to be an engagement of principals. Julius Benn had taken his boys, his charges as well as his sons, to the village church, only to hear the rector denounce the principles of the Reformation.

'Brethren,' he declared, 'Martin Luther cannot but be regarded as an enemy of the true Church.'

For Julius, who usually managed to keep his dissent under restraint — subordinated, he would say, to the main fact of Christianity — it was too much.

Rising in his pew and drawing himself up to his full height ('a noble figure, six feet one in his boots' his son John recorded later), he addressed the thirty or forty youngsters in his care.

'Boys, we leave the church at once, quietly follow me, two and two.'

To the open-mouthed amazement of the congregation of villagers, the little army, not so quiet in their government issue boots, marched out.

A negotiated settlement was reached, though, with the

patron of the living acting as arbiter between the rector, outraged in his church, and the master. The school would continue to attend church, with no attempt to set up a rival chapel, if there was to be no more preaching against the Reformation.

It was hardly an event, in those conservative times, to warm the feelings of those who mattered in the village towards the outsider. When misfortune came upon him he found little support. In his efforts to help his family, Julius made a brief foray into the world of capitalism. Having saved a few hundred pounds he decided to put them to work to pay for the future education of his children. On the advice of a local solicitor he invested his all in a local firm which had taken up an engineering patent — for agricultural machinery, according to one account, for an early form of motor-cycle, says another. If it was the latter it was before its time, but whatever the case, the business failed. Julius lost not only his money but, characteristically, assumed the burden of the debts left by the firm's failure. It took him almost the rest of his life to pay them off. Pay them off, eventually, he did, but that was in the future and future intentions and achievements count for little in the present.

Julius may have been unwise to put all his eggs in one basket, though he had sought the advice of someone supposedly wiser in the ways of business, but that did not prevent his receiving the blame an unfriendly world so often metes out on unfortunates. The committee of the school met, censured him and invited him to resign. 'Gentlemen,' said Julius, 'we leave your house tonight.'

Julius and his sons pushed his by now invalid wife in her bathchair over rutted country roads to an empty cottage belonging to a sympathetic widow, more familiar with misfortune than the gentry on the school committee. The Benn belongings were auctioned and the family returned to London.

It was back from green fields and bigotry to the slum

streets of Stepney and poverty. Not that all the East End was slum. There still remained, cheek by jowl with the crowded courts, squares of pleasant Georgian houses in which lived traders and others who had made their fortunes in and from the Docks. On borrowed money, Julius at first ran a newsagent's business, with the publications of the British and Foreign Bible Society prominently displayed and toys as a sideline. His sons delivered the papers and there was one moment of dire misfortune when John, sent to pay the interest on the loan which Julius had had to raise to pay his own paper bill, found on arrival at his destination that he had lost the money — or perhaps, more likely in the neighbourhood of the notorious Ratcliff Highway, his pocket had been picked.

It was on occasions like that, according to John's own anecdotes, that the prevailing Benn household diet of boiled rice was in peril. Later, by the time of a clash with Bumbledom in the person of a Post Office beadle (which, if there is any foundation in the notion of the inheritance of acquired characteristics, could account for Tony Benn's distrust of civil servants) the Benn diet had risen to the heights of potato pie.

Perhaps it was fortunate that the shop was eventually swallowed up in a rebuilding project. Julius received some compensation and set up a new business, a registry for servants. But these forays into commerce were only a short break in his life of missionary and educational work. The East London Congregational Evangelistic Association put him to work, once again as a missionary, among the poor and vicious who lived in the mean streets around the Ratcliff Highway, Cable Street (at that time not taken over entirely by Jewish immigrants, as it was by the time Mosley's Fascists were parading their provocation through it) and the dockland of Wapping. Arthur Morrison, a minor classic who wrote later in the century, described the vice and poverty of the times in his works *Tales of Mean Streets* and *Hole in the Wall*.

The whole Wapping area, but particularly the Ratcliff Highway and the streets off it, was crowded with pubs, each with its own dancing saloon. Sailors ashore from ships tied up in the Port of London would flock there for drink and sex, only to lose, at the very least, their money, and not infrequently their lives. For Julius's eldest son John it must have been an enormous personal satisfaction when as one of the founders of the London County Council and then its chairman, he saw those saloons closed down and the Ratcliff Highway, once the most notorious street in England, become as safe, if not as reputable, as any other.

Charles Dickens also left us a recollection of part of Julius's area known as 'Baker's Trap', Baker having been the coroner of the time. In one of his journalistic essays Dickens describes how, on his way to visit Wapping work-house, by the swing bridge leading to the island part of the dockland, cut off by the channels of the Thames, he met a figure

. . . remotely in the likeness of a young man, with a puffed sallow face and a figure all dirty and shiny and slimy, who may have been the youngest son of his filthy old father Thames, or the drowned man about whom there was a placard on the granite post, like a huge thimble, that stood between us.

'A common place for suicide,' said I [Dickens] looking down at the docks.

'Sue?' returned the ghost with a stare. 'Yes! And Poll, likewise Emily. And Nancy. And Jane,' he sucked the iron between each name. 'And all the bileing. Ketches off their bonnets or shorls, takes a run and headers down here, they does. Always a-headering down here, they is. Like one o'clock.'

It was Julius's task to prevent desperate girls from taking that header, or to intervene when the frequent fights looked like having a fatal outcome. His imposing six-foot-one figure, as recorded by John, may well have made that part of his task easier than it would have been for less muscular members of the Church Militant. For his work he received a hundred pounds a year, a sum that could have meant relative solvency, even with a wife and six children, eventually to grow to seven, if Julius had not still to finish paying off the debts left by that earlier unfortunate business venture.

Missionary work in the wastes of the East End of mid-nineteenth-century London was probably at least as hazardous as missionary work in the wilds of Africa, with an equal threat from disease as well as violence. Parts of London were still taking drinking water from the sewage-laden parts of the Thames, though progressive doctors were beginning to be convinced that cholera was a water-borne disease, not something carried in noxious vapours in the air, the theory the Royal College of Physicians still officially supported as late as the 1850's. An outbreak of the disease found Julius visiting the sick in their homes and making daily visits to the hospitals. It was no uncommon sight for him to emerge from one of the hovels in his area carrying someone too sick to walk, in his arms all the way to the overcrowded hospital. Eventually he fell sick himself, not from cholera but typhoid. Even that he turned to good account. It gave him time to reflect on what he had seen, to recall his feelings when so often those he had carried to hospital and likely death had been children. He enlisted the support of the wealthy to found the East London Hospital for Children which, though now disappeared, was in its time a landmark in the development of special medical care for children in this country.

For Julius Benn hard times were by no means over. The East London Congregational Evangelistic Association failed for lack of funds. His old friend de Kewer Williams, by then pastor of the Old Gravel Pit Chapel,

9

Hackney, helped to secure his appointment as minister at the Gravel Lane Meeting House in Stepney, though, in good democratic fashion, Benn had to be confirmed in his appointment by a popular election. It was not done without rancour and bitterness. Dr John Kennedy, the unofficial 'bishop' of Nonconformity in East London, who as a simple Reverend had been one of those who invited Julius Benn to take charge of the Star in the East in the early 1850's, never accepted Benn's own claim to the title 'Reverend'.

Gravel Lane had been one of the famous houses of Nonconformity. It had been founded in the reign of Charles II by another of those clergymen ejected from his Anglican living for non-acceptance of Anglo-Catholicism, as had Benn's own ancestor. In the more prosperous days of the beginning of the nineteenth century it had been a fashionable chapel. Each Sunday rows of carriages had waited at the chapel gates. But by the time Julius had been appointed minister, its congregation numbered only the poor, and the collections raised barely enough to meet running expenses, let alone provide a stipend. The only endowment its pastor could count on was a mere three guineas a year.

Julius Benn could not have been quite so bad a businessman after all. On that unlikely basis he carried on for another fifteen years, his reputation growing as his congregation swelled, with not a penny help from any sister churches. It must have been quite a windfall, even though his sons were by then set on the road to fortune, when in December 1882 William Gladstone handed him a cheque for £50 from the Royal Bounty Fund, in belated recognition of his labours among the poor and as an acknowledgment of his contribution to the running of reformatory schools — a paper he wrote at the time he was running the Tiffield Institution won a first prize and was included in a Government Blue Book.

At the same time, William, the son who worked closest

alongside Julius in his mission and the third of the Benn brothers, was married. William Rutherford Benn — Rutherford being the maiden name of Julius's mother — was, according to the Nonconformist newspaper of the day, of the same 'nervous and excitable temperament' as his father.

Like all the Benn children he was hard-working and bright. His speciality was foreign languages and he was employed as a shipping clerk, though his heart was set on becoming a minister too. All his spare time and money went on philanthropic and religious work in what a public appeal was later to call 'that benighted neighbourhood'. A special bond of affection had grown between him and his father.

A month after the wedding, however, William was taken to the Bethnal House Lunatic Asylum in Cambridge Heath. Whatever was wrong, the doctors decided after a few weeks that he had recovered sufficiently to leave but would benefit from the universal specific of those days, country air.

At the end of February 1883 Julius took William on what must have been a rare holiday for father and son. They rented rooms in the cottage of a retired coachman named Marchant at the beauty spot of Matlock Bridge, Derbyshire, and set out to get as much of the country air the doctors had recommended as possible. From local newspaper reports they had an energetic time walking the hills. After a week of this they arrived back at the cottage late on Saturday evening, March 3rd, at the end of a particularly exhausting day, had supper and went to bed. About seven o'clock the next morning Mrs Marchant was awakened by a peculiar knocking noise. She asked her eighty-year-old mother-in-law if she had been rapping, as it might disturb the lodgers. The old lady denied it and, not quite believing her, Mrs Marchant went back to bed. When the Benns failed to come down to breakfast she called them but received only a muttered reply. Mrs Marchant knew the son was taking sleeping draughts and assumed he was still sleeping and that the remarks she had heard came from the father watching over him.

By lunchtime, after going up to the door of the room several times with no different response, she was getting very worried. All she could hear, she told her husband when he came back from chapel, was 'a peculiar hush' broken, occasionally, by the sound of heavy breathing. She had not knocked loudly, she confessed. (It was a common belief then that, as with sleepwalkers, it was dangerous suddenly to awaken anyone who had taken an opiate.) Her husband was not so hesitant. He rapped vigorously at the door and on his third knock it opened.

The *Derby Daily Telegraph* described in detail what then happened:

Mr Marchant was shocked to find at the first glance that a dreadful tragedy had been enacted within the room. The son, who had opened the door, was standing in his night shirt and marks of blood were all down the front of it. The son then pointed his finger to his father on the bed and Mr Marchant saw the deceased lying apparently quite dead.

The son did not make the slightest observation and Mr Marchant, who had been greatly shocked at what he saw, closed the door and ran down stairs. He called upon his family to rush out of the house, as he felt afraid that some further outrage might be committed. The family rushed outside and Mr Marchant went to inform Mr Else, auctioneer, who lives immediately opposite, of what had occurred. One of Mr Else's sons was despatched for the doctor, whilst another went for a policeman. Within a very few minutes Dr Moxon, his assistant Mr Hunter, Sergeant Gee and Police Constable Smith were on the spot and they at once proceeded to the bedroom occupied by the Benns.

On their entrance the son turned round and walked

12

towards the window. Dr Moxon said 'Good morning' to him and Police-constable Smith put forward a chair in which the prisoner quietly seated himself. There was a gash in the prisoner's throat which had evidently been self-inflicted and Dr Moxon at once proceeded to dress the wound and stitch it up. When that had been done the prisoner was removed into an adjoining room and wrapped up in a shawl.

The doctor then proceeded to examine the father who was found to be quite dead. There was the mark of a terrible blow on the crown of the head which, in the opinion of the doctor, was sufficient to cause instantaneous death. The blow had evidently been struck whilst the deceased was asleep, for there was not the slightest mark of a struggle to be seen.

It was some time before it could be seen by what implement the blow had been struck, but eventually, on examining one of the earthenware vessels in the room, it was found to be stained with blood, though not in any way broken or chipped by the force of the blow.

The instrument which the prisoner had used to inflict the wound on himself was a small penknife, which is at the present time in the possession of the police.

During the evening it was deemed advisable to remove the prisoner as far from the spot as was convenient and a brake and two horses were therefore chartered to enable him to be removed to Derby Infirmary. Prior to his removal he was charged with the wilful murder of his father by one of the policemen and in reply he stated 'Yes, I did it'.

On the way to the Infirmary he conversed with the officers, but made no allusion whatever to the crime.

The event, declared the reporter, was without parallel in the memory of any of the residents of that quiet watering place, though he added, 'Of course the excitement is not so great as would have prevailed had the deed been committed in the height of the season.'

At the inquest medical evidence was given that Julius Benn had been struck repeatedly with a heavy chamber pot and that arteries had been severed by the penknife with which his son had vainly tried to end his own life.

From documents John established that his father had been authorized by the asylum doctors to take his son away for a period of rest in the country and that the outbreak in William of what the newspapers bluntly described as homicidal mania was totally unexpected. There had been no question of Julius allowing his love for his son to blind him; the tragedy had been totally unexpected by William's doctors and family alike.

The jury committed William Rutherford Benn for trial but he never came to court. After another attempt at suicide, by throwing himself twenty feet out of a window of the Derby Infirmary, he was returned to the care of an asylum.

Julius's efforts to pay back twenty shillings in the pound on the debts contracted in that unfortunate essay into commerce a quarter of a century earlier, from the meagre proceeds of a life of toil among the poor of East London, left his family destitute in their grief, reported the Nonconformist press. That may have been an exaggeration as far as the financial position of the elder Benn boys was concerned, as they appear to have been able to pay for the best medical treatment for their unfortunate brother. Certainly, though, Ann, the widow, was left without money of her own. An appeal to the people among whom Julius had spent his life of social and religious service quickly raised several hundred pounds for her. Among the names of those sponsoring the appeal was that of T.Barnardo, who may well have found some of the inspiration for his own work for deprived children in that of Julius Benn.

CHAPTER TWO

The Benns and the Literary Scene

John Williams Benn, describing his parents' meeting, said he grew out of his mother's hymnbook. The Benn family fortune, no mean one, came, in part, from between the covers of his sketch pad. In fact, but for that sketch pad, there might have been not only no fortune but no political prominence for the Benns.

Among John Williams's many talents was a gift for lightning illustration and a sense of the theatre. His brother William Rutherford shared his theatrical sense and was also musical. Between them the two boys, when in their teens, gave Sunday School entertainments at the Gravel Lane Meeting House, John Williams providing comic talks, illustrated with his own sketches, and William writing an accompaniment of songs. It was not the cold face of charity the Benns presented to the children of Stepney.

Not that there was no purpose, no propaganda in the entertainment. One Benn success was 'The Trial and Execution of John Barleycorn', written and produced by John Williams for the Benns' own anti-drink campaign, the Old Gravel Lane Meeting House Lifeboat Crew. The writer-producer also took the plum part of Lord Chief Justice, in full-bottomed wig and (mock) ermine-trimmed scarlet gown. Who had the title role is not recorded. Taken, as it were, to the heart of enemy territory, with a performance in the St George's-in-the-East Sailors' Institute, it was a resounding success, no less resounding in that the climax, John Barleycorn's execution, was to the accompaniment of a firework display. The treats and outings enjoyed by those who attended the Gravel Lane Sunday School were the envy of other Wapping children.

Throughout his life the stage remained John Williams's chief relaxation, if relaxation is the word for the intense activity with which he pursued it. No mere theatre-going for him. With the slightest excuse a new production was under way in the Benn household, with all the family pressed into service — to the not unalloyed pleasure, it seems, of some, including his eldest son Ernest.

Relatively impromptu affairs might utilize the billiards table as a stage. Other occasions, such as the annual Christmas play, would see the carpenters in to build a proper one. (That was in later prosperous years.) An ancient cedar tree with a vast spreading branch on the lawn of an Essex country house to which John Williams moved in the 1890's inspired him to an outdoor performance of *A Midsummer Night's Dream*. Most of the youth of the village was coaxed into taking part and the performance was not only well received by the local press but raised considerable funds for the relief of sufferers from a naval disaster.

Often John was not just actor-producer but writer as well, with a particular fascination for classical plays in blank verse, with Grecian plots and settings. It may have been just elaborate amateur theatricals but the originality of the Benn mind produced some innovations which have not been scorned by the professional stage. He got over the problem of the closeness of actors to audience by hanging a screen of green gauze across the proscenium opening. Practically invisible to the audience it yet created an illusion of distance and reality. It also had the side-effect of curing stage-fright in some of the more reluctant performers by making the audience virtually invisible to them. Illusions of depth on a restricted stage were provided by cleverly-lit backdrops of tissue paper pasted on muslin.

It was, however, his talent as a lightning illustrator which came to the rescue of the newly-established entrepreneur when John Williams fell on hard times in those

16

years of the early 1880's which brought such misfortune to the Benns.

He had previously started work as an office boy in the City at the age of eleven and it was then that he had a brush with a Post Office beadle which was to give him the rather jaundiced view of officialdom which stayed with him all his life and survived to his grandson.

Walking down Broad Street in the City of London he kicked a bunch of keys. It bore a name and the address 'General Post Office'. Young Benn wrote to the owner, on his employer's notepaper, suggesting he called to have them returned. The next day a choleric-looking individual appeared and imperiously demanded the return of 'Her Majesty's property'. Young Benn could be locked up for detaining it, and would be if he did not hand over the keys at once.

Far from being overawed the office boy, who had been expecting no more, but no less, than 'thank you', demanded a penny for the stamp for the letter. Furious, the visitor left. The next day, on his employer's advice, John Williams went to the Post Office headquarters. When the owner of the keys appeared he was no longer just an angry, elderly man but a personage, a beadle arrayed in cocked hat, red cloth and gold lace. It was enough to make young Benn quake but, in good negotiating fashion, he raised his demand to a penny ha'penny, the halfpenny being for the notepaper. Furious, the beadle threatened to 'summons' him and summonsed young Benn was. At the court, accused of snatching up the keys as soon as they had been dropped and running off with them, he denied the charge and still insisted on his penny for postage and a ha'penny for paper. The magistrate's comment was blunt, seventeen and sixpence fine or three days in Coldbath Fields, a suitable place of detention for such young rascals as Benn seemed to be. Meekly Julius Benn paid the fine but young John Williams still had a powerful ally, his mother. 'What,' she said, hammering the table

17

with the rolling pin with which she was rolling out the dough for a potato pie — the family had moved on from boiled rice — 'Is a red-faced official bully to disgrace my boy? I'll see the Postmaster-General himself.'

At St Martin's-le-Grand she did not get as far as the PMG but she reached someone sufficiently exalted to cross-question the beadle, get at the truth and compel him to pay over the seventeen and sixpence. It was a story which made the papers under the title 'The Bunch of Keys'. John Williams did not get his penny ha'penny, just an undying loathing for unthinking authoritarianism which he was to describe as 'Bumbledom'. Later in life he used to amuse his grandchildren with appropriate sketches to illustrate the scornful rhyme:

Bumble, the Beadle, you see,
You'd think he's as brave as could be,
   To whack a small boy
   Is to him a great joy,
But anything bigger, not he.

At seventeen, as invoice clerk with a furnishing house, John Williams decided to put his drawing talents to work. He was then paid 12s a week and saw that the designers who drew the articles for which he made out invoices were much better paid for a much more interesting job. He set out to join them, going to art school in South Kensington twice a week. After six months he screwed up his courage to show a sheet of drawings to his employer. To no effect. The boss drew out his own pencil, pointed out errors in the illustrations and said, 'You'll never draw, my boy, it isn't in you.'

But young Benn persevered, arranged to do some work for a small manufacturer, for a very small fee, and one day his employer saw some of those drawings. 'Who did those for you?' he asked. 'Young Benn,' was the reply

18

and his employer, forgetting his earlier verdict, appointed him junior draughtsman with an 8s-a-week rise.

Soon after that, at the age of twenty, he met, through his talents as an entertainer, the girl who was to become his wife, Lily Pickstone. On a visit to his native Hyde an uncle introduced him to the Pickstone family, all agog to see the latest marvel from London — Professor Pepper's Ghost. This was a Victorian magician's illusion which was probably the origin of the phrase, 'it's all done with mirrors'. John Williams offered to demonstrate it. As well as the mirrors he needed a subject, and the young daughter was summoned. The twenty minutes of preparation he needed to produce the ghost also produced for him a bride, though his scruples prevented his sending her a love letter until just before he felt secure enough, financially, to ask her father for her hand. That was in July 1873. He was then chief designer, on £6 a week, to rise to £7 the next year. Soon he was a junior partner, getting £10 a week. Five hundred pounds a year was then the out-of-reach target to which most of the country aspired.

Lily must have been a good manager. Ten pounds a week might have been relative affluence for a young couple but they were soon to be not just a young couple, the family was growing. Even so they had saved £800 by the time John Williams was thirty and on that capital he changed his role to propagandist and publisher. He started his first journal, founding the business which was to be Benn Brothers.

That journal, *The Cabinet Maker*, had perhaps a prophetic title as far as future political Benns were concerned. John Williams's cabinet maker was, of course, the furniture maker and his aim was to see that the furniture it contained was to the best design. This, to Benn's mind, meant harking back to the days before Victorian over-ornamentation. Not as far as the medieval and Jacobean styles which influenced William Morris, but to the eighteenth century, to the times of Queen Anne and Wil-

19

liam and Mary, to Chippendale, Sheraton and Hepple-white. That might generally be considered fairly good taste today but it was not so then, when the main reaction against Victorian gimcrackery was to look to Scandinavia.

When John Williams resigned his partnership, his fellow partners viewed his proposal for pressing the best of English taste on the trade by an illustrated monthly as sheer folly. It seemed they were right. At first hardly anybody wanted it. A fire at the printers which destroyed his books and paper found him not covered by insurance. His £800 had vanished by the end of a year. Benn faced the collapse of his dreams, the return to a humdrum life. His sketchbook came to the rescue.

A chance meeting with the Professor Pepper whose ghost he raised at Hyde pointed the way ahead. Benn already had a considerable reputation as an amateur entertainer. Pepper's advice was the age-old one to the talented amateur, 'make some money at it'. Pepper gave him an introduction to one of those 'polytechnic' institutions which mixed instruction with amusement to a then popular recipe. Benn was an instant success with a lecture on caricature using his own illustrations. Soon he was travelling up and down the country, a sort of semi-educational Rolf Harris of the day, lecturing humorously on a host of subjects, but mainly on Cockney life, accompanied by lightning sketches, occasionally done blindfold, to raise an extra gasp from the audience. It was a huge success. He even came satisfactorily out of one sticky spot when, on his first trip to Scotland, facing a rather dour-looking audience, he found his lecture on 'Noses' had been billed as one on 'Moses'. By 1885 he had chalked up his thousandth performance and recorded an income of £2,000 that year, despite charging so little when he appeared at such institutions as Baptist chapels that it could hardly have covered expenses.

Benn went on in that way for ten years, while *The Cabinet Maker* fought its way to prosperity, editing, publishing and, to a large extent, writing and illustrating the magazine in the intervals between his entertaining. When he did give up the theatrical stage it was only for the political platform. The experience on the one served him on the other.

Long before then he had also made his mark as a publisher and propagandist. Indeed by the end of that first year, when the printer's fire had already swallowed up the Benn savings and he was fitting the second string of entertainer to his bow, he was able to claim there had 'rarely been such a rapid success in the history of trade literature'. The magazine had grown in size and circulation and he had also enlarged its title, to *The Cabinet Maker and Art Furnisher*. That was to indicate more clearly the wider section of people who, he intended, should benefit from his own series of articles on Chippendale, Hepplewhite, Sheraton and the brothers Adam, by means of an illustrated analysis of carving in the Queen Anne period — and by his intense campaign against all he considered to be sham. At a time when boards and rugs were the mark of the gentleman, he argued that the linoleum which covered the floors of most working-class and middle-class homes should be good, honest floorcloth, not imitation marble, tiles or parquet. In the days when flowery patterns spiralled and twined over the walls of middle-class sitting rooms in a bewildering riot of vegetable activity that outshone even the most prolific jungle, he fought for plain colours.

After five years of editing and publishing from a single room in Finsbury Square, a few doors away from the house where lived Benn, his wife, their five children, his mother, sister and two youngest brothers, he moved his business to a four-storey building in City Road. The printing still had to be done elsewhere, for Benn had other, novel ideas for using the extra space. He devised a plan, an early form of franchising, to exploit *The Cabinet Maker's* reputation for making well-designed products of

21

good taste more easily seen and available, all, of course, to Benn's own commercial advantage.

Emblazoned over the front of the building, reaching from roof to just above the ground-floor shop front, were the words 'Cabinet Makers Exchange and Sample Rooms. A Permanent Exhibition of Furnishing Novelties and Materials'. The space surplus to the requirements of the magazine's staff was set out for manufacturers to display their products. Signs on the windows indicated what might be found within — linoleum, carpets, brasswork, pottery, art tiles, domestic fittings and so on. Admission, to those who subscribed to view what manufacturers paid to exhibit, was by member's ticket which also entitled the holder to consult a reference library. The scheme was successful enough for Benn to retain it as a feature of the larger six-floor premises he had specially built in the early 1900's in Finsbury, still in the furniture-making district.

Clearly John Williams Benn had a well-developed entrepreneurial sense, even though, according to his eldest son, he had no personal sense of money, rarely carried any, and had to borrow from his children the shillings he promised to winners of races he organized among his grandchildren. His wife, when they lived in a flat, had to maintain a steady account with the hall porter to pay for the cabs and taxis in which he returned home and, like P.G. Wodehouse's Ukridge, Benn usually had to call on one of his guests to pay the bill when the family dined out. Unlike Ukridge, however, Benn prospered, though not spectacularly, for his political activities, after he left the stage, took precedence over mere money-making.

In 1890 some of his staff, seeing opportunities of their own along the path he had opened up, left him to set up a rival paper on furnishing and decorating. Benn was not to be trifled with in that way, though. He promptly countered with *The Furnisher and Decorator*, published monthly at 2d, which soon saw off the opposition. Less successful was his attempt to spread his ideas more widely, outside the trade and professional circles his existing magazines were aimed at. A woman who wanted to dress well had innumerable papers and magazines to turn to, but if she wanted to learn how to furnish her home and run it well where could she go? Benn decided a new journal was needed, *The House*, which would tell her all she needed to know about everything from drains to drawing rooms, from kitchen equipment to coffee tables, or how to embroider her cushions or choose her curtains. Unfortunately, it proved to be before its time, or, rather, before the colour printing which has helped make innumerable followers of that Benn inspiration into fortune winners for their proprietors.

But is must not be forgotten that the firm was 'Benn Brothers' or, rather, in those early days, 'J. W. Benn and Brothers'. In the very early days it was mainly one brother, Henry, and it was he who recalled how when the first issue of *The Cabinet Maker* arrived from the printers the whole staff, from editor-publisher to office boy, set to work wrapping it for the post. What with the over-enthusiasm of the amateur packers or the weakness of the paste, most of the packages came apart, fortunately before the one horse-cart taking them to the post office, arrived at its destination.

However, it was John Williams's eldest son Ernest, who was to provide the zip and drive that set the firm growing into one of the biggest publishing houses in the country, and who was to show in the highest measure the entrepreneurial side of the Benn character while his father indulged or devoted himself to the political side.

He entered the business in 1891 at the age of sixteen and a half, having failed to matriculate — though an adverse verdict on his maths did not prevent his showing considerable financial astuteness in raising cash for his later ventures — but with the benefit of having been sent, with his brother Wedgwood, to Paris for eighteen months to study art. Travelling may have been no more an adventure for a teenager in those days than now but the prices were different. The third-class return fare from London to Paris was £2 2s (£2.10) and the Benn family habit was to travel by night on the Dieppe-Newhaven route. That saved 3 francs, roughly 3s (15p) — the cost of a French hotel bed. It meant, though, that the traveller arrived at Charing Cross in the early hours of the morning. But that had compensations. Across the road, on the present site of South Africa House, stood an all-night, and all-day, restaurant, Lockharts. A sandwich of two thick slabs of new bread, enfolding an almost equally thick slab of ham, and needing two hands for its manipulation (for a knife and fork was not included in the price), cost 1d. The mug of steaming coffee to wash it down was ½d. For a hungry boy, Ernest was to recall, it made a meal infinitely more satisfying than many expensive ones he was to eat later in five-star hotels and restaurants.

Ernest Pickstone Benn — named after his mother's family — started as an office boy at 5s a week, of which he saved half. His studies in Paris had been intended to fit him for the art work on *The Cabinet Maker*. Two years in the studio proved they had not, and the art and editorial side remained the province of his uncles Henry and Robert Davis. His other uncle in the firm, Julius, who looked after the business side, also took a jaundiced view of his nephew's worth in that direction. When Ernest succumbed to the blandishments of a salesman and allowed a typewriter to be left on a month's free trial, for part of Ernest's job was to write all letters by hand and copy them into the letter book, he provoked a rare quarrel between his father and his uncle. Uncle Julius proclaimed young Ernest was far too dangerous a speculator to be allowed to stay in the business.

John Williams won, and Ernest stayed, becoming a salesman himself, travelling the country, at £3 a week, for six years. When Benn Brothers Limited was registered in

1897 he became company secretary, combining the job with that of advertisement manager.

Ernest's own opportunity to branch out, and the start of a remarkable expansion of the business, came in 1900. *The Hardware Trade Journal* became available and John Williams took the opportunity to set up his son in his own business. Ernest had made the first approaches to the printers into whose hands the journal had fallen, and who wanted to rid themselves of it, but he had less money than his father had when he started *The Cabinet Maker*. Promises to pay in future were not enough, ready money was wanted. His father came to the rescue and subscribed £500, provided Ernest and his collaborator, a young sub-editor on the Journal, enticed £1,000 out of the ironmongery trade. Ernest and his friend had a novel idea for floating the company. Members of the ironmongery trade who invested in the company would get preferential dividends, related to the amount they spent as advertisers in the Journal. Remarkably they found enough people willing to take the chance. The previous owners took 1,500 £1-shares, on condition Ernest bought them back in seven years. Ernest took 2,500 shares as five years' salary paid in advance, his friend also came to terms as part of his future salary. With a nominal capital of £7,000 but actual cash of only £1,500, and a debt of £1,500, the first issue appeared under the Benn colours. In the meantime, his uncles agreed he could remain secretary of Benn Brothers while trying his own venture.

The *Journal* lost just £100 more in its first year than John Williams's *Cabinet Maker* lost in its first year, without the excuse of a fire at the printers. It carried on losing money, though at a lesser rate in its second year. Ernest had no theatrical talents to fall back on, just his financial acumen. He kept afloat by accepting bills of exchange. When one fell due and he was unable to meet it he just had to accept another to repay the first. Everything had to be kept on a tight rein. He had his monthly accounts drawn up by the tenth of the next month, at the latest, ready to be gone through to find more halfpennies to be pared away.

Eventually he won through, with the help of more Benn innovations, such as competitions, daily newspapers at trade conferences, and sketches, by leading caricaturists, of prominent people in the ironmongery trade. Everybody, it seemed, wanted to see the latter, even the subjects. In 1909 the *Journal* was incorporated in what was not yet, but was on the way to becoming, the Benn Empire. Journal after journal followed, including one in Spanish, *El Commerciante Argentino*, published in Buenos Aires, to promote British goods in South America. Sir John Benn — he had by then been knighted — went to Argentina for its launch, to forge the first Benn links with Argentina. Another journal, to do the same job in Egypt, was published in Sanskrit.

By this time John Williams Benn had withdrawn from the active control of the firm. He had devoted himself entirely to politics, leaving business to Ernest. There was a whole series of take-overs of journals, many quite decrepit when they entered the house of Benn, needing careful nursing back to health. Some did not make it but most did. The firm went from strength to strength. When Sir John died in 1922 and Ernest succeeded to the baronetcy, which had supplanted the knighthood, and to the chairmanship, there were eight solidly based journals plus books and directories which had often been acquired with their parent journals. For Benn these books were something of a nuisance. Editors of journals, he thought, should devote themselves full-time to those journals and not have to divert some of their energies to the technical works, diaries and reference books associated with them.

So Ernest set up a separate book department with a bright young man as manager, Victor Gollancz. In 1923 it blossomed into a separate but associated company, Ernest Benn Limited, with Sir Ernest as chairman and Gollancz as managing director. It broadened out into general publishing and soon its list included those two best-selling left-wingers, H.G. Wells and Eileen Nesbitt. Wells made his views clear in his books. Eileen Nesbitt, wife of Hubert Bland, one of the founders of the Fabian Society, rarely, if ever, allowed her socialism to colour her children's books except, perhaps, once, when in *The Magic Amulet* her young heroes and heroines, projected into the ideal world of the future, see a garden notice: 'I know I must not pick the flowers. They are not mine — but they are ours'.

It was not because of the surviving progressive influence of John Williams Benn or even that of Victor Gollancz, soon to start his own publishing firm and to run the pre-war Left Book Club, that two such stalwarts of the Left were chosen to make the Benn book fortune. They just happened to be taken over, with Joseph Conrad and Ethel M. Dell, when the family firm of T. Fisher Unwin was acquired. Wells never allowed his political views to affect his personal prosperity when it came to negotiating advance payments on his books. On some, royalties earned have still to equal advances paid. On the other hand others, like his collected short stories, which is still in print with a total sale of over half a million, go on steadily contributing to the Benn revenues.

To Benn's goes the distinction of producing the first sixpenny library of paperbacks, in 1926. It covered poetry and contemporary drama, soon to be extended to other non-fiction — 'A complete reference library of modern thought' — and sold in millions. Surprisingly, though, the formula failed when transferred to fiction, with the Benn Ninepenny Novels. These were new books, by writers ranging from Elinor Glyn to Sydney Horler, Eden Philpotts to Alec Waugh. They were not the same success. Too well produced, ahead of their time, are two of the reasons given by the Benns. Perhaps it was just that, even at ninepence, they were overpriced by 50 per cent. Just

27

three years later Penguin paperbacks were to be an instant success, even though, initially, they were just reprints, with no new titles, at just sixpence a copy.

Not that Sir Ernest limited himself to publishing books — he wrote them. In good Benn tradition he started as a collectivist. In the First World War, excluded from military service by poor eyesight, he was a part-time Civil Servant, as well as part-time munitions worker at Woolwich, when he was not running his business. He became a passionate advocate of cooperation between business and government to win the trade war which he knew must follow the fighting war. He was in at the founding of the Whitley Councils, to determine pay and conditions in the public service. But this phase did not last, the Benn hatred of Bumbledom was to extend in Sir Ernest's case beyond the obvious bastions of bureaucracy to the whole of State control. In books, pamphlets, in luncheon and after-dinner speeches, on the radio, he never slackened from flaying the propagators of such wicked ideas as nationalization, state control, or any interference with personal liberties.

Of all Sir Ernest's books and pamphlets, one was to make him a world figure overnight, *Confessions of a Capitalist*. With sales of a quarter of a million, translated into eight languages, it created a world storm as it attempted to hold back what was then seen as the inevitable advance of Socialism. Witty as well as argumentative, its flavour is given in chapter headings such as 'Making £1,000 in a Week', 'Whom do I Rob', 'Wealth is Exchange'. While his one-time stable companion was busy with his Left Book Club, Sir Ernest was founding the Individualist Bookshop and the Society of Individualists. He admitted to a steady income of £10,000 a year which, if not the £1,000 a week of a millionaire, was double the income of a prime minister in those days when prime ministers, if no better regarded than today, were better paid.

Benn Brothers claims to have been the first firm to

introduce a five-day week, during the 1914—18 War. That is disputed by Bryant and May, the match firm, but whoever had the honour there were only a few days in it. That contrasts with the 1890's, under the progressive John Williams Benn, when everybody in the firm worked ten hours a day, six days a week, though, according to the young Ernest of those days, the 'bosses' might ease their way through the mornings playing chess in local coffee houses. How far down the scale that went he never revealed.

Sir Ernest also introduced a bonus scheme to enable workers to share directly in the firm's prosperity, one which might still appeal to liberal advocates of workers' participation today. In essence it was simple. Any dividends over 10 per cent paid to shareholders were matched by a comparable increase in wages and salaries. For example, if shareholders received 15 per cent dividends then all employees had 5 per cent of salary as a bonus.

The influence of his grandfather, Julius Benn, must still have been working in him even in the later days of the 1920's when his individualism was at its height. In 1927 he founded the Boys' Hostel Association to provide accommodation for homeless boys in London, as a memorial to the work of his grandfather and father in the East End. The first hostel was opened in Stepney by the Prince of Wales. With a second, in Stockwell, it was to provide homes, over the next thirty years, for 2,000 boys who would otherwise have been left to doubtful lodgings or even the railway arches and pavements. After Sir Ernest's death, in 1954, they were handed over to the YMCA. His successors also sold the large building in Fleet Street which had become the Benn headquarters — it had balanced its special directors' dining room and kitchens with staff games rooms — in order to move the main part of the business out of London, away not only from the smell of wood shavings in furniture land but also the scent of printers' ink, to Tonbridge in Kent.

It has been the individualist Benns, Ernest's sons and grandsons, who have seen Benn Brothers continue to thrive. Not all have been strictly Benns; despite the male chauvinistic sound of 'Benn Brothers', sisters, or at least the progeny of sisters, have played their part. They have continued to operate Ernest's own brand of paternalistic capitalism.

Unions are not recognized in the company and, despite the intense battles that usually go on in the publishing world, from intensely union-conscious workers, backed by unions well conscious themselves of the importance of having every firm tied up in agreements, there has never been any real agitation for union rights. Staff are encouraged to buy shares in the business, with money loaned by the business. It goes without saying that there are such signs of a benevolent employer as season-ticket loan schemes. There are even country cottages available for cheap holidays.

In all this Ernest's own brother William Wedgwood played little part — still less does William's son Tony, except to share the profits which the family firm has maintained even during the most difficult times. Tony's name as a shareholder is hidden behind that of a nominee but he acknowledged his shareholding in the House of Commons Register of Members' Interests.

Whatever Tony thinks of the family firm there is obviously not much family love for Tony among those who run it. The centenary of Sir Ernest's birth and the fiftieth anniversary of the publication of *Confessions of a Capitalist* were used publicly to dissociate the firm from him.

A eulogistic account of Sir Ernest written for the firm's house magazine by the current chairman, Richard Woolley, was 'an emphatic reminder that Mr Anthony Wedgwood Benn's policies do not reflect the principles which have governed the growth of the Benn publishing group. To all our many friends in trade and industry let us state categorically that the publisher Benns, as individuals, are in no position to do more than any other member of the community about the views or actions of the new Energy Minister.' (This was in 1975.) A number of people, he admitted, had asked what connection, if any, there was. It was, quite obviously, an embarrassing question for the descendants of the founder of the Society of Individualists.

CHAPTER THREE

The Proud Londoner

John Williams Benn's theatrical travels did one other thing at least as profound as securing the family fortune. As he moved around the country he became aware of a civic pride which was to launch him into public service and politics. Not his own civic pride, but what he sensed was that of others, of people who were citizens of real cities, not members of the agglomeration of parishes which was all that London was fitted to be in the eyes of nineteenth-century politicians. There was no Greater London Council or London County Council. At the centre was the Corporation of the City of London, at least as much an anachronism then as many consider it today, with its own Lord Mayor, presiding over an area in which few lived, outside the working day, and certainly not those who held office, or even voted; its main justification in the eyes of Londoners an annual circus through the City streets, to which they flocked to watch. The London outside this golden-paved square mile, which dwarfed that within the remnants of the city walls, had been deliberately excluded from the Local Government Act of 1835, which gave all provincial towns powers to run their own

31

municipal affairs. While Birmingham, Manchester and other towns thrived and became models of municipal government that attracted observers from all other countries aspiring to the civilization in which Britain was leading the way, the imperial capital wallowed in the mire, prey for exploitation by all those private bodies nominally providing its 'services'.

As John Williams said later:

Many stay-at-home Londoners did not then realize how backward their city was in municipal development. My lecturing tours had brought me into contact with some of the leading provincial towns and cities, notably Birmingham, and caused me to make comparisons which rendered London government, in my sense, very deficient. To think of the great city of the Empire, with a wealthy square mile in its centre, monopolizing its dignity, hospitality, tradition and wealth, and the districts around this precious enclose at the mercy of some sixty local authorities, Bumbledom rampant, made me long to do something for the unity and decent management of the metropolis. 'Why,' I thought, 'should Lord John Russell's glorious municipal charter of 1835 be available for Little Pudlington and denied to the five million of metropolis.'

The absurdity of the situation was pointed out as early as 1837, by the Commission applying the Act of 1835, but nothing was done until 1856. Then a Metropolitan Board of Works was set up, with minimal powers and no democratic control, leaving untouched the City Corporation, with its privileges, and the many incompetent, sometimes corrupt local vestries. An attempt, a decade later, to convert the Board into a Municipal Council with enlarged powers over the capital's services, foundered in Parliament, a victim of that distrust of Parliament for London government which today seems epitomized by the two

32

buildings diametrically opposed to each other across the Thames, on either side of Westminster Bridge.

Another attempt, two decades later, in 1884, would have made the City Corporation responsible for the municipal affairs of the whole capital, to work by delegating its powers to district councils. It foundered on what has been a continuing bone of contention, control of London's police. The Home Secretary of the time, Sir William Harcourt, whose brain-child that Bill had been, was more concerned by the Irish outrages being committed and the seditious, perhaps revolutionary threat of growing working-class discontent than he was by the lack of London authority. He was determined to remain the Chief of Police which the times had made him, at least in London, and indeed, London's police, unlike those of all other towns, were to remain under the Home Office. While the matter was being argued, the Bill was forgotten in other arguments between Lords and Commons.

In 1888 came the Act which was to give London some degree of local government powers, though only those of a County Council, and only over a restricted area which in no way approximated to the full area of the world's largest municipality. The City Corporation was left untouched, an obsolete appendix where the heart should have been.

But it was John Benn's opportunity. Previously he had been debarred from voting in the City Corporation elections or from standing as a councillor, because his business was just a few yards outside the City boundary, the old City Wall. But now he could fight and win Finsbury in the first LCC elections in 1889, on the side of the Progressives against the Moderates.

The Moderates were conservative. The Progressives ranged from Lord Rosebery, the future Liberal Prime Minister, to John Benn, described by his friend A.G. Gardiner as 'no socialist but a radical who believed in public ownership of public monopolies', and such 'dreamers of dreams' (as their Moderate opponents described them) as John Burns and Sidney Webb. Burns was co-founder of the first Social Democratic Party, the Social-Democratic Federation, and a thorough-going Marxist, as social democrats were in those days. Sidney Webb, who was later to write, with his wife Beatrice, *Soviet Communism, A New Civilization*, had already written a pamphlet, 'Facts for Londoners', for the Fabian Society. Developed into the 'London Programme' of 1892, it was virtually adopted by the Progressives, leading to the charge that they were permeated with Fabianism. While the Fabians believed in socialism, eschewing all profits, the Progressives aimed at the radical municipalization of public services, with profits going to relieve the rates, not to private enterprise.

The responsibilities of the LCC were limited to such matters as main drainage, parks, animal diseases, lunatic asylums, technical education (in which Webb was to play an important role), the safety of theatres, and something entitled 'artisans' dwellings'.

Rosebery was the first Chairman of the LCC, Benn the Progressive Chief Whip. After an abortive attempt to get the Council to demand control of London's police, Benn had more success in the field of artisans' dwellings, which was construed as slum clearance and the housing of the poor. One of the great early achievements of the Council was the sweeping away of the morass of slums which lay between the Strand and Holborn, replacing it eventually with the broad sweep of Aldwych and Kingsway. This, together with the Thames Embankment below it, another achievement of the LCC, is the most visible record of the great changes which the new Council brought in its very first years. From the Embankment, beneath the new roads, ran a tramway tunnel (tunnels and trams were other interests of Benn), carrying water and electricity, both of which were to be so instrumental in changing the life of the Londoner.

Slum clearance, however, was the immediate concern. To those living in the latter part of the twentieth century the conditions of the latter part of the nineteenth are unbelievable. One of the worst areas was around Boundary Street in Bethnal Green, to which Benn called attention with an article and a series of sketches in the *Daily Graphic*. It comprised fifteen acres of collapsing houses, dead-end alleys, noisome courts, in which the death rate was 42 per 1,000 — the inhabitants of this part of the capital of the Empire had a similar life expectancy at birth, 25 years, to that of slum dwellers in Calcutta.

Death rates like that are easily understood in the light of Lord Shaftesbury's account, to a Parliamentary committee, of a visit he made to just such a slum only half a decade before the founding of the LCC. In a low cellar, he reported, 'there were a woman and two children but the striking part of it was this, from a hole in the ceiling there came a long open wooden tube [trough?], supported by props, and through that flowed all the filth of the house above, right through the place where this woman was living, into the common sewer. Nobody paid the least attention to it.'

A consolidation of the Council's powers on housing, drainage, disease and fire prevention enabled it to pull down that and other areas only slightly less bad, and have them replaced by model dwellings along airy streets forty feet wide. Where previously there had been population densities of over 2,500 to the acre, approaching 3,000, the Council had a limit of 342.

Of course, as Moderate opponents of the scheme claimed, it cost money. Owners of the squalid premises in Boundary Street first put in claims for £457,000, or £30,000 an acre, equal to a million in modern money. The Council's valuer cut them back to £266,000. Altogether, Benn argued, the cost to Londoners of rehousing these slum dwellers was one-ninth of a penny in the pound on the rates, falling, as interest payments dropped, to

35

nothing. Surely the prosperous could afford that degree of charity.

Benn also used his pen in the newspapers to illustrate the plight of other denizens of the slums of London, those who had no permanent home at all and relied on doss-houses.

In 1851, Henry Mayhew, in his *London Labour and London Poor* had described a typical lodging house, little different, if at all, from those forty years later:

It is by no means unusual to find 18 or 21 in one small room, the heat and horrid smell from which are insufferable . . . If they have linen, they take it off to escape vermin . . . The amiable and deservedly popular minister of a district church, built among lodging houses, has stated that he found 29 human beings in one apartment and that, having with difficulty knelt in between two beds to pray with a dying woman, his legs became so jammed that he could hardly get up again.

Benn had read Mayhew, but an ounce of experience is worth a pound of theory so he went to savour what the fourpenny doss of the day really meant. Even at second hand, he believed, his experience could help the public and his fellow councillors to understand the plight of the homeless, so he wrote up, with illustrations, again in the *Daily Graphic*, his visit to Blind Con's Doss'us in Golden Lane. It boasted a 'sitting room', where the so-called sheets, strips of greyish calico, hung drying on lines, and where the seat of honour was an upturned zinc pail by the fire, on which Con's deputy Jim installed himself until Con himself came in from the pub next door. The four-pences, naturally, were payable in advance. Benn, fearful of giving himself away despite the tattered rags he wore and the support of his more experienced companion, had to pose as one of the relatively respectable who normally aspired to the heights of a sixpenny doss but, down on his luck, could not find the extra tuppence.

After midnight there straggled in the main body of male dossers, from the many pubs, followed at nearer one in the morning by the women, from the streets. The temporary jollity which came with the drowning of sorrows in the pubs soon vanished in drunken squabbles over the fourpences. Benn wrote:

Sick, both in heart and body as I was, I determined to see the whole thing through and, tapping Jim on the shoulder, I asked him to show us our 'doss'. The price of a pint had made the deputy our firm friend so he went up to show us the room. He led the way up a tumbledown staircase to the second floor and, kicking open a door, pointed to two truckle beds in an unlighted room, saying, 'There you are, boys, I've got you two together'. The door closed and we were in darkness. There was, however, a moon that night and its light through the whitewashed window enabled us to see our surroundings. The room was about 15 ft by 12 ft and there were six beds, each about 2 ft 6 ins wide. In three of them were sleepers, one of whom was snoring drunk.

At about half past one the owner of the sixth bed in the room staggered in. I trembled for fear that he should fall on me, for he came very near, but he managed to find his proper corner. I fell to calculating how much 'Con' was making out of this miniature dormitory. Six beds at 4d=2s, fully occupied 12s or 14s, for a room which let as a tenement would be dear at 2s 6d a week. There was no gas in the house. Four or five common paraffin lamps, worth not more than a few pence each, were all there was for lighting purposes. In the chamber in which I lay there was not a vestige of furniture, except the beds, not even a glass on the mantelpiece.

This is leaving private enterprise to settle the lodging house question, I thought. Here is a blind man, who, for many years, has thrived on the fourpences of·these poor wretches. I know there are superior places, but that such a place as I have described should exist at all deepened my conviction that the London County Council should be stirring in this matter at once.

On leaving at dawn, on the pretext of having to get to work in the docks, Benn asked the policeman around the corner if he had not heard the screams of a woman who had been attacked by Con when she tried to get in without paying and left lying senseless on the stairs.

'Oh yes, sir,' the policeman replied. 'But they can kick up as much row as they like inside, we can't interfere unless we are sent for.'

Doss-houses were inspected, but a coat of whitewash and an occasional scrubbing was enough to see them passed as satisfactory.

Stirred by Benn's account, the Council decided to provide lodging houses itself, the first being off Drury Lane. For a like charge of fourpence, there were decent accommodation, facilities for cooking and laundry, and a quiet place for reading and writing. These houses were the forerunner of the Rowton House, the poor man's hotel which Lord Rowton provided for the Guinness Trust, after paying for the first himself. The LCC lodging houses have gone. Some of the Rowton Houses survive, no longer poor man's hotels but refurbished as ordinary hotels.

But Benn's obsession was public transport. He believed that cheap public transport was the key to the improvement of the life of the Londoner. It would open up new fields for him, literally, giving him the chance of moving away from the slums of inner London. When those slums which were to be replaced by Aldwych and Kingsway were pulled down, he wanted those living there, if they wished, to be moved to the outskirts and given free travel to their places of work. That did not happen, but time

38

proved him right both in his belief that convenient transport would take people to new homes and new lives, and also in his conviction that cheap transport, with halfpenny fares, would still pay profits into the rates.

John Benn has been derided as just an enthusiastic amateur. A professional, goes the argument, would have provided Benn's electric tramcars quicker. The fact is that the professional companies of the time did not, in London at any rate. Outside London it may have been different. Bristol, interestingly, where his grandson Tony was to become MP, was the first British town to have electric trams, in 1896.

One professional at work on London's transport system in those days, and who was to have as profound an effect as Benn, was the American Charles Tyson Yerkes. London is indebted to him for its electric underground trains but it is doubtful if even the most enthusiastic supporter of entrepreneurial affairs would approve of his methods above those of Benn. Yerkes had been a stockbroker and banker in Philadelphia. His forte was the financial take-over, crystallized in his doctrine 'buy up old junk, fix it up a little and unload it on the other fellow'. After a spell of imprisonment he moved to Chicago, to cash in on the American electric traction boom of the 1880s. He did so to no little degree. Giving evidence on his suitability to provide similar services for Londoners he told MPs he controlled 432 miles of electric tramway, 40 miles of elevated electric railway and 47 miles of cable tramway. His lines, he said, carried 300 million passengers a year, no small figure for a town of 1¼ million, giving the people of Chicago a much higher journey rate than Londoners. Theirs was rather crowded travel. 'It's the straphangers who pay the dividends,' Yerkes was fond of saying, forgetting the bribery used to get cheap leases and the Press rumour and innuendo which brought down the share prices of companies he was set on taking over.

In London Yerkes formed the Underground Electric

Railway Company of London Limited, with part American money, part British, and offered to electrify the District railway and build new underground railways. The possible pickings, plus the sight of so renowned a picker as Yerkes at work, drew in rivals, including the great Pierpoint Morgan, working through his London banking firm. The hope that competition might cut the cost was dashed, though, when Morgan withdrew, describing Yerkes's activity as the 'greatest rascality and conspiracy I ever heard of' — praise indeed from the man the world of finance acknowledged as the outstanding master of such matters.

With a capital of £1 million Yerkes embarked on an electrification and construction programme which was costed at £16 million. How to raise the money? His solution was fascinating, not least in the fact that supposedly hard-headed businessmen fell for it. He issued notes with par value in denominations of £100 at 96, to pay income-tax-free interest of 5 per cent and to be redeemed against the company stock — worth just one-sixteenth of the face value of the notes. The total assets of the company were only worth a quarter of the notes' value. Inevitably came trouble. In 1905 an angry meeting of note-holders sent Yerkes speeding back to New York, not to his wife but with his current mistress, for Yerkes, at over 70, was still a great womanizer. There he died. Despite his apparent great wealth — he bequeathed a fabulous art collection to a museum — he turned out to be bankrupt, and the art went to pay his debts. The American novelist Theodore Dreiser turned the life of Yerkes into his three-volume indictment of American capitalism, *The Financier*.

Despite all that, despite the losses of the note-holders, London got its electric railways. Yerkes electrified the District and Inner Circle and built three tube railways in five years, less than the time it took to build one London tube in the 1960's. Admittedly, in comparison with the speeds achieved on the railways, the underpowered trains were rather slow. His technical expert justified their 16 mph by saying the human body would not go faster, it could not be treated 'like a bullet out of a gun'. However, Lots Road power station stands to this day as a memorial to Yerkes, as it continues to power the London Underground.

Ironically, the underground railways of Yerkes, the privateer, survive as the mainspring of the municipally-run transport system for which Benn fought, while the tramways on which he built his ideas have vanished. From the beginnings of the LCC he was a member of the Highways Committee, then vice-chairman, finally chairman, but all the time the spokesman on tramways. In transport London had lagged behind, not just other capital cities but provincial centres here and in the USA. In the mid-century, it had pioneered underground city railways, with the cut and cover tunnels of the District and Metropolitan lines, soot-caked from the steam trains, serving the wealthier areas just north of the Thames. All most Londoners had, though, were a few horse omnibuses and horse-drawn trams. There were thirteen tramway companies, with not even a standard gauge between them, but the time was fast approaching when, under the Tramways Act of 1870, municipal authorities would be able to buy them out. One other great disadvantage for the Londoner working in the City was that the trams were not allowed to cross the bridges, so people living in such popular centres as Camberwell — about the limit, then, of daily travel — had to face long walks along the Embankment and across the bridges before queueing for the trams — if queueing is the word, mostly it seems to have been a mad scramble in which the weakest went to the wall, or walked. Above all, of course, there remained the disadvantage of the slowness of the horses. Benn set out to put it all right. It proved to be a long and difficult task before the triumphant day came when, in top hat and morning dress, he collected the halfpennies and issued the tickets for the royal party on the inaugural run of the electric tram. That tram was to be linked, by chroniclers of working-class life, with the gas stove as doing more to improve that life than any other turn-of-the-century development.

The Moderates were the self-appointed protectors of the private companies which were busy manipulating profits to boost their valuations for any purchase price. In no position to prevent motions to purchase being passed, the opposition councillors realised they could make those motions inoperative by merely staying away, thus reducing the total number of votes below the legal minimum. Then in the mid-1890's, after the Prime Minister Lord Salisbury had swung an election by a personal attack on the 'socialism' of the LCC, a hung council held up the purchase.

Two attempts to get Parliament to agree to trams crossing the bridges foundered, the first in the Commons, the second, after scrambling through the Commons by two votes, in the Lords. But a change of electoral fortunes, in 1898, led to the first trams with the legendary 'LCC Tramways' on the sides running on eighteen miles of South London tramway on 1 January 1899. The municipally-run trams set off to forecasts of disaster. The company which had previously run that system had the reputation of being extremely well managed. The Council, said their opponents, would lose money. Those forecasts grew even more confident when the Council's first act was to bring in a six-day week — the unfortunate tram-men, it seemed, had been working sixteen hours a day, seven days a week, while they lasted, to bring their families a living wage. That cut in hours, with no loss of pay and even a rise for lower-paid workers, would cost £13,300 in the first year, it was said. Despite those predictions of doom there was a credit balance of £53,000 at the end of the first year. One-fifth of that went on cutting the hours worked in a

42

day from 11¼ to 10, to produce a 60-hour week, and on free uniforms, the rest went to the rates. Ratepayers and tram-men were both benefiting, to say nothing of the passengers.

For those passengers one of the first benefits was a cut in fares. The LCC had already insisted, in 1891, on cheap fares, at a halfpenny a mile, for workmen. Under LCC administration there came a twopenny workman's return, for any destination reached before 8 a.m. Fares at ½d up to 1,600 yards, 1d up to 2½ miles, 2d up to five miles and 3d above were reckoned, on average, to save LCC Tramway passengers ½d a journey compared to those travelling by private trams.

But electricity brought the change that was to transform the Londoner's life. A contemporary commentator, Charles Masterman, who lived in Camberwell, described a journey by horse tram in 1890. After fights to get on, with the very young and the old being squeezed out, those who gained the interior spent the time crammed tight together, unable to do more than gaze at their neighbours' dismal countenances by the light of smoky oil lamps, for anything up an hour of purgatory. But by 1905 there were 'fast lines of electric trams, brilliantly lighted, in which reading is a pleasure, hurrying us from the bridges in half the time. Each workman has an hour restored to his life.'

Not only that, families were leaving the squalor of Camberwell. Fast trams meant they could move out to four-room cottages in the distant fields of Hither Green and Tooting, even to have gardens of their own. The unknown sight of 'To Let' notices appeared around the hovels of Camberwell as owners were forced to modernize, renovate, clean and decorate before they could hope to find new tenants.

No wonder hundreds of thousands turned out to make 15 May 1903, a fête day, as *The Times* reported, when the first electric tram ran from Westminster Bridge to

Tooting. All in white, with pink cushions on the blue seats, decorated with evergreens, it was boarded by the Prince and Princess of Wales, the future King George V and Queen Mary, with their children who at once sought out the front seats on the top deck that were to become perennial favourites of small boys and girls. After Benn had collected the fares — Royalty, apparently, got even better rates than workmen, for their halfpence covered the full distance of just under six miles — the tram set off at the head of a procession of fifty in the normal LCC livery of purple. All along the way shops were closed, buildings were decorated and the crowds cheered and cheered. The procession took its time. Despite the immense power of the trams, with two 35hp engines each, speed limits made the journey last 45 minutes, but at that it was probably not much slower than the same journey by car or bus in the rush hour today.

But electric trams were not all smooth running for Benn. There was the problem how they should pick up their electricity. He was for the conduit system, as used in the USA, with a shoe running in a groove in the railway, within the track. Though more efficient and less bother than overhead lines, it was dearer, and that, naturally, was seized on by the Opposition. Mostly Benn had his way with conduits. It was a third system, of studs, which could have not only cost Benn dear but also placed restrictions on the whole system of public debate on matters of public concern, which is the essence of democracy. Just as his grandson was to do, in opposing the principle of obligatory inheritance in the peerage, so John Williams Benn found himself in court, fighting for the principle of democratic debate and, of more immediate personal concern, against the loss of a great deal of money. Studs — intermittent electric pick-up points, set in the roadway — would cost only £10,000 or £11,000 a mile, against the £17,000 for continuous conduit, said the Moderates. So, when they took control in 1907, after an election in which the Progressives had been attacked as Wastrels, notably by the Northcliffe press, they had studs installed on an experimental length of tramway in Mile End Road. In the first three weeks nearly a thousand of the studs were found to be live, a horse which kicked one was killed, tramcars caught fire and people gathered from miles around to watch the nightly show of fireworks. One burst of sparks was accompanied by an explosion which hurled an iron cover twice the height of a tram into the air. Benn leapt to the attack, in the *Daily Chronicle*, in *The Times*, and in speeches within the council chamber and outside. The experiment was stopped but the inventor and his engineer colleague sued Benn for libel. In a now notorious verdict the court found for them and levied damages of £12,000 and costs against Benn. A quarter of a million in modern money, it was an impossible sum for a man who, however successful his family business, had never taken a personal fortune from it. Equally outrageous was the demand that he pay over £5,000 at once. Uproar followed in the legal and political world. If the verdict stood, no public man would ever be able to level a public criticism on a matter of public concern without looking over his shoulder for the private dagger in his back. The verdict was overturned on appeal; criticism of 'jerry-built tramways' was criticism of the Moderates, not the inventor, criticism of an inventor's invention should not be regarded as defamation of the inventor — the original judge should have known better, ruled the Lord Justices.

There was one battle, however, that Benn lost which many Londoners may now wish he had won — tram subways. He argued that trams should run just below the road surface, in tunnels which would carry all town services. The ridiculous business of digging up roads to get at sewers, water pipes, gas mains and the like would be ended simultaneously with road congestion. Yerkes had similar sub-surface ideas for his trains, but schemes were sunk by complaints about the disruption such tunnels would cause to existing pipes.

Out of office, though, Benn was to see his tramways spread all over London, to Hampton Court and Uxbridge on the West, Purley in the South, Enfield in the North, Dartford and Chadwell Heath in the East, in other words throughout the *real* area of London, not the reduced, administrative county allowed to the LCC. Trams did not, however, appear on what would have been the most profitable routes, in the City and West End, but even without these they provided a steady income for the rates. Fares remained cheap. Benn's workmen's returns had become part of London life; from 19½ million in 1906 they grew to 81 million in 1919 and 96 million in 1933.

Already, however, a cloud had appeared on Benn's publicly-owned transport horizon, the privately-owned bus. It was to be many years before it supplanted his electric trams, and probably it would never have done so but for the Second World War and the inflated maintenance bills imposed on the tramways after it. Any advance made by the bus in the beginning, Benn claimed, was due to unfair advantages, to the support of the Moderates who, natural supporters of a privately-owned rival to their own public system, held back on tramway extensions, and due to the argument, since taken up by railway supporters, that the road-using vehicle did not pay off the costs of the wear and tear it inflicted on its running surface, while the tracked vehicle did. When a committee was set up in 1913 to inquire into the bus versus tram question, Benn produced what he thought were unassailable arguments: To carry the same number of people as the Council's 1,400 trams, it would take 3,211 buses; the trams, with proper safety intervals, occupied 17 miles of street route, the buses would need 32½ miles; if the 512,653 people carried by trams had to pay the extra fares demanded by buses they would be mulcted of an extra £640,000 a year. The committee agreed. Trams, they reported, had 50 per cent more seats, they could accelerate and decelerate faster and had a higher speed, they were less prone to accidents, cost less to run, did not damage the roadway, and could run in fog and snow, when buses could not. The one advantage of the bus was its flexibility — and that advantage has since outweighed all other arguments.

Benn's trams have now gone, however much the nostalgic may regret it, however much some transport authorities may point to their continuing, indeed growing role in other countries. Even Benn's workmen's tickets have gone. He would relish the fact, though, that London's public transport is now even more firmly in the hands of London's government than he ever expected to achieve, and he would feel not a little affinity with the GLC leaders who find themselves in conflict with the government on the other side of the Thames in their efforts to subsidize fares. In his day, he might point out, it was the fares which subsidized the ratepayers.

Benn had a hand in all the early achievements of the LCC. With John Burns he fought for and won the principle of direct labour, when the Council felt it was being overcharged by contractors — in those days direct labour proved the cheaper. With the beginnings of home supplies of electricity he proposed the Council should be a mass supplier of cheap power to boroughs, instead of each individual borough having to make its own expensive arrangements. The power station built at Greenwich for his trams, the counterpart of Yerkes's at Lots Road, was to have been the nucleus of an overall London generating system. Benn's plan failed and to get what he thought best, he had to move from his normal stand on public ownership of public monopolies. His hopes of municipal control having faded, he supported a Bill for a private company to have the overall control he believed necessary for an efficient, cheap supply.

London owes its modern water supply, the equal of any

city in the world, to the labours of Benn and his colleagues. Today when any air traveller flying into Heath-
row can see how well provided London is with reservoirs,
when the only real reason for ever limiting supplies in
times of drought is to save upsetting less well-served citizens elsewhere, it is hard to realize that in Benn's time
most summers brought shortages and cut off supplies, and
one in three threatened a water famine.

A number of companies shared the spoils as water
charges rose steadily through the nineteenth century,
while their own costs generally fell. After a period of
cut-throat competition those north of the Thames had
succeeded in partitioning out their customers and had
become a series of monopolies. South of the Thames
there was still the occasional area which had two suppliers, even, sometimes, to the extent of opposite sides of
a street having different mains. This situation provided
a bonus, above the rewards of competition, when
brighter-than-average doctors noticed that those fortunate
households which got their water from a company which
had moved its intake upstream above Teddington Weir
had fewer cases of cholera, in one epidemic, than those
whose water still came from where sewage washed up and
down the Thames. Previously it was accepted the disease
came from 'bad air and miasma' and the leaders of the
profession still held rigorously to that view for a few years
more.

In the 1890's most samples of London water submitted
for analysis showed higher than acceptable numbers of
intestinal bacteria, showing the presence of imperfectly
filtered sewage. The Council could still be told, in one
debate, of one court in Poplar where 86 people lived in
ten rooms with but one water tap between them, turned
on for only four hours in the 24. A councillor told how,
when he turned on his own tap after supplies had supposedly been restored, a worm three inches long wriggled
out.

Throughout that decade the struggle went on to buy out the private water companies. It was a matter on which the City Corporation, which had lost its own control of London water three centuries before, was at one with the Progressive leadership of the Council, even to the extent, on one occasion, of inviting them to dinner — Benn and Burns stayed away. Sometimes Moderates joined with the Progressives in the plan to bring water under municipal control and Benn managed to get a two to one majority for this even in the hung council of 1895. But when that happened the Government proved an insurmountable obstacle. Eventually the council had to accept the handing over of water to a separate public body as the best it could get, the LCC paying almost all the costs and having less than a quarter of the seats on the new body. All the time, of course, the private companies had been raising their price. In the 1880's they had asked £27,000,000 for assets put at £12,250,000. The price eventually paid in 1902 was £47,000,000.

Benn was Chairman of the LCC in 1904. After the Progressives lost power in 1907 he was Leader of the Opposition for his remaining years. On his death in 1922 he was the sole survivor of the original council formed in 1889, having served continuously all that time.

First knighted in 1906, Benn was made a baronet in 1914 and his baronetcy was to reveal another talent in him, for heraldry. When told, after two years, that he must have a coat of arms and that the standard fee was £70, he designed his own. Back it came from the College of Heralds with a large red hand emblazoned across it, the sign of the order of baronetcy. It was a sad thing, commented Benn, that he, a lifelong teetotaller, should, in his declining years, have to advertise Bass bottled beer.

CHAPTER FOUR

Into Parliament

John Williams was also the first of the Benns to sit in Parliament, though it must be admitted that the stir he created there was nothing to that caused by the manner of his arrival. He had the advantage of a family connection when he accepted a Liberal invitation to stand, in the 1892 election, for St George's-in-the-East. In this constituency lay the Cable Street area where his father had been so loved a figure and where he had made his first reputation as a Sunday-School-outing entertainer. But against him was a man who, if not loved as Julius had been loved, was enormously respected. The Rt Hon C. T. Ritchie was admired, and liked, as one of the most enlightened Conservatives at a time when enlightenment was not necessarily the first quality among Conservatives to spring to mind. Even Benn's position as an LCC member of rapidly growing reputation was as nothing against Ritchie's as President of the Local Government Board. Indeed Benn could be charged with a political form of parricide in tackling him, for it had been Ritchie who had been author of the Local Government Act which had brought the LCC into being.

'A bold man' is how Ritchie described Benn, 'a forlorn hope' was the pre-contest verdict by even Liberal papers. Perhaps, though, they underrated the regard in which the name Benn was held. 'A friend in every alley, a welcome in every court' was what the young challenger found canvassing. He drew on his childhood memories when he wrote his election address, calling for reform. All his emphasis was on matters to relieve the life of the poor. Perhaps they, the pundits, underestimated the mood of the Stepney working class, the appeal of Benn's support for trade unions to fight employers of sweated labour, for a shorter working day, for electoral reform under the cry 'one man, one vote' — a man could be temporarily dis-enfranchized in those days just for moving from one par-ish to another. 'Better drains' struck almost as strong a chord as 'better homes' among those whose support he sought. When told he had no support among respectable people he replied, 'I aspire to the honour of being the member for the back streets'. He did not aspire in vain. Perhaps also Ritchie's appeal had been overestimated. After all, it was known he had been by no means a warm and loving parent to his offspring, the LCC. He had even refused it pocket-money in the form of a petty cash account, in a then famous squabble with Lord Rosebery. His vote against equalization of rates, when poorer areas were proportionately overcharged, and his support for the landlord against the tenant had roused the ire of some of his erstwhile supporters. On the other hand Benn's attack on the demon drink, when one in five business premises in the area was a licensed drinking house, made for a stormy campaign. At the height of the election fever gangs of roughs stormed Benn meetings — Lord Rosebery pre-sented his rising young protégé with a gold chronometer to replace the watch stolen in one scrimmage. From the Liberal leader Gladstone came another souvenir, after the count, a message 'Brave Benn', for Benn got in by 398 votes, with 1,661 to 1,263, and Ritchie was the only Cabinet Minister defeated in the election.

In Parliament, Benn admitted later, he was not a great talking member, though, of necessity, a great walking one. After two years in the House he told his constituents he estimated he had walked between thirty and forty miles in and out of the lobbies. Parliament, he suggested, might take a lesson from the LCC on how to conduct its busi-ness. Even if he had not talked all that much himself he had taken note of others who did. During the previous year three members had been on their feet, asking questions or making speeches, almost 1,500 times, one 429 times, a second 532 and the third 533 times. If all members had exercised their rights in such a way there would have been 300,000 speeches and questions that year. In fact, he calculated, all the average back-bench member could expect for a year's speechifying or questioning was an hour and a half, though the one with 533 appearances had clocked 44 hours.

Benn was not a great one for matters of general politics or affairs of state. He was more likely to make his voice heard on such topics as allotments for the unemployed, pointing out, of course, how well the LCC had done in such matters. Optimistically, when the House was discussing plans for the Thames Conservancy, he promised fly-fishing near, if not actually off, the Terrace 'in a few years' as a result of the Council's pure river policies. It was 80 years before the LCC was organizing fishing parties in the Thames. But he was a little more accurate about the future of the telephone than the then Postmaster-General, Arnold Morley. Benn looked to the day when ordinary people would order their groceries by phone. Nonsense, replied Morley, it was a luxury and could never be brought down, like the penny post, for the use of the masses. Benn was once again objecting to a private company's monopoly of what should be a public service and was demanding the Post Office should allow London to provide its own telephone service.

The next election, in 1895, was real Eatanswill stuff. The relatively mild-mannered Ritchie had departed the scene, to find a seat elsewhere, and his place was taken by someone of an entirely different mould. This was Harry Marks, would-be newspaper tycoon, proprietor of the *Financial News*, whose own financial affairs had left others feeling bruised on both sides of the Atlantic but who had been taken up by the Conservative Party — later it was to drop him hurriedly when the scandal grew too great. Gladstone was gone and the Liberals were due to take a hammering, but Benn trusted in the loyalty of the poorer section of the 3,000 electorate to the Benn name. If contemporary reports are right, Marks found a more basic appeal than that to their hearts and heads, one to their stomachs. He doled out tickets for free meals at the Marks soup kitchen. There were attempts to blacken Benn's name by a series of court cases over the previous election, all of which failed, and Benn was probably misguided in replying to calumny by quoting Marks's own clashes with the law. At the end of a campaign rowdy even for these days, Marks was home by four votes. Benn demanded a recount. This time Marks's majority was eleven, but 24 votes were held back for a decision by judge. Benn petitioned for a reversal of the result, claiming that votes had been cast by Marks agents falsely claiming to be voters and that Marks had also bribed and treated real electors. From court records it seems he had a strong case. Marks admitted handing out soup tickets and general over-spending. The whole matter was so befogged, however, perhaps because Marks spent £10,000 on his legal costs, that these peccadilloes were disregarded. The Court considered more serious a counter-petition against Benn that he had failed to charge for a room in his house used for the election. Benn had unwisely acted as his own agent and probably did not know all the niceties of electoral law, but it hardly seems to have been a matter of great moment that he failed to increase his election costs by paying rent to himself when his total expenditure was well inside the allowed limit. Some of his followers had been so misguided as to put a stiff backing on photographs of Benn, thus turning them, in the eyes of the learned judges, into banners. Photos were allowed, banners were not. In the event Benn was excluded from standing again at St George's-in-the-East for seven years.

Naturally, the Liberal *Daily Chronicle* was outraged that Benn's actions were regarded as so gross while

Marks, who had admitted 'spending money right and left, standing drinks, sociable evenings at the Conservative Club, soup tickets by the thousand', got away with it. But even *The Times* expressed its concern at an abuse of the law.

Benn was obviously tough. Even after such treatment he was back in the electoral field again two years later. His seven-year disbarment only applied to St George's and a by-election came up in Deptford, regarded as a very safe Conservative seat. It was Benn's doubtful privilege to find himself playing the leading role in a new type of electioneering, one to loom large in the coming century, pillorying by newspaper. Marks's feelings for Benn had not softened, perhaps he regretted that £10,000. At any rate he had acquired the *Sun* newspaper — described contemporaneously as 'an evening newspaper of a suitably gutter type' — which he later transferred to that other entrepreneurial pillar, Horatio Bottomley. Day after day it came out with violent attacks on Benn, mostly seemingly libellous. The climax was one not even reached by Northcliffe and Rothermere in the heyday of their striving for political influence, a free copy, on the morning of the election, devoted entirely to attacks on Benn.

Even so Benn cut the Tory majority by over a thousand. It was John Burns who, in trenchant turn-of-the-century oratory, set down why, in the eyes of Benn's workers, that Tory majority had not been turned into a Liberal one. Standing precariously on top of the carriage in which he and Benn had been travelling away from the count, halted by a crowd of indignant supporters, he declared; 'This election has been won by a newspaper owned by blackguards, edited by scoundrels and with the mark of the beast on every page'.

The Khaki Election of 1900 found Benn in Bermondsey, suffering from the handicap of lack of enthusiasm for the South African war at a time when the nation was in a jingoistic frenzy, already celebrating victory, albeit prematurely. Again, too, he had to face Marksian intervention, this time in the form of a last-minute pamphlet, allegedly an account of his political life.

A mixture of vague approximations to the truth with downright lies, it illustrates why the Benns appear to have a hereditary dislike of the Press. The grandson might find familiar one claim against his grandfather, that he was no poor man but, in reality, a wealthy capitalist, but not such other charges that he was against trade unions uniting in self-defence, was for the House of Lords and favoured fat pensions for the wealthy. It may have been enough to turn the tide again. Benn lost by 300 votes but again cut a Tory majority in an election which had found Liberals swept away like thistledown in a summer breeze.

The pamphlet had the hallmark of Marks and Bottomley but it bore the imprint of McCorquodale's, the printers. From them Benn exacted damages of £300 and costs.

That seems to have made Marks and Co pause to think. At least Benn was given a fairly easy run by the Press the next time he stood. The best it could do, and that in the respectable, though none-the-less anti-Benn *Daily Telegraph*, was to call him an 'adventurous cockney carpetbagger'. Perhaps it was simply that they thought his cause was hopeless, for the by-election he fought in June 1904 provided as sensational a Liberal win in its day as Orpington was to do half a century later. The difference was that it signalled a Liberal majority to come in the general election which followed in 1906.

Benn had been invited to fight an apparently hopeless cause at Devonport, which was to have connections, also, with another great political family, the Foots. He could not fight that on the local issues of London, the most he could hope was that his record on fair wages at the LCC would help him with the dockyard workers. Against that his opponent, a local man and a big employer, by no means unwilling to point to his own importance in providing jobs, had the Tory record of heavy expenditure in rebuilding the Navy.

Benn took the orthodox Liberal line, emphasizing electoral reform, including the abolition of the vote of the House of Lords, but with one Benn addition — temperance. Incredibly, in a town of rum naval tradition he made it a main plank of his campaign. He was not a 'bigoted teetotaller', he declared, just a total abstainer who objected to the Government's feather-bedding of the liquor business, a feather-bedding to be further softened by a Bill then before the House.

'What have the licensed trade done that they should be petted and aided and abetted by the Government?' he asked in one speech. 'Are not the butcher, the baker and the candlestick-maker as respectable and as useful as the vendor of strong drinks?'

Again it was a matter of private monopolies, the breweries, to which he objected. 'I deplore very much that the old days of the respectable publican who was proud of his house and of the way he kept it, and who saw that it was a place of refreshment for man and beast, in the proper sense of those words, has been superseded by the great liquor syndicates.'

The question for Radicals and Democrats, Benn argued, was whether they or the licensed trade should rule the country. At the moment, if the proper label were hung over the House of Commons it would read 'Bung and Co's Entire'. That should be pulled down and 'Under entirely new management' put in its place.

That is just what happened. Benn won, a feeble, last-minute attempt to raise the old St George's disqualification issue, in a reprint of an article in the local *Western Morning News*, being quashed by a simple reference to the damages awarded after Bermondsey. When news of Benn's majority of over 1,000 in a total poll of 13,000 reached the House there were calls of 'Resign' and Asquith, who had taken over as Liberal leader, declared it was notice to the Government to quit or at least give up its attempt to mollycoddle the brewers with its new Licensing Bill. Despite that the Tories held on, to push through their Bill, but when they went to the country they suffered their worst electoral defeat ever.

Devonport may have sent Benn back to the Commons but it was the role of 'member for the LCC' which he quickly resumed. Understandably, perhaps, when education came up for debate in the Commons he spoke on the burdens the Conservative Education Act of 1903 had put not on the local Devon council but on the LCC. He was, by then, Chairman of the Council. The handing over of voluntary schools to local councils, and their taking on the work of the School Boards, was, he implied, a continuation of Tory tactics to discredit the Progressives by making them put enormous new burdens on the ratepayers.

An architect had surveyed the 438 schools the Council was made to take over and found only 64 satisfactory and a quarter of the total so bad it would be impossible to bring them up to LCC requirements. Ninety-two would have to be closed at once, so would parts of 26 others. The Council would have to find 70,000 new school places, at a cost of £224,000 a year. The total cost of the Act to the Council, which had never asked for it, would be over half a million a year. The Government should help the Council and its ratepayers.

The cost of running the LCC was obviously a worry to him. The theme ran through his speech when he took the Council's Chair. Office accommodation was a growing problem. The Council had far outgrown its original premises in Spring Gardens. Its departments sprawled around in a score of buildings and the rent bill had risen fivefold to £26,000. There must be, he declared, a County Hall worthy of London's Council. He was to see it, though never as an MP looking south across the Thames from the terraces of the House of Commons, an infuriating spectacle to those Tory MPs who, like one in a letter to the *Daily Telegraph* in June 1982, call for its powers to be returned to the Palace of Westminster, for the clock to be turned back a hundred years. At least if Benn had seen his original proposal come about they would have been spared the sight. He wanted a County Hall as part of the splendid new Kingsway the Council was building in place of the slums it had swept away.

In that same speech, Benn expressed his concern about new slums. In one prophetic section he condemned the coming ghettos, the way sections of the populace were being herded into special districts. It was not division of race which worried him, but the divisions of class, the way the customs of centuries, during which rich and poor had lived almost side by side, were being broken. The wealthy, he protested, were pushing the slum dwellers out of their districts, into those already burdened with an excess of the poor.

With what might be considered another foretaste of the future, he used for his peroration those lines of William Blake which have become a battle hymn for the Labour Party:

I will not cease from mental fight,
Nor shall my sword sleep in my hand,
Till we have built Jerusalem,
In England's green and pleasant land.

For it was to become apparent, if not to John Williams then to his son, William Wedgwood, ('Wedgie' Benn), that the nineteenth-century radicalism in which the Benns were steeped no longer fitted the Liberal Party, their place was with the Labour Party.

Why the name 'Wedgie' is a bit of a mystery, and Tony, if he knows, is unwilling to throw light on it. There is a vague family connection, through marriage, with the pottery family, through a town clerk of Stoke who was an offshoot of the Wedgwoods. But that goes back five generations and seems hardly strong enough to have established as firm a grip as it did, until Tony severed it. That would also smack of a sense of family connection which seems a little too snobbish for John Williams. Like John Williams's own second name it may well have come not from the female line of the family but from an admired fellow-member of the Congregational Church. To a strong Congregationalist, who eventually saw his equally strongly religious, but Anglican wife join the field, such an origin may well have given the name a lasting appeal which was so obviously imparted to John Williams's second son.

'Wedgie', who had benefited from his trips to Paris by acquiring a first-class degree in French at University College, London, at first worked in the family publishing business. After a few years, in 1906, the irresistible call of politics, for a Benn, took hold and he left his brother Ernest to join his father in the House of Commons. His arrival there was doubly delightful for John Williams because his son came representing his old seat, from which he felt he had been cheated, in the streets, at the poll and in court, St George's-in-the-East. Wedgwood Benn did a round of jobs as parliamentary secretary, at the Treasury, Board of Education and the Admiralty and, after retaining his seat in 1910, a year, like 1974, of two general elections, was made a Junior Whip. By then his father's parliamentary career had ended. John Williams lost Devonport by 140 votes in the first of the 1910 elections but had the satisfaction, in the second, of reducing the Tory majority at the then seemingly cast-iron Conservative certainty of Clapham, a seat his son had asked him to contest.

William Wedgwood Benn was small, determined, possessed of abounding energy. It was not for nothing that Winston Churchill nicknamed him 'The Pocket Hercules'. Earlier, however, he had been known as 'Buttons' for his juvenile appearance, agile movements and his eagerness to serve his political superiors as he bounded around the House on the duties of a Junior Whip.

When war came in 1914 he quickly decided that running the National Relief Fund, a follow-up to the work he had done organizing relief for families during the dockers' strike of 1912, was not enough. Despite his size he obtained a commission in the Middlesex Yeomanry and soon found himself in the Near East for a personal war which reads like instalments of a *Boy's Own* serial. After a fairly orthodox introduction, fighting on the heights above Suvla Bay at Gallipoli, he joined the Egyptian Royal Naval Air Service as an observer. There he took part in the pinpoint bombing of the Baghdad railway, won a DSO for his part in the sinking of an enemy ship and survived not only the ditching of his plane in the Mediterranean but also the sinking of an improvised aircraft-carrier by shore batteries. Unorthodoxy was his way. Like 'Popski' in the Second World War, from whose barely authorized activities grew the Long Range Desert Group and the Special Air Service, Benn formed his own private army, of French sailors, for long-range guerrilla activities behind the Turkish lines, then, putting his men's skills to their proper use, indulged in a little privateering in the Red Sea.

It was impressive enough for Lloyd George, always ready to use the propaganda value of a war hero, to offer Benn the job of Chief Whip when he temporarily returned to England in 1916. Anybody who could keep such a ragbag in order in the Near East would have little trouble controlling MPs, Lloyd George must have thought. But Benn had returned just to train as a pilot and had other plans. He returned to the Mediterranean, this time to Italy. There he organized another novel departure in warfare, the first parachuting of secret-service agents behind enemy lines.

Apart from his DSO, 'Wedgie' earned the Distinguished Flying Cross, two mentions in despatches, the

Croix de Guerre, the Italian War Cross, the Italian Bronze Medal for Valour and was made a Chevalier of the Legion of Honour.

His nickname now, among his constituents, was 'The Man with Seven Decorations' and though, according to that list it should have been eight, seven was enough to have considerable electoral value. He had already proved himself a most able electioneer, speeding around his constituencies, holding far more street-corner meetings than anyone else would have considered possible, summoning an audience by the simple medium of ringing a handbell. Lord Hailsham, or Quintin Hogg, who owed to Tony Benn his opportunity to renounce his peerage and return to active politics in the Commons, was forestalled in his discovery of the political advantages of the handbell by Tony's father.

'Wedgie' quickly resumed his political career, though not as MP for the familiar family scene of East London. He found that St George's had been merged with another constituency. He stood down in favour of a fellow Liberal, and instead, went north to Leith, to a seat he held through three more general elections. In his second spell in the House he proved to be one of those MPs who might well have awakened his father's statistical interest during his quieter first spell. His fervent radicalism was becoming an anachronism in the Liberal Party. Some of his opponents found him prejudiced and emotional but he earned the encomium, from Lord Halifax, a very orthodox Tory who was to be Foreign Secretary and a candidate for the premiership, of being 'one of two of the best Parliamentarians of my time'. The other was Lord Winterton, who outstayed Benn in the Commons to be Father of the House.

However good a Parliamentarian he was, he was not so steady a party man, at least not in the eyes of Lloyd George. The man whom the leader once wanted to be Chief Whip proved an intolerable burden to his later whips. Benn had been an Asquith man, resentful of Lloyd George, and was more often to be found voting with Labour than with the Liberals. Eventually, in 1927, he joined the Labour Party.

In his statement of explanation he declared, 'For some time I have questioned the truth of an economic outlook based on the theory of private enterprise and free competition . . . The substitution of public service for private profit is no new ideal for me who was brought up by my father to believe in the municipal socialism of the London Progressive Party of 1889.'

Perhaps those were different days, perhaps politicians were readier to admit that the electors' votes were cast more for a party than a person, perhaps Benn's principles were made of sterner stuff, but, unlike more recent examples of changing allegiances, Benn resigned his Liberal seat before assuming his Labour colours.

'This decision,' his statement went on, 'involves the honourable obligation to resign my seat. I have always recognized that obligation as being unconditional.'

Not that that made much of an interruption to his career, though the Leith Labour Party already had a candidate. He was soon back in the House, although he had to travel even further north to find a constituency, this time in North Aberdeen, where he won a by-election in 1928. Soon he was sitting immediately behind Ramsay MacDonald, often whispering into the Labour leader's ear, and high office was predicted for him.

In the Labour Government that came to power after the general election of the following year he became Secretary of State for India, the first Benn to be a cabinet minister and privy councillor. He started under the handicap of a controversial political trial at Meerut, shrugged that off by promising India dominion status, stood by the law to order the arrest of Gandhi when he began his campaign of civil disobedience, but saw his release for the talks with the Viceroy which led to the Delhi pact.

Wedgwood Benn had proved himself a firm minister of principle in a government not renowned for that quality. By the time the London Round Table talks took place, however, Benn was out of office. He refused to go with Ramsay MacDonald into his National Government, remaining loyal to the Labour Party. That loyalty cost him his seat in the landslide general election which followed. Defeated again in 1935 he got back to the House in 1937, in time for the bitter disagreements on how best to resist the rise of Fascism and Nazism which coloured the next two years.

He joined up immediately on the outbreak of war. He had been forty at the end of the First World War, he was over sixty when he reported for the Second as the most decorated pilot officer in the RAF. The slight, elderly figure, with an RAF raincoat buttoned across his chest, drew a few puzzled glances from the fledgling officers at the induction meeting but puzzlement turned to admiration when, one of the welcoming officers failing to turn up, he unbuttoned that raincoat to reveal three rows of ribbons and gave an hour-long talk on the European situation.

Despite his age 'Wedgie' got himself on operations, earning another mention. He was found out, officially grounded but given the rank of air commodore as part of the branch of the RAF devoted to boosting its image. By 1942 that was truly taking coals to Newcastle. Benn was called to the Lords as Viscount Stansgate to strengthen the Labour representation there. Not that that was the end of his war effort. His work in the First World War was recalled and he was made Vice-president of the Allied Central Commission in Italy.

After the war he was Secretary of State for Air in the first post-War Labour government, but only for a year or so. When it was decided to merge the separate services in a Ministry of Defence he resigned. After that he reverted to the back benches and to the radical views of his

63

youth. His was the voice of the Liberalism of his youth and of his father. It was also the voice of parliamentary democracy. For ten years, from 1947, he was World President of the Inter-Parliamentary Union.

Witty, enthusiastic, a good speaker, Wedgwood Benn earned deep friendships and respect but beneath an often urbane exterior lay deeply held convictions which could drive him to belligerence in debate. Like many small men he could be very peppery. He once provoked Winston Churchill into one of his better parliamentary retorts: 'The honourable gentleman should not generate more indignation than he can conveniently contain!' On the other hand he once had the better of Lloyd George, whom he had provoked into describing him, in a variant of the Churchillian tag, as a 'pocket Moses'. Quick came the reply, 'Ah, but I never worshipped at the golden calf.' For once the golden-pocketed as well as golden-tongued Welshman, a wizard in financial matters as well as parliamentary, was left speechless.

When he died, in 1960, Viscount Stansgate left £36,837, after estate duty of £9,983, in trust to his wife for life, then to be divided equally between his sons Anthony and David — David is a barrister.

In its obituary of him *The Times* wrote:

Few could rival his knowledge of procedure or match his mastery of the niceties of debate. His sharp brown eyes could pierce to the heart of any sham; they could also blaze with righteous fury and twinkle with fun. He was relentless in exposing shoddy argument, hypocrisy and inconsistency. With a vivacity which could electrify the dullest debate he had a galvanic effect on the House of Lords.

But, however galvanic, it is debatable now if his effect on the country, including the House of Lords, was longer lasting than that of his elder brother Ernest, discounting, of course, his effect through fathering Tony. That, however profound it turns out to be on the country, has been revolutionary on the Lords.

While 'Wedgie' stuck to radical liberalism, moving from the Liberal to the Labour party in the process, Ernest developed his more personal form of libertarian liberalism, which almost took him into Parliament in the safe Conservative seat of East Surrey in the mid 1930's. While 'Wedgie' stuck to the Labour Party during the Great Depression, Ernest was busy attacking swollen state expenditure, proclaiming what would now be accepted as purest Friedmann-Thatcherite monetarism. The individualist movement he founded could have had the banner 'The State the Enemy'. If today the concept of personal liberty is so fashionable, prevailing over the concept of personal duty to society, it is due in no little measure to Ernest Benn, to the societies he founded, the twenty books and eleven pamphlets he wrote, his regular journalism, all in the cause of the freedom of the individual.

'Wedgie' also stuck to the religion of his forbears. Religion shared his life with politics. His wife shared his religious life, perhaps to a greater degree than she shared his political one.

Margaret Eddie Holmes was the daughter of Liberal MP Daniel Turner Holmes, returned for Govan, Lanarkshire, in 1911. She paid her first visit to Westminster the following year, at the age of eleven, having to sign a solemn undertaking, with her mother, that they would make no disturbance in the House, for the suffragette movement was then at its height.

Whatever her views, at that tender age, of woman's place in politics, Margaret was far more concerned, throughout her life, with what she considered to be woman's rightful place in the Church — in the pulpit. Wedgwood Benn was already a rising young MP but, of course, a Londoner and not among the group of Scottish Liberals she met. Ten years later he was, and he and Margaret were married in a fashionable wedding at St Margaret's, Westminster. He, a Congregationalist, held any religious abhorrence he might have had of those surroundings well in check for the occasion. His wife was then still an Anglican.

When he became Secretary of State for India she, at 32, was by far the youngest Cabinet Minister's wife. Out of office and out of Parliament, in the mid-1930's, Mr and Mrs Benn travelled the world, meeting political and industrial leaders. Perhaps it was a spiritual sense, rather than a political or industrial one, which enabled her to see deep into Henry Ford, into the well-spring of his personal self-satisfaction, which seems to have escaped other observers.

'Do you believe in reincarnation?' she asked.

'Yes, madam,' he replied, taking life anew at the question. 'I believe I've been on this Earth millions and millions of times before.'

His present position, he made her feel, represented the accumulated success of his previous achievements.

When, as Viscountess Stansgate, she accompanied her husband on his travels as head of the Inter-Parliamentary Union, she met Eisenhower, Nehru (she had already met Gandhi when he was in London), Nasser, Ho Chi Minh, Chou en Lai and many other world leaders. But it all seems to have left her unmoved, or rather did not take one scrap of her attention from matters less worldly but more important in her view. In the 1930's she had studied the Bible in Hebrew and Greek, at King's College, London, as part of a theological course, proving able to read from the Hebrew Tanach to Ben-Gurion later. She knew too much Hebrew to be a Zionist, commented that non-Zionist founder of Israel. She was already deeply involved in the interfaith dialogue between Christians and Jews. Already too, she was at odds with the Anglican leadership over the ordination of women.

While she was still in her twenties, Margaret braved

the head of the Church, then Archbishop Davidson, in his lair at Lambeth Palace to receive his description of himself as a 'firm feminist in the secular realm, essentially opposed to the priesthood of women'.

She was a founder member of the inter-denominational Society for the Ordination of Women. During the Second World War she was able, under the Chaplain's Department, to work on the religious welfare of women in the Forces. After the war, when her husband was Secretary of State for Air she won a notable victory when the Reverend Elsie Chamberlain was appointed the first woman chaplain to the Forces.

But it was the Church of England's inflexible position not only on the ordination of women but the whole ecumenical movement in the late 1940's and 1950's which found her joining the Congregational Church of her husband. For twenty years she was happy there but, in what outsiders might think a bizarre move away from her previous efforts for Church unity, she objected when, in 1972, Congregationalists voted almost three to one for union with the Presbyterians. The basic principles of Congregationalism, she believed, as Tony has reported, would be submerged beneath a new system of remote control. So she gathered around her a band of opponents to the merger, to form the Congregational Federation. She became its president and, in a triumphant conclusion to her fight for the feminine movement in the Church, was the first lay-woman to head a Christian denomination.

It was to that redoubtable man and woman, each of strong if unusual principles and both utterly determined in their application, that Tony Benn was born — then, of course, Anthony Neil Wedgwood Benn — in 1925. He was the second son. His elder brother, Michael, was directed as positively by his mother towards the ministry as he was, by his father's title, to the Lords. Both boys followed their father into the RAF but Michael, a pilot, was killed in 1944.

CHAPTER FIVE

Peggy: An Interlude With Someone Not So Well-Known — As A Benn

One afternoon towards the end of the year 1905, a serious-looking girl of thirteen was day-dreaming behind the starched lace curtains of the front room of one of a row of Victorian red-brick villas in Wimbledon, in south-west London. She may have been imagining herself the great actress she was convinced she could be, despite her rather plain looks. Perhaps she was just wondering what colour this year's party frock, with its elegant smocking, might be, due soon to arrive from her rich relations, the Benns. Her thoughts, though, were not so far away that she failed to notice and wonder about the shabby, elderly, bearded man who was picking his way along the pavement outside, looking at house numbers. As he turned into the front gate the girl ran to open the door.

'Are you Peggy?' he asked. 'I have a message for you from your father.'

'I'm Peggy,' replied the girl, 'but my father's dead.'

'He is very much alive,' said the stranger. 'He sends you his love.'

Then, as the girl looked in disbelief, he added, 'Your father's shut up in Broadmoor.'

At that he turned and walked away, leaving the girl conscious that something terrible had happened to her, though what she did not know.

'Aunt Bessie,' she asked her guardian who had come downstairs to see who the visitor was, 'what's Broadmoor?'

For Aunt Bessie the moment had come which she had been dreading for years. As she had vowed to do, if this happened, she told her.

'Broadmoor is the asylum for the criminally insane.'

'My father is not dead, why did you tell me he was,' said the now weeping girl as her weeping aunt took her into her arms.

'His is a living death,' were the aunt's words of explanation, the girl told the very few closest to her in later life.*

Perhaps it was that experience, rather than anything in her heredity which caused the girl to suffer herself, thereafter, from bouts of depression which sent her into the care of nursing homes 'to get fit for the world again', as she used to say, between films and plays.

Despite that she was to grow up to become perhaps Britain's best-loved actress, Dame Margaret Rutherford. Charles Chaplin called her 'my favourite actress'. To Donald Wolfit she was a great tragic actress as well as a great comedienne. Royal princes and princesses were to bring her piles of autograph books, from their school friends, for her to sign. Dining at Buckingham Palace she was to be allotted the special place, for a lady guest, alongside the Queen's consort.

But then it is no wonder that, being a Benn, she had the determination as well as the talent to overcome what might have seemed impossible odds.

William Rutherford Benn, then 27, had been married to Florence Nicholson, 24, at All Saints, Wandsworth, on 16 December, 1882. Florence's parents were dead and one of her sisters had committed suicide by drowning. The strong character in the family was Bessie, her unmarried elder sister, Florence's bridesmaid. Florence was herself a frail, romantic, unworldly girl who had fallen in love with William the poet, not William the man.

Florence was quite unprepared for the physical side of marriage and soon doctors were consulted about the husband's strange moodiness and irritability. They blamed

* As reported by one of the very few, her adopted daughter, Dawn Simmons.

69

his incipient breakdown on failure to consummate the marriage and gave that diagnosis on the medical reports which accompanied him to the Bethnal House Asylum, where he was sent on the family doctor's advice, while Florence returned to her sister Bessie's Wimbledon villa.

That first stay in an asylum was short. His second was to last seven years. After one appearance before a magistrate on 27 March, 1883, charged with murdering his father, he became so incoherent that he was removed to Broadmoor without any further legal proceedings. Doctors reported he would never recover his sanity, the Home Secretary ordered his removal and the case against him was abandoned.

After those seven years, though, the Broadmoor doctors decided their previous opinion was too pessimistic. He was fit to be discharged, into the care of his brother, John Williams Benn. Florence had been writing to him almost every day and they set up house in Balham, changing their name by deed poll to Rutherford. William resumed his occupation of silk merchant.

Their earlier marital troubles were evidently past. On 11 May with Aunt Bessie acting as midwife, Florence gave birth at home to a daughter, to be named Margaret Taylor Rutherford.

Local records show the Rutherfords continued to live at the house in Dernton Road, Balham, for the next two years. Then they disappeared from the neighbourhood and, according to an account attributed to Aunt Bessie, the little family moved to India. Florence wrote to Bessie of William's efforts to 'redeem himself'. He was devoting himself to the poor, nursing the sick through cholera epidemics in the slums of Madras and Delhi, just as he remembered his father doing in the slums of the East End of London. Among the many letters Margaret received in later life from admirers was one from an Englishman who recalled first staying with her father in Delhi and then being nursed by him through an attack of fever in Madras.

That letter was found among her treasures when she died. Margaret herself said she could only remember the heat and the white pony which her parents gave her on her birthday — her sixth birthday she later recalled, wondering what had happened to the animal.

Florence became pregnant again and at once was restless and disturbed. They were, so it has been said, still in India and William telegraphed to Aunt Bessie, asking her to come. Before her bags were packed, though, a second cable came, saying Florence and her baby were dead. Three months later the distraught father, clutching his small daughter by the hand, appeared at the Wimbledon villa to tell Bessie her sister had hanged herself.

That story is Margaret Rutherford's. In her autobiography she just refers to being sent home to Aunt Bessie after the death of her mother, her father dying tragically, shortly afterwards. To her closest theatrical friends, including her understudy Lucy Griffiths, she confided that her mother had hanged herself. The mature woman's memory, though, may just have reflected the nightmares born of the small girl's confused understanding of what was happening.

A death certificate has been found recording Florence's death at Aunt Bessie's Wimbledon home, in the presence of her husband. The cause was given by a local doctor as 'nervous exhaustion, four years, weak heart'. The date was 22 May 1896. Margaret was just four years old.

William may have gone back to India, after a holiday in Paris, given the bereaved husband by the Englishman he had nursed in Madras. Benn family records suggest he was there in the later 1890s, even suggest he had a child there. By the turn of the century he was back in England, for, in October 1902, he was admitted to another asylum, Northumberland House. Fifteen months later, again showing homicidal tendencies, he was back in Broadmoor. There he stayed until 1921 when, in poor health after a stroke, he was moved to the City of London

Asylum, near Dartford, Kent. He died there, from pneumonia, on 4 August that year, aged sixty-six. On his death certificate his address was recorded as 4 Berkeley Place, Wimbledon — Aunt Bessie's home.

One possible way out of the confusion which fits what few facts we have, and Margaret Rutherford's recollections, is that he did not go to India until after Florence's death. For the two previous years when, according to the Benn records, he had 'disappeared from Balham', his home was in Wimbledon. Florence had given up the task of trying to run her own home in her state of nervous exhaustion.

Peggy may have been given a sixth birthday present of a pony in India. William's efforts to redeem himself by working among the Indian poor, the help he gave a sick Englishman may, as the Benn records suggest, have been in the late 1890s, not earlier in the decade after the move from Balham. In that case might not the story of the pregnancy, the suggestion of 'another child', and the death of his wife relate not to Florence but to Margaret's step-mother, to the second wife he took to look after his little girl? If that was so, the records will be in India. All we have in England is the death certificate of Florence, William's medical records and death certificate, the letter from the Englishman who gave his friend a holiday after his bereavement and the rare but consistent stories Margaret told only to those closest to her.

Success did not come easily to Margaret Rutherford and, without the Benn capacity for fighting for what she believed in, it would never have come at all. She was into her thirties before she got her first, abortive, start on the stage. At 39 her ambition, to be unfulfilled, was to play Juliet and she was in her forties before finding herself in the first of those supposedly funny roles of somewhat dotty ladies which have the touch of pathos and tragedy which marks out the great comedian or clown.

Like many little girls Peggy had a passion for acting.

The highlights of her young life came on visits to the home of her cousin Graham, later to achieve academic fame himself as Professor Graham Nicholson, where she took part in the family theatricals. Graham was not always so keen. Peggy's first triumph came on one occasion when he failed to carry through with his role of Fairy Prince. Peggy played it as well as her own part of the Bad Fairy. It was the latter part which brought praise from a professional in the audience. Her words — 'that child has great powers, you have to be really good to be as bad as that' — sent Peggy happy to bed.

About this time a doctor decided that Peggy had a weak back, so Aunt Bessie made her lie stretched out on the floor every day while she talked to her in French. To that the actress later ascribed her good carriage, her ability to wear period clothes and her impeccable French accent.

But Aunt Bessie also delayed her niece's entry into her chosen profession by sending her to a very proper private boarding school, Ravens Croft. This was run by two sisters, the Misses Margaret and Isabelle Mullins at Warlingham, Surrey then, later, in Sleaford, Sussex. Peggy was an honoured student. Her name still appeared on the prefects' board years later when the school had moved again to Eastbourne, but the Misses Mullins were decidedly not of the opinion that young ladies should become professional actresses.

Peggy's talent, they decided, was for playing the piano. For six years she studied to pass the Associate examination of the Royal Academy of Music. Then it was back to Wimbledon as a music teacher.

One can picture her — she has drawn the word-picture herself — on her bicycle, her music-case over the handlebars, hurrying along, head down, skirts flying, exactly as she appeared later in so many films. In her first really big West End success, as Madame Acati, the medium in *Blithe Spirit*, a part Noel Coward rewrote for her, she made her entry cycling wildly to the front of the stage

73

without ever once, she proudly declared, going over the footlights.

While teaching music Peggy herself was taking elocution lessons, for her acting ambitions were unshaken.

Soon after her father died Aunt Bessie died too. With the small legacy she received, Peggy quit teaching music, took a room next to Holloway Prison and began her assault on the London stage. Later, she was regularly to entertain the prison inmates, as one of her own Benn-like good works — once, at the request of the governor, changing the poem she was to recite from *The Shooting of Dan McGrew*, which she thought women, disillusioned with men, might like, to *The Lady of Shalott*.

On the stage Peggy had a quick but short-lived success. Lilian Baylis took her on as a trainee actress at the Old Vic School. Peggy was then 33. Her first part was as the Fairy with the Long Nose in a Christmas entertainment in December 1925. Then she read the lines, off-stage, for a mute Edith Evans on stage — which resulted in one spiteful (Margaret's own adjective) critic noting how Edith Evans's elocution had improved. Then she was on stage with Edith Evans, as Lady Capulet to the famous actress's nurse, in *Romeo and Juliet*. But after eleven small roles in nine months Miss Baylis decided there was no longer any room for her trainee, a decision she was later to admit was very wrong.

So it was back to piano teaching and amateur theatricals in Wimbledon. A professional actress, taken to see Peggy giving her own elaboration of the part of a comic maid, said, 'I don't know whether Peggy is a good actress or not but she is lovable and will make people laugh, and that is very important.'

For her next assault on the stage Peggy made her headquarters in the YWCA. A succession of small parts, 27 in one year, saw her no nearer the West End. Tyrone Guthrie saw her and told her to 'bombard me' with applications for parts.

Bombard him she did, but to no effect, until she heard the rising young producer was working on a play, *Hervey House*. After turning her down once he relented and found her a part. Guthrie is often given credit for launching Peggy but Donald Wolfit had earlier given her the part of Aline Solness in Ibsen's *The Master Builder*. When, two plays after *Hervey House*, which had flopped, she played Aunt Bijou in *Spring Meeting*, Guthrie was to have directed her but, in fact, it was John Gielgud who shaped the performance that was to make her a star. Aunt Bijou was the first of those strange old ladies, delightfully and humorously vague on the surface but with an underlying sense of the tragic reality of the world, which she was to play to perfection.

After that Gielgud offered her the part of Mrs Prism in *The Importance of Being Earnest* and Noel Coward rewrote Madame Arcati with her in mind. In between, to show that she was more versatile than some might now give her credit for, she played Mrs Danvers in *Rebecca*, singled out, in a star-studded cast, for the way she conveyed to the audience why that woman was so consumed with hate, exciting their sympathy if not their understanding. What had been said of the eight-year-old girl was even more true of the woman on the verge of her fifties — 'You have to be good to be so bad.'

From that she went on to become the most popular of actresses, as loved as she was admired. At one time no film seemed complete without her. This is not the place to recount her career, but the starting of it illustrates vividly those Benn qualities of determination and application which were to appear equally in her uncle's grandson, cousin Tony. Also, like other Benns, she thought she had a duty to help the poor and needy.

The Benns also loved her. They never forsook her demented father but never mentioned him to her, in case, as Tony told her adopted daughter Dawn, after her death, she did not know. She, of course, did.

75

In her turn if anybody made an adverse comment on Tony in her presence she would, without revealing she also was a Benn, draw in those double chins and her craggy features would freeze into a withering look that, wordless, would immediately silence the offender.

CHAPTER SIX

The Younger Years

Cousin Tony should have been an actor, Margaret Rutherford said, more than once. That is one of those remarks which at first takes one by surprise and then, after consideration, the surprise left behind, takes one by its truth. At least, if he had, he might have been as universally loved as was Cousin Margaret herself. He could have been the ideal juvenile lead, never ageing, playing his parts more and more to the manner born. His charm, his looks, his way with words would have assured him a succession of roles which would have endeared him, above all, to conservative middle-aged women who, instead of seeing him as a menace to their ordered way of life, as they now do, would have gone in coach parties to applaud him. To any aristocratic role, of course, he would have brought not only his own noble title of viscount — as an actor he would hardly have embarked on overturning the constitution to lose it — but also a natural ease of manner which is the mark of true, not man-made, nobility.

Perhaps if not an actor an advocate.

It was not only Tony's way with words and his pleasing appearance but the way he chose and marshalled his facts and argued a case from them, in a 22-hour speech, which

76

led a judge to advise him that if he was to be deprived of his chosen profession of politician he could make quite a career at the Bar — that was after the same judge had rejected those carefully marshalled facts and closely reasoned argument to disqualify him, only temporarily as it proved, from that chosen profession.

Since then millions have been able to observe and assess those skills for themselves, through television interviews, some ever-ready to be persuaded, others seeking the slightest flaw so they can satisfy themselves the case being argued is nonsense. Even in these days of prejudice nourished by propaganda, though, there are some who listen and watch with a relatively open mind seeking to see, through the actor and the impassioned advocate, to the mind of the man behind.

They will observe the quiet confidence with which he argues his case, but then all politicians must give the appearance of confidence, though some are less quiet than others. There will be no doubt about his way with words, their ordered, unhesitating flow, by no means the words of an advocate who has been rushed in preparing his case and has a nagging doubt about the correctness of his brief, rather those of the great actor who, though word-perfect in a part, still manages to convey to his audience that he and they are sharing an experience that has come fresh and new. They will observe the good manners, how he sits quietly listening as the interviewer unravels his question, never interrupting, not even when, as sometimes happens, it is the interviewer who stumbles and needs help in that unravelling. Then they will notice, if watching carefully, that, as the question ends, it is as if a spring has been released. The gaze which may have been downcast as the question was being absorbed, is lifted and livens. The relaxed pose becomes alert as the words begin to flow. Above all the eyes gleam with an animation which the insular British might find a little foreign to their idea of a professional politician, one expected to balance argument against argument to determine small advantages. Convictions so intensely held, as revealed by the light in those eyes, may awaken suspicion in some and at the same time, to others, inspire equal conviction.

Of course it was inevitable that it was to be neither acting nor advocacy but politics — perhaps a combination of the two — that was to exercise those gifts. It was not just a matter of heredity but of environment. It could be that the bump of Bennery, of passionate absorption in radical politics and equally passionate concern with the deprived, underprivileged and inadequate — in plain English, with the poor — is even bigger in him than it was in his father, grandfather and great-grandfather.

There may have been a Norland-trained nanny in the nursery for young Anthony and his brothers, but that was only befitting a moneyed family in which the mother was as occupied by religious matters as the father was by politics.

The house itself, on the site of his future Ministry of Technology, far enough along the Embankment from the Houses of Parliament to give an MP a brief, lung-filling walk before taking up his duties yet near enough for him to be summoned for any emergency, was suffused with radical politics, right down to the basement. There Tony's father kept in meticulous order the card index which gave him immediate access to any in a vast collection of facts which might, some day, prove of vital political value. Then it was regarded by fellow MPs as just another indication of Benn eccentricity. Nowadays it would be seen as a sign of dedication and good sense, even if a little old-fashioned. It is the habit of the present Benn MP of tape-recording all interviews to have a check against future reports which causes some colleagues to smile. His own basement is full of tapes as well as files of constituency letters and his speeches, back to boyhood. Not, though, that his photocopier has pride of place. His wood-working tools show that he is not so single-minded in his interests as some think.

Next door lived other radical thinkers, Sidney and Beatrice Webb, stalwarts of the Fabian Society. Though radical they also had their roots in a much more conservative level of society, Beatrice, as renowned for her beauty as for her intelligence, having been wooed by Lord Asquith.

It was inevitable that the Benn boys should go to the local school, not to a Westminster council school, well back from the river in Pimlico, site now of one of the better comprehensives to which Caroline, Tony's wife, gives so much of her time, but to the older establishment across the road from the Palace of Westminster, hard by the Abbey of Westminster, Westminster School. Already on its roll were six prime ministers and, by enrolling him there, the father must have had ambitions that his younger son would be the seventh — the elder boy, he knew, was more taken with his mother's interests.

It was the elder boy who shone, a high flyer in whose shade the younger brother went relatively unnoticed, so the story has passed down to the present generation of masters. While the school magazine records Michael's progress to the dignity of Head of Home Boarders and School Monitor it has little to say of Anthony.

The school magazine does reveal a temporary move towards double-barrelling the family name, an intrusive hyphen appears in the entries not only of M. J. Wedgwood-Benn but also of A. N. Wedgwood-Benn. Of the latter it mentions an occasional minor sporting occasion, as when he lost in the first round of the Junior Sculls, and two appearances on the school stage. He was 'Second Gentleman' in a performance of *School for Scandal* and 'Plush, a Westminster Boy' in a Dick Whittington pantomime. The leading role was apparently bespoke, for other reasons than acting ability. It went to a boy named Richard Whittington who later found his own commercial prominence in a company with headquarters not in London but Chicago.

Tony, it seems, showed just enough of his brains in class to avoid attracting undue attention one way or the other, either as a dullard or as a shining example to his less mentally alert contemporaries. For there was then no doubt of his mental alertness or the novelty of his ideas among the general run of the boys, be they sons of well-to-do MPs, purveying at second hand the orthodox views of the troubled thirties when not everyone, certainly not every MP, realised Europe was on the brink of war and of unbelievable changes; be they the sons of lawyers or businessmen; or, as occasionally happened, a foreign diplomat's offspring. The son of Ribbentrop, the German ambassador, soon to become Hitler's foreign minister, was there for a while, sometimes delivered in his father's supercharged Mercedes, and not all his schoolfellows would have rejected out of hand his view of where the real menace to Europe lay — further east than Germany.

Young Benn was not among them. There are early records of his opposition to Hitler, as well as to the appeasement policies of the premier Neville Chamberlain and his Foreign Secretary, Lord Halifax, in the minutes of the school debating society. Such views might find some support among public schoolboys not of the Left, but when he got onto the subject of socialism, state the minutes, 'he argued against many odds and was heckled by all'.

'A lively, friendly boy' is how a senior master of the time recalls Tony. The headmaster, John Christie, remembered his 'liveliness and manners' and found him an 'awfully nice boy'.

'A lively, ebullient character,' is the description given by another Westminster boy who went on to be an MP, Neville Sandelson. 'There was no doubt, even then, that he would make a mark on public life. Even then his ideas seemed a little unusual.'

All stress the liveliness of Benn the boy and, according to another future MP among his contemporaries, his liveliness could sometimes be painful to others. Not all his disagreements were settled in the debating chamber. Like most small boys, perhaps rather more than most, he would sometimes have recourse to violence, an argument could lead to a fight. 'He was a bit readier with his fists than most,' according to that authority.

Perhaps that got the violence out of his system early, leaving no atavistic urges to stop his progress to the view that parliamentary democracy, not revolution, must be the road to socialism. Nowadays the violence is the violence of words, the vehemence with which he expresses his views. But he was vehement at school too, during the one lesson each week when he really shone, when he could be counted on to speak more often and longer than anyone else. That was the Current Affairs period when the master, as well as the pupils, would be amazed more by the extent of the thirteen-year-old's knowledge of social matters than by his conviction that he was utterly right, the only one, in that company, to be right — no bright young teenager worth his salt could ever believe otherwise.

In its Westminster home, in the year or two before the war when Tony was there, the school could run to a junior debating society. He became its secretary, impressing the master in charge more by his organizing ability — particularly when he prevailed on his father to allow the use of the splendid family home for a debate and to provide the hospitality suiting hungry schoolboys — than for his skill as a speaker. During the war, when the school was evacuated, away from its dangerous position alongside the Houses of Parliament, such activities withered. An attempt to revive the Debating Society foundered for lack of support. All the school could run to was a Political and Literary Society, to which the young Benn was elected in 1941.

His development as a debater was to get its great stimulus at Oxford. Between school and university came wartime service, neither as dramatic as his father's nor as tragic as his brother's, though he became a pilot officer in the Royal Air Force Volunteer Reserve and went on for a spell in the Fleet Air Arm as a sub-lieutenant. He has lately preferred to emphasize his time in the lowliest of Air Force ranks, as an aircraftsman, second class, a foible which has brought jibes from researching reporters.

He reached Oxford in 1947 and there met another destined to rise high in the Labour Party, though perhaps not as high as he might, if his abilities had been no greater but his personality had been possessed of a little more Benn-like charm. Anthony Crosland, who was to die in 1978, when Foreign Secretary, was Tony's tutor — except that there could only be one Tony in Crosland's circle so Benn was translated into a 'Jimmy'. The suitability of names might make a subject for a philologist's thesis. Do people grow to be like everyone's concept of their names? Or does the fact that names are bestowed by parents mean that there is some hereditable suitability? It is difficult to think of either Crosland or Benn as 'Jimmies'. 'Jimmies' are Callaghans or, from the pre-war era, Thomases, bluffer, heartier characters, not so deep, perhaps, as 'Tonies' or even 'Harolds'. Crosland was Tony, so Benn happily accepted his renaming. He was probably too polite to do otherwise and politeness is not a description which one would apply readily to Crosland.

Crosland was one of those academics who appear to belie the Shavian dictum that 'Those who can do, those who can't teach.' Crosland 'did'. He reached high Cabinet office, but then, one wonders, what did he actually 'do' in that office? His achievements do not spring to mind. His widow Susan has excused him by saying he had jobs like Environment Secretary in which it is difficult to shine noticeably, but that was not always so. His was the academic brain which found its place in Cabinet discussions

— he liked people to think of him as the intellectual of the Labour Party, and they did — but he was without the radical drive which leads political campaigns. The journalist who, piqued at his air of superiority at a press conference, described him as 'supercilious with little to be supercilious about', was being unjust, but Crosland could upset people.

He inclined to the left, but not too far. He had earlier attached himself to Gaitskell. Benn has quoted his comment on the role of the journal *Tribune*:

. . . to be the expression in popular form, and to as large a public as possible, of the views of the Left and Marxist wing of social democracy in this country. Its policy must be that of those who believe that the present leadership of the Labour Party is not sufficiently Socialist.

When, however, Crosland stood in the leadership election on Harold Wilson's retirement he came bottom of the poll, with 17 votes. Foot was accepted as the Left's main challenge to Callaghan, the centrist, with Healey to the right, but in that first ballot many MPs were prepared to vote according to their personal preferences and do their vote-switching later. Benn himself received twenty more votes than Crosland and despondently Crosland told Susan the result was 'very bad'. Some MPs thought he had been rude to them but he himself was hurt by the result.

When they were both Cabinet Ministers 'Jimmy' was a regular visitor at the Crosland home, near his own in Holland Park, leaving his bike propped against the kerb while he sauntered in, still wearing his bicycle clips. In public Crosland would say he was devoted to Benn, adding, 'nothing the matter with him except he's a bit cracked'. In private, according to Susan Crosland, he could be harsher in his comment, though still, apparently, devoted.

When the Benns, Tony and his wife Caroline, managed

83

to find a smile while others were closer to tears at the Crosland home after the 1970 election, Crosland explained to Susan, 'He's happier in Opposition. There's no other time he can make his move' (to take over the party). 'We all know he occasionally lies but no one doubts his sincerity in seeing himself as a messiah. The trouble with fanatics, why one should never underestimate them, is they're so assiduous.'

To the question 'Do you think he'd ever succeed?' Crosland replied, 'Over my dead body.'

On another occasion, after Susan had been called in to hear Benn's views on the origins of the Labour Movement and the way ahead, she said, when Benn had gone, 'It's so odd. He has this astonishing command of language. He speaks in perfectly shaped prose. The history lesson was fascinating. Yet I haven't the faintest idea what his conclusion meant.'

'Not surprised,' commented her husband. 'The conclusion was meaningless.'

Benn worked for his degree, an MA with Honours. More to the point, though, for his future, was his presidency of the Union. That brought him to the notice of someone who was to be a considerably greater influence than Crosland in his life, including his political life, his wife, Caroline.

Debating teams from British universities had gone to the USA almost every year between the First and Second World Wars, at the invitation of the American Speech Association. The visits were resumed after the war and in 1947 it was Oxford's turn. Benn, as president, was an automatic choice. The team of three was made up by the treasurer, Edward Boyle, later to be a Tory Cabinet Minister, and Kenneth Harris, new Deputy Chairman of the *Observer* newspaper.

In just under five months, lasting into 1948, the team visited 60 universities, debating, principally, the motions 'This House approves the nationalization of basic industry', 'The best way to preserve peace in the world is by the Anglo-American alliance' and 'This House prefers vocational education to education in the arts'. Sometimes the Oxford team proposed the motion, sometimes it opposed. Once, recalls Harris, when Benn had missed a train, Boyle had to propose the nationalization motion — 'Edward was not too keen on it.' Benn had an excuse for missing that train. All the organization of the tour was the Oxford President's responsibility. Money was short and he kept daily accounts, meticulously, according to Harris. Benn the assiduous accountant is an unexpected role and it apparently so delighted Benn that he has preserved the accounts as carefully as he then kept them.

Arguing the case, for or against as the occasion demanded, was his chief task, though, and in that he excelled. He proved himself not just a good speaker — 'one of the half dozen best, on his day the best,' is Harris's current opinion — but an extremely powerful debater. The two are not synonymous. It was Benn's ability to listen carefully to the other side, to note and reply to their points, without ever being aggressive, that marked him out.

He went down remarkably well with his American audiences and not just because of his power over words.

'He was very good-looking, very youthful-looking, very pink and white,' recalled Harris. 'Everybody said he looked so very English.'

In Cincinnati lived the De Camps, like the Benns a family with a history of religious persecution, descended from Huguenot immigrants. Like the Benns they were addicted to meaningful second names, preserving the maiden names of wives. Like the Benns they were prosperous middle class, but with a prosperity greater and longer established.

Among them was a young woman of Tony's age, Caroline Middleton De Camp, daughter of a wealthy lawyer. As a child she had had the reputation, among her playmates, of being strong-willed, bossy and ambitious. At an age when the affections of most girls are still centred on their dolls she had announced that one day she would marry the President of the United States. She proved to be extremely bright, graduating first from Vassar, the chosen seat of learning for America's most wealthy, liberated and socially acceptable girls, and then gaining a second degree at Cincinnati.

Cincinnati, known variously as the 'Athens of America', for its European appearance, and 'Porkopolis', for its place in the commerce of the mid-West, had not been on the debating team's itinerary, though the Ohio State University, Columbus, had been. Some of Caroline's friends had heard Benn debate and, perhaps more to the point, seen him. When Caroline decided to go to England to continue her studies into the English stage, to produce a lengthy MA thesis on the conflicting roles of Ben Jonson and Inigo Jones in the production of Stuart court masques, she was told she must meet the charming, handsome, intelligent orator who had sent so many feminine hearts a-flutter.

She did. As she said later, 'We met on Monday and were engaged on the Saturday. He proposed on an Oxford park bench.' Tony has put the interval somewhat longer, nine days. With a romanticism equalled only by the Benn determination, Tony decided that as well as the girl he must have the bench. The council's reaction was predictable. Sell one of our benches. Can't be done. There's no precedent for it. But, as others were to find, it is a Benn forte to establish precedents. The bench now stands in the garden of his house in Holland Park Avenue, the only spot, Caroline has told her friends, where he can quietly and contemplatively relax.

Caroline had forsaken her prospective president for a prospective premier. In the USA, a country rather more amateur in its approach to politics than even the United Kingdom, it is more difficult to identify a future president.

One might have to pick a Hollywood actor, a peanut farmer, a lawyer, a soldier. At least in Britain the choice narrows to one of a few hundred parliamentarians. By this time, too, Caroline had had it pointed out to her that she was getting far too radical. She had moved further from the days when, ten years old, she shocked her wealthy Republican relatives by announcing that she was a Democrat — 'I couldn't see why we should have money and other people not,' she later explained. She shocked others even more when she took her brilliant young husband back to America and sat proudly by as he demolished some of the local Cold War shibboleths about Russia at a meeting arranged for him. 'At least he gave his little talk at the Jewish Community Centre,' recalled one of the outraged Cincinnati folk, as if that reduced the offence.

It was as bad when she declared Britain's Nationalized Health Service was 'just heaven' and predicted that one day America, too, would know the joys of socialized medicine. 'We've never had a doctor's bill,' the young mother told other young mothers who knew how expensive the joys and pains of childbirth could be.

In the matter of education the boot did appear, for a while, to be on the other foot. 'Why does she send her children to such a fancy school instead of a public one,' asked one of her home-town neighbours, after Caroline had brought her children on a visit, using 'public', of course, in the American way to mean a state school. At that time the two elder boys were going to the Westminster Preparatory School. But Caroline was conscious of the discrepancy, even of her sons' clipped English accents.

'The children are coming home with notions of their own — and England's — superiority instead of more democratic ideas,' she confided to a friend, and the friend got the impression that such notions would be 'whacked out of them', a promise, which if Caroline did make it, would have shocked some of her later, progressive, educational colleagues.

As for Westminster School, the Benn boys were soon to leave it. When the time came for the eldest boy to leave the preparatory school and enter the main school both he and his brother were moved to Holland Park Comprehensive. Unkind parliamentary colleagues of Benn, particularly some on the Labour benches, have suggested that the move only took place after the eldest boy had failed his entrance examination. But that would not have been an insuperable obstacle for the son of an old boy, he would have had another chance. That failure — if failure it was, as both boys were reported by the school to be 'intelligent and adaptable' — could have been only a temporary aberration. After winning prizes for music at Holland Park he went on to take a degree in economics and then do a post-graduate course in American studies.

Did Tony tell Caroline, on that park bench, of his political ambitions? Then a radio talks producer on the BBC's North American service, he was already set for his career in Parliament, taking over from Sir Stafford Cripps as a Bristol MP in 1950, the youngest MP in the House. Whatever they may have discussed on that park bench since, it seems unlikely that politics intruded then. It was no political marriage of convenience. It was a love match, a marriage of true minds, in the eyes of those who attended the wedding at the Episcopalian church in Cincinnati in June 1949. But there is also no doubt that it proved a marriage of like minds.

'It is a very close marriage, Tony relies a lot on her opinions and support,' said the wife of one of Labour's Front-bench spokesmen, who added, 'She's very family orientated. She always knows the names of your children.'

The gossip among politicians is that 'Caroline is to the left of Tony and their children further to the left of them both.' That would not be unusual in left-wing families but all the evidence is that Caroline's role in her husband's political life is supportive rather than formative. Except perhaps in education, where Mrs Benn's activities excited the suspicions of Norman St John Stevas in 1977, when the Queen's speech disclosed that a promised Bill to strengthen parental rights in the choice of schools had been dropped.

'Who is the Education Secretary?' he asked. 'Is it Shirley Williams or is it this lady who has apparently killed it off? It is bad enough to have Macbeth in the Cabinet. We don't want Lady Macbeth around as well.'

On a more mundane level it might be thought that one of her foibles as a fervent feminist might upset most marriages.

'The man who has done most to liberate woman is Kellogg. Any man can pour milk over a plate of cornflakes and spare his wife the task of cooking dinner,' she once said, without any perceptible trace of a smile. One of her sons has said that the Benn household once went two days on cornflakes when Mrs Benn was particularly busy — without the complaints that might be expected from husbands more devoted to the table. Tony has said that food never bothers him. His regular daily lunch from the House of Commons cafeteria is a square of cheese, a sausage roll, an apple and the inevitable mug of tea. He once confessed to drinking 18 pints a day. According to the Tea Council, which gleefully worked out that it would take 1¼ tons of the caffeine-laden leaf to brew the 29,000 gallons he would consume in 40 years, it is one trait which he shares with Brigitte Bardot, the actress. She demanded 80 cups a day when film-making. But, as she left half of each cupful to get cold, her true consumption, at about 40 cups, was much the same as 18 pint mugs.

Back home in Cincinnati, Caroline once described her role as a supportive political wife in the fifties when, as a loving wife and mother, she was having and raising her

family of four. She found time to accompany Tony whenever he went on his campaigns.

'I would sit on the platform with him and make little
talks of my own on his behalf. I also addressed many
women's groups.'

It was an experience which caused her some tremors,
for she is by no means as confident a speaker as her
husband.

'Now, however,' she added, 'I canvass the homes. I like
that much better. It gives me a chance to get close to the
people and I no longer have to be afraid that the audience
will heckle me as happens at some public meetings.'

She is happier writing than speaking. Her novel *Lion
in a Den of Daniels*, written 'quite quickly' in 1960 and
published in 1962, is seen by many of her friends, particularly in America, as revealing of herself.

Like Caroline, her heroine Lydia Brightbrook, speaks
in a breathless manner, is an American living in Europe
— though married to a somewhat stolid American — and
finds England decadent.

'That's not knocking Britain,' Caroline explained, when
admitting she shared that view. 'We both think decadent
countries are much nicer.'

Lydia comes from a family of wealthy aunts and
'stuffed-shirt' uncles and finds herself in London mixing
with Left-wingers, homosexuals and, that group of people
with many of the characteristics of politicians, journalists.

Not all English attitudes she observes strike a chord
with Lydia:

'What a low ebb!' she exclaims at one point. 'In love with
a husband. How could I possibly stay in Europe and hold
up my head with honour? I guess I'd have to go, yet how
could I face the only alternative, Hank's Uncle Walt's
office.'

The book was reviewed with considerable civic pride

by Frederick Yeiser, literary critic of *The Cincinnati Enquirer*, the paper on which Caroline's brother, Graydon, was political writer. Yeiser thought of it in terms of the stage, a mélange of *Up in Mabel's Room* and *Gentlemen Prefer Blondes*. It made him recall with affection those earlier days when he and his friends were young and gay.

Caroline worked for a while as a children's story-teller on the Jackanory TV programme in the mid-sixties, chosen, she said, for her mid-Western accent. Equity protested to the BBC over the employment of a non-professional.

Her attention and her time were being more and more absorbed by the problems of education in England, as she saw them. Too little depended on the abilities of children, too much on the opportunities open to them and the expectations of their teachers. The American system was more democratic and more efficient. When next she wrote a book it was in collaboration with the noted educationalist, Professor Brian Simon of Leicester University. Entitled *Halfway There* it was a history of the comprehensive movement in Britain. The title indicated the authors' opinion that much remained to be done. It appeared in 1970, the year Edward Heath chose as Education Secretary a rising young woman in the Conservative Party, Margaret Thatcher, who was to display her determination and cost-cutting propensities by stopping free school milk in face of public outrage.

Mrs Benn had her own brush with Mrs Thatcher over comprehensives. Education policy had changed from being just pro-grammar to profoundly anti-comprehensive, she charged in 1973, quoting the rise in the rate of rejection of applications for schools to be recognized as comprehensives from 4 per cent at the beginning of the Thatcher ministry to 26 per cent.

Caroline has been a devoted worker in the cause of comprehensive education, carrying out surveys, writing pamphlets, doing the office chores, even, despite the tremors it still brings, speaking in public.

In one survey she canvassed the views of middle-class parents whose children had moved from independent to comprehensive schools. Half, it proved, had made the switch from financial necessity, which certainly was not the case with the Benn children. Caroline reported she was well pleased with the effect of the change on her children and many of the parents she questioned thought the same. She found teaching standards in comprehensives higher than in private schools, with younger, more energetic teachers. Sports and art were better provided for, but discipline was worse than in private schools. Some parents and children condemned the mixing of pupils from widely different social backgrounds but she quoted approvingly the boy who said, 'some boys had Cockney accents and you thought they were big bullies and you didn't mix with them. Then you realized they were perfectly decent people and very nice and they're all my friends now. I was snobbish before. I did not realize you could have a Cockney accent and be good at school work.'

Her campaigning style and American origins can have some surprising consequences. Accompanied by a GLC legal adviser she once went to see a police superintendent to protest about the damage done by outside vandals at one comprehensive. After listening, unconvinced, to the policeman's explanation of the difficulties she said, 'In America, if this happened, we'd have armed police patrolling the perimeter.'

She has been no more a Labour Party puppet than her husband has. Having been co-opted onto a London education committee to boost Labour's influence with her authority on comprehensives she proceeded to vote against Labour and with the Tories on the very first motion put. Her colleagues were as taken aback as the police superintendent had been.

The Labour Party was obviously not nearly as radical

in its educational policy as she would like. When Reg Prentice was in charge in 1975, she said progress towards comprehensives was no faster than it had been under the Tories. Just after St John Stevas called attention to what he thought her excessive influence on that policy, she was criticizing the continuing subsidising of public and independent schools, under a Labour Government, to the tune, she calculated, of £135,000,000 a year. Thirty-two million went on paying school fees for the children of military personnel, mostly officers, posted abroad. Other ranks used British forces schools, which were reported to be excellent. Why could not officers' children? Allowances averaging £1,500 were paid for 1,887 children of Foreign Office personnel. In Washington, Embassy children went to expensive private schools, by courtesy of the British taxpayer, while the President sent his to the local state school. Apart from the money from central funds another £40,000,000 was spent by local authorities on private school fees. Money spent that way was undermining the comprehensive system.

She was certainly at one with her husband over the question of titles. As she declared when her father-in-law failed, in 1955, to remove the prospect, or threat, of one from his son and daughter-in-law.

A peeress's tiara? Not for me. Titles belong to fairy tales. I don't believe in honours someone else has earned. But I'm chiefly against it because it threatens my husband Anthony's career as MP. I certainly don't want deference from anyone. I would be terribly embarrassed if someone called me to the head of a queue because I happened to marry the son of a man who had earned a title. I hate to see people being shown preference myself. I feel real mad when I see private patients go straight in to see a doctor when I have been waiting in an outpatients' queue for hours.

There is bound to be a reform. You people scorn Continental titles. Well most Americans, apart from wealthy daughters with nothing to do but collect the best titles they can find, think yours are about as out of date as you think Continental ones.

She, was of course, a wealthy daughter herself. Her mother died in 1974 — her father died in 1961 — leaving over two million dollars. A third of the estate, amounting to £172,000 after American tax, was put in trust for Caroline's children.

Large as the De Camp family fortunes may be, she has not brought conspicuous wealth to the Benn life-style. The popular press made much of the discovery, in 1974, that she, Hilary and her two younger children, Melissa and Joshua, were holidaying on a private yacht in the Aegean, just after the Labour Government had cancelled a good-will naval visit to Greece in protest against the lack of democracy there. The yacht, claimed the *Daily Express*, cost £200 a day, excluding food and drink. It turned out, though, that Caroline was the guest of an old school chum, the Canadian sister-in-law of the French banker who owned the yacht — and also one of those scorned Continental titles, the Baron Alain de Gunzburg.

Whatever those American dollars do for her children one of her American traits has added to their lives. Stephen and Hilary share her love of baseball and, with her, are enthusiastic fans of the Cincinnati Reds.

In a letter back home in 1975 she wrote:

Steve, Hilary and I are bleary-eyed because we stay up each night to catch the World Series. Here that means going to bed early and setting alarms for 2 a.m. and turning on the Armed Forces Network Radio station. It also means keeping awake until 5 a.m. which is about when they end.

One night I got up at 2, listened, but went back to sleep when I thought we'd won because we were 5-1 ahead. But Boston caught up and it went into extra innings. Steve was awake for the whole of that game and was furious when the extra innings meant the game ran into the dawn programmes from Eastern Europe and the broadcast was overlaid by interfering stations.

The only thing we could do was wait until the US Embassy opened and call the poor Marine on duty there to find out how the game ended. But he was used to it.

CHAPTER SEVEN

The Fight to Stay a Commoner

The Hon. Anthony Neil Wedgwood Benn ('Hon' as the son of a Viscount) was returned Labour MP for Bristol, South-East, on 30 November 1950.

Bristol had had a history of radical politics stretching back to the philanthropist Edward Colston, in the early part of the eighteenth century, and Edmund Burke, in the middle of that century, on to Sir Stafford Cripps, Benn's immediate predecessor.

Cripps was also considered too radical by the official leadership of the Labour Party. He is remembered now for his Popular Front campaign in the later 1930's, to build up resistance against Hitler, in which he was prepared to cooperate with Liberals and dissident Tories rebelling against Munich appeasement.

Before that, though, in 1934, when Labour was breaking with its pacifist past to support League of Nations sanctions against Italy, then engaged on an imperialist incursion into Abyssinia, he declared, 'if war comes before the workers of Great Britain have won power that war will be an imperialist war,' and promptly resigned

95

from the party's National Executive Committee. In 1936 he was of the opinion that if socialism was the answer to the world's problems, as he believed, then it was essential to push on as hard as possible to achieve it. To that end, he advocated a 'British United Front of the Working Class', to bring together the Labour Party, Independent Labour Party and the Communist Party to defeat the National Government. That was by no means to the taste of the official leadership, whose opposition to Communism has always been as clear cut as its support of socialism has been clouded. The NEC first saw to it that membership of the Socialist League, a left-wing intellectual group mainly financed by Cripps, was declared incompatible with that of the Labour Party. However, the journal *Tribune*, launched to help forward the Cripps ideas, did survive.

The NEC later announced that any member of the Labour Party appearing on a public platform with any member of the ILP or Communist Party would be expelled. Cripps challenged this decision at the 1937 conference. That amalgam of trade unionists, MPs and local party workers overwhelmingly defeated his motion, but the constituency parties, later to make Benn their darling, showed their support by re-electing him to the NEC.

Cripps's membership of the party survived, but in 1938 when, after Munich, he declared the need was for 'strength to maintain the rule of law internationally', and refused to withdraw his programme for a Popular Front campaign, he was expelled.

Cripps, born in 1889, was the fourth son of the first Baron Parmoor, who was to renounce his Conservative family origins to become Lord President of the Council in the Labour Government of 1929. His mother was the sister of Beatrice Webb, wife of Sidney Webb, President of the Board of Trade in that same Government.

At first Cripps shone as a scientist, part author, at 22, of a paper on chemistry read to the Royal Society. He

96

then read for the Bar, becoming the youngest King's Counsel in 1929. In 1930 he joined the Government as Solicitor-General, though he did not get his Bristol seat for another year. He proved to be a lucid and cogent speaker, rather than a master of the higher flights of oratory, and amazed MPs with his grasp of complex facts as when, for example, he had to deputize at short notice for the Chancellor of the Exchequer in a financial statement.

After his expulsion from the Labour Party, when he continued to sit as an Independent, he was out in the cold until Churchill, on taking over from Chamberlain, made him Ambassador in Moscow. He stayed there for two years, increasingly disillusioned by the lack of readiness of Stalin, possibly an even greater master of the complex fact than Cripps, to pay much attention to his proffered views. When he returned to Britain in 1943 he served for a while as Leader of the House. MPs found him too harsh a disciplinarian, whether because of what he had learned from the Georgian in Moscow or because of his naturally ascetic outlook, and Churchill had to move him to the Ministry of Aircraft Production. With post-War austerity he came into his own, first as President of the Board of Trade, then as Minister of Economic Affairs and, finally, as Chancellor of the Exchequer.

By the 1950 general election he was in ill-health. He stood and was re-elected with an enormous majority of almost 20,000. By October, though, he was forced to resign both his office and his seat. Two years later he was dead. Reports of the enormous personal wealth of this dedicated socialist proved exaggerated. Though he had been said to have made a fortune from the complexities of patent and compensation law, with an income, at its height, of £40,000 a year — eight times a prime minister's salary — he left only £5,000.

With their experience of the child of one socialist Lord, Parmoor, radical Bristolians saw nothing wrong in taking another sprig of the socialist nobility to their heart, the brilliant young offspring of the Viscount Stansgate. Benn had Cripps's commendation — 'a true Socialist who is as keen a Christian as I am myself.' Though he could not hope to repeat the massive Cripps majority at his first effort, Benn got home by around 13,000 votes.

'People will not believe me,' he has said and, of course, nobody does, 'but my ambitions were wholly satisfied when I entered the House of Commons.'

He chose the Iron and Steel Industry Bill debate in February 1951, for his maiden speech, hardly the non-controversial occasion usually preferred. Benn's was a model of his later speeches, a well-mannered logical analysis, flavoured by wit and analogy. The people and steel had at last been married, went one analogy, after a long period of not very reputable cohabitation: 'If I may misquote the marriage vows, "For better, for worse, for richer or poorer, until the advent of the Conservative Government doth us part" . . . "That which Parliament has joined together, let no man put asunder".'

'A most admirable and able speech,' declared the Conservative, Sir Ralph Glynn, who followed him.How refreshing Sir Ralph was to observe in a comment which gains piquancy when recalled over the years, to have such sane remarks made from a Socialist point of view. We are given great hopes for the future, he said, adding a prophecy perhaps not wholly fulfilled, 'We shall all gladly cheer as he goes up the ladder of success in the House.'

When Labour moved into Opposition in 1951 Benn quickly became a prominent Back-bencher and it was as a defender of the rights of Back-benchers that he had a notable tussle with the Speaker, W. S. Morrison, in 1957. He had had one exchange, the previous year, during a Suez debate, when one Tory described him as 'Nasser's little lackey'. Such a remark addressed to him, the Speaker, would have been grossly out of order but it was not on the list of forbidden words when bandied between

Members, ruled Speaker Morrison. Benn resented that the Speaker was not prepared to resent the application of the remark to him, though he would have resented it himself. There was, Morrison pointed out, a proper form for expressing such resentment against the Speaker.

Benn chose not to take that course on a personal matter but, in circumstances which he felt hit fellow-members, tabled a motion of censure in July 1957. It was over Standing Order 9 and the procedure for raising urgent business by moving the adjournment of the House. Gladstone had had the procedure tightened in 1882 when it was felt Irish MPs were abusing it to raise Irish matters. The question now was whether it was too tight. The principle had been invoked by MPs on 73 occasions since the end of the war but only eight applications had been allowed.

Benn's disallowed application had been over the despatch of British troops to the Gulf Sultanates of Muscat and Oman. It was not a matter of urgency, ruled the Speaker, because, although the Foreign Secretary had admitted, to Benn, that the decision to commit them had been taken, none had yet been committed. Incidentally, we now know that on many occasions since then, under Tory and Labour Governments, British soldiers have been in action there unbeknownst to the British public or to British MPs.

The Government was perturbed enough by Benn's action to put a three-line whip on their MPs. In fact Benn quickly made it known he was not pressing the motion to a vote, just providing an opportunity for Back-bench MPs to put their point of view — the party system might limit the way MPs might vote but it did not limit their right to speak.

In talking about that Standing Order, he said, they were talking about Back-benchers. Front-benchers could decide the business to be talked about:

They are in the privileged position, reading every day

from a menu of their choosing, as they lounge on the couches beside the banqueting table. But the Back-benchers here are a hardier race. We have to grub for our food. A Parliamentary Question is all that we get and it is a job very often to get the chance to ask a supplementary. We have to hope that we shall get the evening Adjournment; we have to ballot for a Motion. We have, when we believe it urgent, the security of Standing Order No 9.

If the Speaker took away or limited that right, Benn argued, he would be damaging the Back-bencher's battle to win a place in the House from the Front-bencher.

'It was,' recalled Reginald Paget, a lawyer MP who seconded Benn's motion though he disagreed with him on Muscat, 'the most brilliant parliamentary performance I have ever heard.'

Older MPs looked askance at the brashness of the young man with the temerity to challenge the Speaker but a number of Back-benchers took the opportunity to air their complaints and trust that the Rules Committee would look at them. There were Conservative MPs among them. As Benn had pointed out, their feet might be shackled when it came to walking into the voting lobbies but not their tongues when speaking in the House.

In the course of his speech Benn had pointed out that discussions on party discipline were not unique to Britain. Referring to a famous dictum by Mao Tse Tung, he said he was only one of a thousand flowers asking permission to be allowed to blossom. That brought a rueful comment from R. A. Butler, Home Secretary and Leader of the House, that the eloquent Benn had hardly been unable to blossom through the past months and years, 'in fact we regard him as a somewhat luxuriant wood in this Assembly.'

For Benn had made his mark in Hansard. Like his father, he would have been one of those MPs noted by his grandfather. He was regularly taking up a full page of

100

entries in the annual index to those proceedings of the House, an amount hardly approached by any other Back-bencher and more than the Leader of his party, Hugh Gaitskell.

His days as a Back-bencher were numbered. He was already effectively boss of Labour's television operations, described by the experts as 'splendidly televisual, boyish, straightforward, suave and sincere.' His own description of himself about that time was 'a left-of-centre-keep-calmer with a strong radical bias.' By the end of the decade he was spokesman on transport. Despite his rapid advance and the promise of greater things to come, however, there was a move to take him from the House to Labour Party Headquarters, as a replacement for the party secretary, Morgan Phillips, then about to retire. For over Benn's parliamentary future hung the cloud that he was not, like Cripps, a younger son of a peer, but the eldest surviving son and heir to a seat in the Lords which would disqualify him from the Commons.

When William Wedgwood Benn acceded to the urgings of Attlee that it would strengthen the Labour Party in the Lords if he accepted a peerage, he might not have considered the effect it would have on his second son. His elder son was destined, by his mother, to the church and a title would be no barrier there. But both sons were destined by history and their father's war record to the RAF and Michael was killed.

Tony was now the heir and his dislike for the hereditary peerage was as great as that of Mark Twain's Yankee at the Court of King Arthur, in that masterpiece of anti-establishment satire — for more personal reasons if for the same general ones.

Mark Twain's Yankee objected to the idea of hereditary rule:

'What nation,' he asked, [when persuading the "freeman" how unfree he was], 'with a free vote in every man's

101

hand, would elect that a single family and its descendants should reign over it for ever, whether gifted or boobies? . . . What nation would elect that certain families should be raised to dizzy summits of rank, to the exclusion of the rest?'

What the younger Benn objected to was that, belonging to one of these dizzy families, he was denied the right of being elected to rule.

He might well have objected further because he was disbarred by a viscounty, a bit of an upstart title, which originally carried no hereditary powers of rule. There were no viscounts in Arthurian Britain and only barely in the feudal medieval times which Twain was really pillorying in his book.

The oldest English rank of nobility is Earl, probably brought here by the Danes, the defeat of whose jarls brought Alfred the Great his first victories in the campaigns which laid the foundations of England. Canute instituted the rank of earl for those who administered his authority over an area covering several counties. Later the territorial association was with one county, making it the equivalent of the Continental title Count. Even in Britain, of course, the feminine of Earl is Countess. Feminists uncertain of their attitude to titles might note that an earldom was inherited originally under the rules of succession of fiefs, which meant it might pass to a woman — though her husband then took it in his own right.

The oldest title, though not in England, is Duke, taken by the barbarian enemies of Rome from the Roman 'Dux', or leader, the high military commander with large territorial responsibilities — and barbarized, some might think, by being made hereditary. Baron was already a Germanic title, for one holding land, with its feudal military responsibilities, directly from the King. It was not introduced in England until the fourteenth century, then used for those summoned individually to Parliament. A

Marquess originally was responsible for a march, or border territory. In England it was also a fourteenth-century introduction.

A viscount was originally, on the Continent, the son or younger brother of a count, and indicated the title he had just missed or to which he might aspire. In England the vice-count was historically the chief aide to an earl (count), a magistrate or sheriff. It was not until 1440 that Henry VI used the title to mark out a new rank of peerage, below that of earl but above that of baron, by conferring it on John, Baron Beaumont.

In those supposedly rigidly feudal times there was, some might think, something a little more democratic, because less irrevocable, about becoming a peer than in the 1940's, in the middle of the great crusade for the democratic way of life, when Wedgwood Benn was elevated to the Lords. Those who found it too heavy a burden could give it up, taking care, of course, not to upset the Sovereign in doing so. There was almost a set form of words of renunciation:

I beg your Majesty's august consideration of the hardships of your Majesty's poor subject. Great have been the honours conferred upon our lowly family by your Majesty's illustrious father [ancestor] of happy memory; yet I am constrained to beg humbly of my gracious Sovereign that my lordship hereditary may be taken back into that fountain of honour which is your Majesty's most excellent self. Great and grievous are the difficulties which attend upon my entering into the enjoyment to this lordship, with the enumeration of which your poor servitor fears to weary your Majesty's royal ear . . .

The petitioner would always maintain, of course, with proper emphasis, that whatever happened he would remain the most devoted, 'the most loyal of your Majesty's faithful subjects'.

It worked. There is no record of any Sovereign being so upset by the ungracious return of that ennobling gift that he had the petitioner thrown into the Tower to think better of it. Between 1232 and 1660 nearly a score of peerages were resigned. Some peers did so because they decided they could no longer afford the honour and, paradoxically, perhaps to make up for the free board and lodging they would no longer be expected to provide the royal court on occasion, were fined. There is one example, however, of one petitioner, a distinguished soldier, Guichard D'Angle, who did rather better. He was a boon companion of Edward III in the Wars in France and was rewarded for his skill and bravery with an earldom. On the battlefield, though, he had been too concerned with winning, not enough with looting or taking prisoners able to afford fat ransoms; a true knight, he was, after the heart of Conan Doyle's Sir Nigel. Back in England, after Crécy and Poitiers, he found his earldom just could not be lived up to, it sent his personal cost of living soaring faster than an ordinary post-war inflation. In 1378 he petitioned to be relieved of his burden. He was, with the additional sweetener of a pension of £1000 a year, sufficient then, he may have thought wryly later, to make even an earldom supportable.

Sometimes a little pressure was put on a less unwilling holder of a title to relinquish it, or at least swop it for another. Henry VII's uncle, before the Tudors came to the throne, had to give up the Earldom of Pembroke after an earlier Tudor failure, though he later became Earl of Huntingdon. About the same time came the only case of a peerage being annulled by Act of Parliament, when one of the Nevills, George, nephew of Warwick the Kingmaker, paid the penalty of also picking the wrong colour rose by losing the Dukedom of Bedford in 1470.

That sort of thing was more recent history in the seventeenth century, more relevant too, at a time when Parliament and Crown were in dispute. Thrice the House of

Lords made judgments designed to ensure that the Crown should not bring the Lords under its control, by pressure on it or on individual peers, culminating in a ruling of 1678 which stated that a title could not be given up nor otherwise extinguished except for treason.

With that in mind William Wedgwood Benn did consult his elder son before accepting his viscounty. Michael had no objection. The second son, Anthony, was not consulted. Perhaps a hint of the reason why came unwittingly from the then Lord Stansgate when explaining the matter to the House of Lords later. His sixteen-year-old schoolboy second son was 'a bit of a chatterbox'. Whether he was trying to prevent the leaking of a secret or just fearful of the torrent of words which would inevitably come, he did not make clear. Anyway he did not escape the torrent. Anthony read of it in the newspapers and, said his father, 'was angry and abused me'.

The father did his best to make amends when Tony entered Parliament with the awful prospect of being removed from the Commons not by the ballot papers of his constituents but by the roll of parchment, the letters patent of the Stansgate viscounty.

In 1960, with his father then in his eighties, Benn made quite clear how awful the prospect was to him, when describing how the semblance of power differed from the reality. At the State Opening of Parliament the Queen sat on her throne, around her the great officers of the realm, Lords in their ermine robes, judges in their long wigs, and the bishops representing the power of the medieval church. Tony observed:

The Commons stand in business suits beyond the bar and the ordinary public can only watch it all from the public gallery. Yet the reality is very different. Today, real power resides in the public galleries with those who have the vote. They pick the MPs who stand below them. And those MPs have curbed the Lords and have converted the Crown into a symbol of our national sovereignty.

Power lay, be it noted, not even in the Commons, but where the public sat. The House of Lords, with few powers left, was just an assembly where 'elder statesmen of the nation who have given great service can meet to talk over matters of state and tender their advice, based on a lifetime of public service.'

In contrast, the Commons was 'bursting with vitality':

Every MP comes to Parliament on a surge of popular support. He is refreshed every weekend by the political life and interests of the people he represents. He is kept in touch with the realities of life and the problems it throws up by his constituents who come to him for help. The individual relationship that exists between an MP and those who send him there is the lifeline through which the Commons draws its vitality and power.

Anyone interested in politics, anxious to play some part in the great political decisions of the day, must necessarily be in the Commons. There was no comparison between the two Houses of Parliament.

There was, Benn declared, 'no greater honour that can be conferred upon any man or woman in Britain today than to be chosen to be an MP'. It was not just a question of power, he made clear, but the work, sometimes exciting, sometimes humdrum, of an MP:

A lifetime as a common back-bencher would be infinitely preferable to any honour or any ministerial office that the House of Lords might make possible.

It is no wonder that, feeling like that, he had already taken steps to see he stayed in the Commons and had begun taking them almost as soon as he arrived there.

His first attempt, and the first of a series of precedents he created in his battle, was to attempt to renounce his right of succession by a Personal Bill in the House of Lords. As published, in December 1954, it provided the line of succession should be through the next heir male, Tony's eldest son, Stephen Michael, then three years old. No similar use of the Personal Bill procedure could be recalled, it was pointed out at the time.

An explanatory note recalled the circumstances of Viscount Stansgate's elevation to the peerage. It, and three others, were not political honours or rewards but measures to strengthen the Labour Party in the Lords, where its representation was 'disproportionate at a time when a Coalition Government of three parties is charged with the direction of affairs'.

In the course of a 90-minute plea, when his claim was considered in February 1955, he argued that the case should be tried on its own peculiar merits — just as all peerage cases had been in the past, he insisted — and so the history of the creation of his title would be relevant. He went further back into history, to recount some of the cases we have already referred to, the classics of peerage renunciation. He also found one novel one, an unprinted Act of 1549, involving the then Lord De La Warr and his nephew and heir William West.

Moved by most un-Benn-like feelings, the young West so wanted the title his uncle showed no signs of vacating in normal fashion that he decided to speed matters up with poison. Narrowly escaping with his life the uncle petitioned for the boy to be removed from the succession. Parliament was so horrified it put all the lurid details of the poisoning into the preamble to the bill.

'If you are anxious for me to follow precedents exactly,' said Benn, 'I could always attempt to poison my father.'

All that provoked from William Wedgwood was a smile of parental pride. His son had made a magnificent case, he said afterwards.

'That I suppose, is all the more reason why the House of Lords will not want to lose him.'

For the noble lords constituting the Personal Bills Committee which had had to be appointed to consider the matter had decided that it was too personal. If Benn's petition was allowed then there might be a widespread desire for similar relief. Not unlikely, commented Benn. There were nine members of the House of Commons facing disqualification on becoming peers — a hazard they shared with convicted criminals and madmen. Then, said the Lords, it might be a matter of concern to the nation, to be treated generally. That would not have cut much ice with Benn, who could recall that the distinguished politician and lawyer, Quintin Hogg, faced with the disaster of being booted upstairs to the Lords — also as a viscount, Hailsham — had asked the Labour Prime Minister Attlee to initiate legislation and had been refused.

For his next attempt Tony was officially an onlooker, behind the Bar of the House of Lords. Having failed in his personal bill he had immediately had a public bill introduced, officially to give effect to an instrument of renunciation signed in his constituency, South-east Bristol, in the presence of such parliamentary witnesses as Aneurin Bevan and Clement Attlee, that former premier who had declined to act in the case of Hailsham.

It transpired that he had the support of another and even more illustrious prime minister.

Lord Stansgate, making amends for his 1941 dereliction of duty to family parliamentary aspirations, had argued his son's case in a whirlwind of tempestuous oratory. His was a brand unlike his son's, more fiery, passionate, perhaps lacking in similar measure that apparent appeal to calm logic and intelligent analysis favoured by other distinguished Parliamentary debaters, such as his own son and Enoch Powell.

At the end he produced, dramatically, what should have been his ace of trumps, a letter from Sir Winston

108

Churchill. He, be it remembered, declined the customary earldom bestowed on former prime ministers — in his case it had been suggested it should be a dukedom, like that of his illustrious ancestor Marlborough — contenting himself with a knighthood and the knowledge that he was not standing in the way of the political ambitions of later Churchills. In a note to his Chief Whip on 18 March 1945, he had written 'It is a terrible thing for a father to doom his son to political extinction, which must happen to many that have not had time to make their way in the House of Commons.'

That had led Tony to write to Churchill earlier, asking his support, to be told that it was impossible for the Prime Minister, as he then was, to come forward in support of an individual Member of Parliament, no matter how right his plea might be.

After Churchill left office Tony wrote to him again. The reply, from Chartwell on 9 April 1955, a fortnight before the Lords debate, read:

My dear Wedgwood Benn,
    As I wrote to you confidentially in September 1953, I certainly feel that yours is a very hard case, and I am personally strongly in favour of sons having the right to renounce irrevocably the peerage they inherit from their fathers. This would not, of course, prevent them from accepting another peerage if they were offered one later on.

Yours sincerely,
Winston S. Churchill.

Stansgate's performance may have been a tempest but the issue in the governmental view was a side wind and change should not come from side winds, said the Lord Chancellor.

His reply was a set of variations on the theme that this was an important constitutional issue which should not be dealt with on the appeal of an individual. What was wanted was those 'full and frank deliberations' which those doubtful of change always propose as a brake on the more impetuous.

It was within the functioning of an ordered constitution that true liberty alone lay, he said. Politics was the most fascinating but the most cruel of all occupations. No one was indispensable. Despite Mr Benn's excellence as a House of Commons man he could not be differentiated from any other heir to a peerage.

The theme, or the variations, or both, offended Stansgate's ear. Almost hopping with fury he declared he had never heard a speech which filled him with so much despair.

Even thought the House voted firmly for the Government view, by 54 votes to 24, it was obvious there was considerable doubt as well as concern about the matter. Lord Hastings, holder of one of the most ancient of titles, while not denying Mr Benn's right to renounce, declared that this should be final. Peerages should not become convertible commodities, otherwise the appropriate supporter for a coat of arms would be a jack-in-the-box. Lord Samuel saw the whole thing as an infringement of personal liberty and even a breach of Commons privileges. The Lords had no right to remake a man's life against his will. A king could abdicate but a peer, apparently, could not.

That, for most people, would have been that, but it was not for Benn, even though it had to be that until his father died, in November 1960. That very night, he disclosed later, his pay and allowances as an MP ceased — 'I received my cards'. In exchange he posted off to the Lord Chancellor the Letters Patent of the viscounty.

Could he renounce or could he not? Was he disqualified from the Commons automatically on the death of his father or was he not? Could a decision of the Lords in 1678, in its own self-interest, without reference to the

Commons, be binding on the Commons? Those were questions to delight constitutional lawyers, to be argued over and savoured and, after three centuries, to be answered only because of the persistence of Benn. Not that the answers were to bring him much satisfaction, however much they fitted his suspicions of what they would be.

On the death of a Lord in Parliament — it was the possession of that red velvet seat in the Upper Chamber, not the family estates in Essex which was at issue — the heir did not receive the writ of summons to that place until he produced his predecessor's death certificate and his own birth certificate. Until he did so, Benn contended, however much he might be considered a peer he certainly was not a Lord in Parliament, refused the right of being a Commoner in parliament.

Secondly, the House of Commons (Disqualification) Act drew up a list of offices and places that disqualified from membership and declared that no member of the Commons, or candidate, could be forced to accept a disqualifying office. Was a peerage an office or a place? If it was an office it was covered by the bar in the Act. If it was a place, as, admittedly, the Letters Patent described it, then it could be that the terms of the appointment of the law officers, the Attorney-General and Solicitor-General, also disqualified them or, alternatively, made it possible to sit in both Houses.

Then there was the paramount point for so avid a defender of Commons paramountcy, could the Crown prevent one elected by his constituents taking his place?

Benn described himself as 'not a reluctant peer but a persistent commoner' and hinted that he might be as persistent as that other fighter against orthodoxy and tradition, Charles Bradlaugh, and fight — and win — election after election until Parliament accepted the decision of the electors. Bradlaugh's battle had been over his determination, as an atheist, not to take the oath but to affirm. That, as it turned out, was the course Benn had to take,

111

though officialdom knuckled down rather more weakly than its Victorian predecessor.

Interestingly, when asked how he wanted to be addressed, he then replied 'Anthony Wedgwood Benn', the more plebeian appeal of Tony Benn was not yet established.

A Select Committee, chaired by R. A. Butler, then Leader of the House, deliberated long on the matter but when it reported in the following March it found against Benn on every issue. He was Viscount Stansgate — though it referred to him as Mr Wedgwood Benn — he could not renounce his peerage, he was disqualified from sitting in the Commons, a summons to sit in the Lords would not involve Commons privilege, the committee did not recommend a Bill to enable him to remain a member of the Commons.

That last point, the question of an enabling bill, was only passed by Butler's casting vote. All other points were passed by six votes to four but on that the four Labour Front-benchers, Hugh Gaitskell, George Brown, Chuter Ede and G. R. Mitchison were joined by Conservative MP Sir Kenneth Pickthorn, who asked for that one to be deleted.

The one gleam of hope for Benn, which he must have then thought a very faint one at the end of a very long tunnel, was the statement that the Committee's terms of reference did not require it to express an opinion on whether there should be general legislation on the right of peers to sit in the Commons.

The Committee's report quoted, approvingly, one of Benn's own witnesses, Michael Foot's brother Dingle Foot QC MP that, in the eyes of the law an heir must become a peer as soon as succession was established, but rejected his contention that the validity of that law was questionable.

Another of Benn's witnesses was Dick Taverne, then a young Labour lawyer, with an expertise in medieval law. Later he was to be the controversial Labour MP for Lincoln, whose advocacy of the Common Market brought him to loggerheads with Benn, when Benn was chairman of the party, and who, eventually, after a brief spell as Democratic Labour MP following a by-election in 1974 and the formation of a party which won control of Lincoln Council, was ousted in the 1974 October election.

Not that recourse to medieval history was of much help to Benn. If fourteen peers, or sons of peers, had sat in the Commons in the fourteenth and fifteenth century that would not invalidate what had become settled law since, said the Committee. Anyway, it turned out, they doubted Benn's witnesses' history.

The committee preferred the more recent precedent of the MP for West Edinburgh of 1895, Viscount Woolmer, who, on succeeding to the Earldom of Selborne, objected he wanted to stay in the Commons. He had been refused. Later, Benn was to argue, forgetting for the moment his medieval witnesses, that 1895 was too old hat. Parliament should bring itself into the twentieth century, the later twentieth century.

Not that Benn got much help from the support of the peer coming first in non-Royal precedence, the Duke of Norfolk, who declared, 'it may be that some of our methods are today out of date'; nor from that of the Lord Great Chamberlain, who had suggested to the first Lord Stansgate that his heir might be seconded to sit in the Commons, as the heir of Churchill, if he had become a Duke, might well have been. Perhaps, after all, it was a pity that Churchill did not accept that Dukedom, no precedent could be refused one of such prestige.

A more general comment, which was to come up again and again in later actions, was one which Benn might find abhorrent in these more race-conscious times. It came from Lord Saltoun who wrote:

Is it not absurd that a man can come from foreign parts,

113

settle and make a fortune here, become naturalized himself or his sons, and then aim at the posts of the greatest power in our land, with all his predilection for human sacrifice, ritual prostitution and witchcraft latent in his blood, while those who have been part of our nation for centuries and undergone great sacrifices from age to age are debarred from even competing?

Benn's next move was to petition to be allowed to speak from the Bar of the House of Commons. The House had before it the report of its committee rejecting his claim and also a motion for the introduction of a 21-line bill, the Peerage (Renunciation) Bill, which would make it possible for peerages to be renounced for life. The one thing that proved was that the Conservative party was divided. Viscount Lambton, one of several of its own MPs faced with Benn's position, was one of the proposers of the bill.

The Government won the day, rejecting the bill, approving the report and refusing Benn's request to speak, but only at the cost of the opposition of at least fifteen of its own MPs, plus that of the political correspondent of the most ardent of its supporters in the Press, the *Daily Telegraph*. His verdict was that justice had not been seen to be done and he quoted approvingly the comment of Liberal leader Jo Grimond that in courts, when the evidence seemed to point one way, nobody said, 'do not bother about a trial. Just sentence the chap behind the scenes'.

The best speech of all, unheard in the Commons, was printed at length in the papers of the next morning. It was Benn's. The law should allow the privileges of peerage to be renounced for the rights of commoners, it went. All contrary objections rested on the assumption the British constitution was so precariously balanced on a pedestal of tradition that any real change would threaten its stability. Benn continued:

114

. . . to believe that, is totally to misread the whole history of Parliament — rich with examples of brilliant innovations and studded with new precedents that have shaped our destiny . . . Our ancient pageantry is but a cloak covering the most flexible and adaptable system of government ever devised by man. It has been copied all over the world just because it is such a supreme instrument of peaceful change. In Parliament tradition has always served as a valued link, reminding us of our history, never as a chain binding us to the past. To misunderstand that would be to misunderstand everything that this House has achieved over the centuries.

The vote meant that South-east Bristol no longer had an MP. There had to be a by-election. No one appeared to be in much doubt that Benn would do a Bradlaugh and stand. During the debate that debonair but principled and highly individualistic Tory, Gerald Nabarro, declared he would campaign for Benn and hoped the Conservatives would not put up a candidate. Benn could stand, if his nomination paper was in order, ruled law officer Sir Reginald Manningham-Buller, but even if he topped the poll he would not be allowed to sit, votes cast for him would be votes thrown away.

Thrown away? That was not the view of the electors. When the returning officer announced the figures, the following month, he reported a vastly increased majority, of 13,044 for Benn, compared to 5,827 at the previous General Election, a swing of over 13 per cent to him from his Conservative opponent Malcolm St Clair.

Armed with that authority from the electors Benn tested the defences of the House, as it prepared to sit the following Monday, under the Churchill Arch, leading to the Commons Chamber. He had already made his entry, as a member of the public, through St Stephen's door, his brilliant red tie lighting his way.

That tie did not dazzle Mr Victor Stockley, who rejoiced in the title of Principal Doorkeeper. Their exchange, beneath the Arch went:

Mr Benn: I have a certificate here which returns me as the member for Bristol, South-east.
Mr Principal Doorkeeper: You cannot enter, sir.
Benn: On whose instructions?
P.D.: By Mr Speaker's, sir.
Benn: Are you instructed to prevent me entering by physical force if necessary?
P.D.: I am, sir.

Whereupon Benn, with his escort of two Labour MPs, turned and left. It was, as observers suspected, a playlet prepared if not rehearsed. Benn had been in the House already that day and seen the Speaker.

Inside, the House debated first a motion by Hugh Gaitskell that Benn be admitted and heard. The electors of Bristol had made their view overwhelmingly clear. Of course it might not just be their view on renunciation of peerages which was made so clear, but their view of the Government, in which case it was not Benn who should not be there but Government ministers. He quoted the *Daily Express* for the view that 'public opinion overwhelmingly favours changing the law to enable peers to sit in the Commons if they so wish', and for the questions 'why are ministers so stubborn?' and 'why the insistence on delay?' Answers, suggested the *Express*, might be found in the 'able, brilliantly attractive, roly-poly figure of Lord Hailsham, Lord President of the Council and Minister for Science', then as maverick a member of the upper councils of his party and a candidate for leadership as much feared by orthodoxy as Benn was to become in the Labour Party.

As tit for tat R. A. Butler replied that if Attlee had given a favourable response earlier to Hailsham they might have had him in the Commons — 'no one would

116

be happier than the Government to have him here' —
and, by implication, Benn.

After that motion had been duly defeated, with some
Conservatives voting against their party, Butler proposed
that 'Anthony Neil Wedgwood Benn, otherwise Viscount
Stansgate, be not permitted to enter the Chamber unless
the House otherwise orders', amended by George Brown
to read that 'the oath be administered to Mr Anthony
Neil Wedgwood Benn and that he do take his seat'.

The issue, of course, was never in doubt; the amend-
ment defeated, the motion approved, and the matter left
to the Electoral Court, St Clair having already presented
his petition that he be declared elected in place of Benn.

One rebellious Tory contribution came from Lambton.
It was beyond contention, he said, that unless the House
of Lords was reformed it would have no future. The
Government side, who wanted the retention of a two-
Chamber Government, were saying the House of Lords
was not going to be reformed at present. Had there ever
been such an absurd situation? In retrospect it was a
noteworthy speech.

It was indicative of a growing view in the Lords itself,
where the revolt was proving stronger than among Tory
Commoners. Even the Marquess of Salisbury, that pillar
of Lordly Toryism, had said he thought there was a case
for exceptional treatment of a peer with a career in the
Commons behind him.

Once again Benn had a speech to be handed out to the
Press if not delivered to the House. In it political commentators found echoes of his predecessor as a Bristol
MP, that fighter for Parliament's rights and people's liberties, Edmund Burke:

My sole authority [for claiming the Bristol South-east
seat] is that the electors of that constituency have deci-
sively chosen me to represent them here.

We, who are members of this House of Commons, do

not sit here at the whim of the Crown or by courtesy of the Lords. We do not come here at the discretion of Mr Speaker or even by consent of the House — and least of all by virtue of any personal merit. We sit here because we have been elected by our constituents and for no other reason whatsoever . . .

I come now not as a supplicant for special favours but as the servant of those whose will must be sovereign. What happens to me matters not at all. But their right of free choice is of tremendous constitutional importance and it is my clear duty to defend it — whatever the consequences for me may be.

The monetary consequences, it may be said, were to prove considerable.

Nowadays some political commentators might look critically on the sincerity of such a speech. At the time none did. Perhaps they were less cynical times — times when ministers were expected to resign if their departments were in disrepute. Certainly Benn was winning not just the admiration of his colleagues and people generally for the manner in which he was conducting his fight but their affection for his behaviour and his youthful likeableness.

Benn had listened to the debate from the public gallery. To the suggestion that he might do so from the peers gallery he replied with just a look.

'He nothing common did or mean upon that memorable scene,' quoted the *Telegraph*, adding, 'King Charles was at least given a hearing.'

CHAPTER EIGHT

The Constitution Overturned — 'A Victory for Common Sense'

The stage then moved to the High Court in London, before two judges, Gorman and McNair, sitting as the Electoral Court. Leading for St Clair was Sir Andrew Clark, leading barrister in the Chancery Division, a renowned advocate, with a gravelly voice, in the direct line of descent from Dickens's Sergeant Buzz-Fuzz. Mere solicitors and lesser barristers scuttled from his path as he made his way about the corridors of that gloomy Gothic edifice — it was before the removal of London grime from the walls turned it into a soaring triumph of Victorian architecture — and even judges could expect no more than a condescending nod, when off their benches. Benn could have had the pick of Labour lawyers but chose to represent himself, developing a 'peculiar type of advocacy as if he had been doing it all his life', one of those lawyers commented admiringly afterwards.

Clark, who said at the outset he would call the respondent 'the respondent', to avoid controversy over his name and title, told the court five points of law were at issue.

Was a peer disqualified by the common law of Parliament from being a member of the House of Commons? If he was, could he effectively renounce his peerage? If he could, had the respondent done so by merely writing his renunciation? The fourth point was whether the House of Commons (Disqualification) Act of 1957 had altered the common law; the petitioner, St Clair, said it had not affected the privileges or disabilities of a peer in any way. Finally there was the question whether or not St Clair was entitled to be declared duly elected, if the court found for him on the previous points.

On the fifth point Clark submitted the respondent's disqualification was 'notorious and common knowledge' in the constituency. Express notice had been given to electors that he was, prior to polling, and therefore their votes were thrown away. They must be treated as void, leaving St Clair at the head of the poll. The fact that the matter had had to be brought before the Electoral Court for a decision on the matter of disqualification was, seemingly, irrelevant to the claim that the electors should and, indeed, must have known the law before the Court decided.

Perplexing though that might be to the lay mind it turned out in the end to be the view of the Court. When, at one point, Mr Justice McNair pointed out that the one thing the electors did not know was the decision of the court, Clark charged them, the electors of Bristol South-east, with perversity — though he was quick to point out that perversity did not have to be proved.

The vital point of disqualification was, seemingly, a matter of common law — if not of common knowledge where the people of Bristol were concerned. The law relating to the peerage of England, its rights, privileges and disabilities depended entirely on custom. There had, until then, been no decision of a court of law on the question and there was no express statutory disqualification. The common law had to be ascertained from decisions of the Houses of Parliament, themselves and their committees, and also from the writings and opinions of authoritative authors.

Peers of the realm, declared Clark, 'being bound to serve the state in a capacity incompatible with the character of a representative of the people, composed a distinct and separate part of the constitution and had always been deemed ineligible to sit and incapable of sitting in the House of Commons.'

Going back one hundred and sixty-six years, to one of those authoritative authors, Simeon on Elections, pub-

120

lished in 1795, was long enough to establish common law, said Clark, thereby countering the medieval research done by Taverne, by others in Benn's army of researchers and by Benn himself.

Benn, or the others, had done later research also, it proved. He had already interrupted Clark earlier, gaining sufficient of Clark's approval to be addressed as 'Mr Benn' as, said Clark, he knew the respondent wished, to say he was not contesting points three and four. Now he had Clark somewhat at a loss when the counsel quoted the distinguished authority on Parliamentary law, Halsbury, in his *Precedents of Proceedings in the House of Commons*, first edition, in support of his view that a peer became disqualified on succession.

Benn broke in to point out that there was a vitally important footnote in the second edition which entirely contradicted the sense of what was reported to have been said, by a certain Speaker, in the first edition. When Clark admitted he had not seen it Benn handed him a photograph. Clark, after studying this, declared it was not relevant, it referred only to remote heirs, not to successors to a peerage by lineal descent. McNair took a different view. It meant, he said, a fresh election should not be ordered until the member had been called up to the House of Lords.

If that gave Benn renewed hope of victory that hope was misplaced. No one would ever suggest, of course, that the dispassionate view on any subject of one of Her Majesty's judges would ever be coloured by the jaundiced reception of a piece of High Court humour. A short while before, though, Sir Andrew had made a joke on the difference between 'Scotch', used primarily by Scotsmen to describe their national drink, and 'Scottish', a joke which had not been happily received by the Scottish judge.

One authority on law, but not language, had referred to a 'Scotch peer' in discussing disqualification.

121

A Scottish peer might not like to be called a 'Scotch' peer, commented Clark, but by doing so one might avoid the unfortunate error *The Times* once made when a Scottish peer's personal habits, his liking for Scotch, was indicated by the printer leaving out the 'c' in 'Scottish'.

Perhaps he had forgotten Mr Justic McNair was there, but, primly, the judge responded that the disqualification of Scottish peers was one of the grievances against the Act of Union.

But it was that Scottish peer, Lord Woolmer, and his case in 1895, when he was found by a Select Committee to be automatically disqualified, which proved the backbone of Clark's case. Though Parliamentary committees could not change the law, it appeared they could make abundantly clear, through their pronouncements, what common law was.

Understandably, even for an MP practised in oratory, Benn was nervous when he rose to open his case. He spoke rapidly. He fluttered his hands before him, reported observers. But as he warmed to his subject his nervousness went. His first concern, in his speech, was democracy, the will of the people, in his view the sovereignty of the people. To suggest that they, in this case the people of Bristol, were not concerned above all else for their representation in Parliament, to suggest that they were more concerned with having a demonstration than electing an MP was monstrous.

He had accepted nomination for the disputed election, he declared, because he believed that a Member elected to Parliament had a first duty to those who sent him there and cou'l not accept disqualification save by common offence against the law of the land. Solemnly he declared:

I would have been betraying the interests of my constituents had I allowed anyone other than them to remove me from the Commons. I had to go back to them to say 'do you still want me?' . . . I believe this case will give the opportunity for the first judicial examination of the rights of electors.

With the rights of the electors went the duties of the elected. The Court would have to balance those electoral duties against the moral duties which Sir Andrew had read into the Letters Patent of a peer. The House of Commons regarded those electoral duties so highly that no MP could resign them, only disqualify himself.

The question, of course, was whether he was disqualified by the fact of becoming a peer. He said he was not, but agreed his whole case rested on his contention that only a writ of summons to the House of Lords would disqualify a peer from the House of Commons.

This was an unusual election case. There were no charges of corruption or bribery, as in earlier cases. It was the first time someone had appeared in the dock, in effect, in an electoral court on a charge of 'peerage'. The petitioner himself, he pointed out, was himself an heir to a peerage and, therefore, separated from the disqualification he wanted to impose on another by a single heartbeat. St Clair was heir presumptive to the seventeenth Baron Sinclair.

'I come from a Parliamentary family which for three generations has been seeking to make the House of Commons its hereditary home,' said Benn. He would not be arguing on the validity or otherwise of his instrument of renunciation but renunciation was his intent.

'I wish to renounce the Viscounty of Stansgate and in that wish I am supported by every member of my family. We all feel that the Viscounty of Stansgate, having been created as a matter of State policy, should now be extinguished.'

The disqualification of peers, he submitted, was based on incompatibility of parliamentary service, not on status, and that incompatibility of service arose with a writ of summons and not before. Writs of summons must be claimed from the Crown and no right or duty to attend the House of Lords arose until one was issued.

He cited his own authorities for that view, argued against Clark's interpretation of his authorities and produced one novel suggestion. As the question whether the writ was the instrument of disqualification was the crux of the matter then, in order to avoid any possibility of conflict between the decision of the House of Commons and the decision of the Crown — that conflict, after all, had been the source of the seventeenth-century rulings — the court should lay down as a matter of law that the issue of the writ was the sole determining matter. It should then apply to the Lord Chancellor for a certificate on the matter. Clark thereupon interrupted Benn. That was only a possible solution if the Court ruled it had no jurisdiction. It was not a procedure arising naturally, even from the authorities quoted by Benn.

What Benn was arguing was that the Crown was the sole fountain of honour, questions of succession could be determined only by the appropriate constitutional machinery, by the Lord Chancellor himself or, in disputed cases, on a reference from the Crown to the Committee of Privileges. On their decision the writ of summons would be issued. He had taken no steps to prove the succession, no writ had been issued and, therefore, the Court had no jurisdiction.

It was not an argument which appealed to the Court. If that were the law the Court could not decide the matter it had been told to decide. The question of succession, the judges ruled, would have to be determined by the Common Law. The writ, they conceded, was the crux of the matter but the truth was its importance had declined. Originally it was everything. The King summoned his councillors by it. The fact a man was called to one Council conferred no right on him to attend subsequent Councils, still less did it confer that right on his successors. Only with the rise of the Barons did it confer a hereditary right

124

to sit in the House of Lords. The appearance of Letters Patent, in 1387, had changed things. It was the Letters Patent, ruled the Court, that conferred the right, the writ just gave time and place. But, by the way the judgment went, it had taken a further four and a half centuries for that to be established in the Common Law. By the early nineteenth century, but, seemingly, not before, the writ had ceased to be the only method by which the disqualification by status could be established, the judges ruled.

As for renunciation, it followed that a peer had no right to renounce. Those medieval peers who had renounced had been wrong, even the King, it seemed, had been wrong to accept renunciation. A ruling by the House of Lords Privilege Committee in 1907, on a claimant to a defunct Earldom of Norfolk, meant, said the judges, that the Earl of 1302 had been wrong in surrendering his earldom to Edward I in 1302 and Edward II had been wrong in granting a Charter in 1312. That Charter was invalid. This to lay minds might seem perplexing. A fourteenth-century King was the law, yet a fourteenth-century King had transgressed the law. It seemed to involve a degree of transubstantiation beyond even the powers of a medieval king. Henry VIII, no doubt, would just have changed the law, if it had been brought to his notice.

Despite all those complexities which the Court itself had taken a week to resolve, the Court ruled the electors of Bristol should have known the respondent — noticeably, the Court still avoided using the title Viscount Stansgate — was disqualified. Mr St Clair was entitled to the seat.

The one point the judges found in favour of Benn was on his conduct of his case. Judge Gorman recalled that in the course of the 'delightful manner' in which Mr Benn had conducted his case, once again the judge avoided mention of the viscounty, he had used words to the effect: 'I had intended to make the House of Commons my career. It may be that I shall now have to get my living in some other way.'

His Lordship thought that there might be some other way.

'Indeed,' he said, 'having heard the magnificent way his case has been conducted by Mr Benn this Court has not the slightest doubt that there is another way.'

Kind words but it was the actions which hurt and continued to hurt. It had been a costly experience for Benn. Not only had he lost his seat and his career, he had been ordered to pay the costs of the action. Sir Andrew had described as 'extraordinary' Benn's suggestion that it had been a matter which needed to be settled in the interests of the community and therefore he should not be called upon to pay. There were no pennies from Heaven, said Clark. The Government was not bearing the costs. Why should Mr St Clair have what Sir Andrew called 'the enormous expense' of fighting the petition.

Some years later Benn revealed the St Clair costs came to £7,500, a very large sum in those days, the equivalent of at least five times as much in the early 1980's. It took him years of hard freelance work to pay it off.

But with MPs on the Government side supporting Benn, Noble Lords with the bluest of blood, with never a tinge of red, supporting him, and the newspapers supporting him, it was a ruling which could not survive to become established law — that an MP was automatically sacked on the death of a peer to whom he was the heir. The will of the people, of the majority, even when it included peers, among them newspaper peers, who could not vote, must prove sovereign.

Even before St Clair took his seat in the Commons a few days later, at the beginning of August 1961, promising Benn, it transpired later, that he would give it up if the law on the renunciation of peerages was changed, the step had been taken to change the law.

Butler had already announced a Select Committee

126

would consider the composition of the Lords, the rights of peers to sit in either House and to vote and possible changes in the law on the surrender of peerages. For good measure it was also to consider the question of payment to peers who carried out their parliamentary duties, or indulged their parliamentary privileges. (So those Labour lords who find their peerages a satisfying extra to their pensions owe Benn some degree of thanks for that.)

Would it be able to consider the total abolition of the Lords, asked Jo Grimond, then Liberal leader. Butler parried that. It would depend on the meaning of the word 'composition'. If anyone wanted to give evidence to the Select Committee on that meaning that, he presumed, would be in order.

The Times forecast it would take at least a year for the Committee to report and another year for parliamentary and public opinion to crystallize on the matter. On the first point it was right. In December 1962 the Committee reported in favour of the right to surrender a peerage for life only. A surrendered peerage should remain dormant until the next heir had to decide, himself. A peer who surrendered should be able to vote in parliamentary elections and to stand himself, but a surrender should be irrevocable. Having been defeated in a bid to sit in the Commons the one-time peer should not be able to go back to the Lords. The right to surrender should be retrospective, those who would have wished to exercise such a right if it had existed when they succeeded should now be given an opportunity to exercise it within a reasonable time.

The proposal on retrospective rights, from a Labour member, Mitchison, was carried by a single vote, by eleven to ten. A majority of the Conservatives on the Committee voted against, but it was a memorandum from Lord Hailsham, Leader of the Lords and Lord President of the Council, which appears to have carried the day. It had been argued that the right to surrender should be

127

available only to those who had not applied for a writ of summons, on the grounds that a line had to be drawn somewhere and that was an obvious point, the one where a peer had himself taken the step to sit in the Lords.

That was a specious argument, declared Hailsham. It would disqualify those who had thought it their duty to comply with the existing law and to undertake the social and moral obligations of the holder of a peerage and qualify those who, from apathy, neglect or a desire to flout the law, had not complied. Naturally there were some in Westminster who thought they saw an element of personal interest in Hailsham's counsels.

Another memorandum by Hailsham did not get the support of the Select Committee. He did not see any advantage in people having to opt for life. Few at the age of 21 knew whether they would wish to enter the Commons at 40 and those who did know were not necessarily the best. There might be virtue in lifelong vows in religion and matrimony, though they were sometimes onerous even there, but it was taking the romantic outlook too far to make them part of a political mysticism. Peers should not move backwards and forwards at will, like a horizontal yo-yo, not because of any advantage but because such behaviour was ridiculous and some of the ridicule would attach to Parliament. He suggested either a ten-year choice or one for the length of the current Parliament plus the next, whichever was the shorter.

'No,' said the Committee. Surrender must be for life and the decision must be taken promptly, within a month for a peer already in the Commons when he succeeds, six months for a peer already succeeded when the law is changed, a year for all others.

'A victory for common sense' was Benn's response. Cautiously he pointed out that the battle had not yet been won and would not be won until the law was changed.

But changed it was, and in less than the year predicted. The Government had already drawn up a bill on the lines recommended. On 31 July, 1963, just two years after the Electoral Court had divested him of his proud title of elected MP and ruled he was hereditary Viscount Stansgate, he was sitting in the gallery of the House of Lords to hear the Royal Assent given to the Peerage Act with the words *'La Reyne le vault'*, words redolent of Norman autocracy but on this occasion signifying his own victory for the democratic principle over the autocratic hereditary principle.

Benn took off as if a starting pistol had been fired, reported onlookers. With his wife and mother struggling to keep up he sped down the stairs to hand to Sir George Coldstream, the Clerk of the Crown in Chancery, an Instrument of Disclaimer, his renunciation of the Stansgate Viscounty, witnessed by his wife, Caroline. Placing his right thumb on the seal he said, 'This is my deed and my act.' Sir George had a draft of the Lord Chancellor's receipt to hand and proudly Benn told political correspondents, 'I am the first man in history who, by Act of Parliament, is prevented from receiving an hereditary peerage. I am statutorily immunized.'

At a celebratory party he held up a phial of his blood to show there was no blue in it. Recalling that gesture, one of the guests at the party, Tory MP Peter Kirk, who had helped in the renunciation campaign, recently commented, 'Sadly he has since lost his sense of humour.'

Soon Benn was back in the Commons, St Clair having stood down, with an increased majority of over 15,000.

His renunciation was quickly followed by those of other reluctant peers and wishful commoners. Lord Altrincham became John Grigg again, Lord Hailsham was once more Quintin McGarel Hogg.

The Prime Minister, no doubt the last premier to sit in the Lords and the first to reverse the normal process by being translated from Lords to Commons, ceased to be the Earl of Home. At 3.05 p.m. on 23 October 1963, allowing three minutes for the disclaimer document to be carried from 10 Downing Street to be registered in the House of Lords, he reverted to the Rt Hon Sir Alexander Frederick Douglas-Home.

The terms of his renunciation, under the then established law, contrasted with the flowery appeals to medieval monarchs by those anxious to be relieved of a burden:

Peerage Act 1963

WHEREAS I, THE RIGHT HONOURABLE SIR ALEXANDER FREDERICK DOUGLAS-HOME, Knight of the Most Ancient and Most Noble Order of the Thistle, succeeded to the peerages described in the Annex hereto on the date specified in that Annex, and desire to disclaim the said peerages for my life under the above mentioned Act:

AND WHEREAS I attained the age of twenty one years before the said date:

NOW THEREFORE, I, the said Sir Alexander Frederick Douglas-Home, in accordance with the provisions of the said Act, hereby disclaim the said peerages for my life:

IN WITNESS whereof I have hereunto set my hand and seal . . .

The annex listed six peerages, the Earldom of Home, the Lordship of Dunglass, the Lordship of Home, the Lordship of Hume of Berwick, the Barony of Douglas and the Barony of Hume of Berwick.

Some genealogists said they were puzzled. The original Lord Hume of Berwick, they pointed out, was only a remote relative of Sir Alec's family, who had accompanied James I to England and was rewarded with the title in 1604. If it had been included in case it had descended, said the editor of Debrett's, then it was strange that Sir Alec had not included the Earldom of Dunbar, conferred on Lord Hume of Berwick the following year.

No one followed that up to decide if, after all, Sir Alec had been in error while he sat in the Commons for the next ten years and should have been in the Lords as the Earl of Dunbar instead. He returned to the Lords with a life peerage in 1974.

Not all disclaimers were from political motives. One, at least, was to disembarrass the holder of the same problem which so upset Guichard D'Angle in the fourteenth century. Charles Fitzroy, the 60-year-old fifth Baron Southampton, one-time man about town and night-club owner and a descendant, on the wrong side of the blanket, of Charles II, renounced his peerage to cut living expenses. Wherever he went, as a peer, he said, he had to pay more. He also wanted to get away from hangers-on. He explained:

To get away from the snobs I had to leave home at Ascot for weeks on end. I tried living under an assumed name in a hotel in Wales, but the truth soon leaked out.

Some of the fools actually thought I owned all Southampton, including the river Test. One woman asked me to send her a salmon the next time I fished 'my' river. To teach her a lesson, I bought a frozen Canadian salmon and sent it to her. But you can't freeze out a snob. The absurd woman did not know the difference.

The eighth peer to renounce was the Earl of Sandwich, who, as Viscount Hinchingbrooke, had been a distinguished member of the Commons before Benn. He had objected that the Select Committee report, and the Act, did not go far enough. He condemned the report as 'partial', 'inadequate', 'tailormade to the needs of Mr Wedgwood Benn' and 'unnecessarily republican in character'.

A memorandum he had submitted, he complained, had been ruled by the Select Committee as outside its terms of reference — thereby, it seems, fulfilling Jo Grimond's

131

fears about its lack of readiness to consider House of Lords reform.

The Lords, went the memorandum, contained more disinterested and experienced members and its debates were on a higher level than those of the Commons but there remained the latent danger of sudden and capricious rearguard action by 'hereditary backwoodsmen'. What he called 'this disabling factor to the prestige of the House' needed to be removed by reducing its numbers to those who were, in general judgment, reliable councillors. The Royal prerogative to create peers and peeresses should continue and in all cases they should be hereditary. But only the first generation would automatically sit in the House. Those of the second and subsequent generations would be eligible to be elected for life by an Electoral College of peers, as Irish peers had once been. The College would meet at the end of each Parliament. Eldest sons, on succeeding, could continue to sit in the Commons until elected for the Lords. No one, of course, should be a candidate for election to both Commons and Lords.

The tenth peer to renounce raised another problem which had not been settled by the Act, that of courtesy titles used by wives and descendants of peers, sometimes lesser peerages held by a peer, such as a viscounty held with an earldom or, at the least, the prefix 'Honourable'. Lord Lambton disclaimed on the death of his father, the Earl of Durham, but wanted to remain Viscount Lambton, the name by which he was known and, more important, the name under which he had been elected to Parliament. He was, he declared, fighting for others. He would at least remain Mr Lambton if he lost his courtesy title but Lord Balniel, if he disclaimed on those terms, would have to appear on the ballot paper as Robin Lindsay, quite unknown to his electors. The Earl of Dalkeith would appear as Walter Scott, more familiar but not in an electoral context.

Hailsham had suggested to the Select Committee that

132

it should be left to the choice of the person whether he continued to call himself by his hereditary title when he renounced. It was a title which no one else could claim during his lifetime. Retained it did no one an injustice, abandoned it affected only the person concerned. The Marquess of Salisbury, a former Conservative Leader of the Lords, had attempted to get that written into the recommendations. Peers, he proposed, should be able to divest themselves of their parliamentary status while retaining the use of their titles. He was roundly defeated. On courtesy titles the Committee recommended that they should cease to be used by wives and descendants of peers who renounced. When the Act came to be written, though, nothing was included on the matter. It was lamely suggested, later, that it was thought this would follow automatically.

It did when Home renounced. His children gave up their titles. Later the Earl Marshal, the Duke of Norfolk, advised by Mr G D Squibb QC, Norfolk Herald Extraordinary, quoted as the highest authority by Sir Andrew Clark at the time of the Electoral Court, ruled that children could keep courtesy titles. Home's children did not change their minds. They had given up their titles from 'love, favour and affection' for their father, they declared.

Lambton, said to be the least snobbish of aristocrats, who had supported Benn at the 1961 by-election, asked, in 1970, for a bill to enable him to continue to use the title Viscount, as when he was elected. James Callaghan, then Home Secretary, refused. Debrett's pointed out that if he were allowed to use the title there would be two Viscount Lambtons, himself and his son. Two years later, though, the Lord Privy Seal, Earl Jellicoe, ruled in the Lords that no legislation had been passed preventing the use of courtesy titles. The Speaker, Selwyn Lloyd, ruled Lambton, then Joint Under-Secretary for Defence, could use his courtesy title. Labour indignation resulted in the matter being referred to the Committee of Privileges.

From that came a recommendation that he should be plain 'Mister' again. The use of the title was against the spirit of the Peerage Act.

Whatever the spirit of the Act, the opinion of the Crown Office in the House of Lords is that courtesy titles may be used.

'The Act did not forbid it. A peer has a month to renounce. In that month his child might get to like his new name. Why should he have to go back to his old one if he does not want to,' said one of its senior advisers in a surprisingly human approach to the matter.

There were no courtesy titles attached to the Viscounty of Stansgate but Benn's children were quite entitled to describe themselves as 'Honourable' if they so wished.

Lambton's situation had been quite different. He wanted to carry on with his old title after renouncing. Parliament had ruled that this could not be done in Parliament. Outside Parliament it was a different matter.

'Anyone, of course, can call themselves whatever they wish. Any of us can ask to be addressed as Duke or Earl, providing we do not do so with intent to deceive or defraud.' (Don't call yourself the Duke of Wapping in order to impress your bank manager, is that adviser's advice.)

Benn's own campaign to change his name was not over. He had lost the aristocratic Stansgate but there was still that interloper Wedgwood, even if not attached to Benn by a hyphen as when he was at school. Anthony, too, did not fit the image he wanted. There was still some way to go, another fight to be won, before he achieved the proletarian 'Tony Benn'.

In 1974, with Labour back in power and Benn back in the Cabinet, word was passed around among political journalists that he wished to be described as Tony Benn. Some complied, some did not. Some inquired at his Department and found a memo had been passed around, instructing that he was to be plain 'Tony Benn'. It was some years before the last of the editors of newspapers and news agencies relented and allowed him what is, after all, the right of every person, to be addressed as he wishes.

All, apparently, except *Who's Who*.

When he first appeared in those august pages he was the Hon Anthony Neil Wedgwood Benn. Then he became a Privy Councillor, to appear as the Rt Hon Anthony (Neil) Wedgwood Benn, with Neil relegated to brackets.

As an important public figure his entry ran to a good three inches, with those idiosyncratic touches which are expected of those filling in their *Who's Who* forms. His education 'continued after university'. His recreation was 'staying at home' until, in the natural order of things, it became 'staying at home with the family'. For years it stayed virtually the same, one addition perhaps showing his own assessment of the really important thing he had done in the first Wilson Government — 'recommended establishment of GPO as a public corporation and founded GIRO' it went. About the same time that appeared, in 1971, his recreation changed to 'family and politics'.

In 1974, when the word was going around that he wanted to be just 'Tony Benn' the only concession *Who's Who* made was to drop the '(Neil)'.

In 1976 it was still describing him as 'Benn, Rt Hon Anthony Wedgwood MP (Lab) Bristol SE, Secretary of State for Energy'. In response to that insistence on the rejected name, Benn added only one thing for his entry, his address, the House of Commons.

The next year his entry vanished altogether.

Whatever the promptings that led him to pare his name down to the fundamental essential of the surname Benn and the basic forename Tony, there can be no denying that replacing that for Viscount Stansgate was a considerable achievement.

When the Peerage Act was passed the *Guardian*, in a leader headed 'The Wedgwood Benn Act', found it reassuring that 'the combination of an attractive champion, a unanimous press, overwhelming public opinion and a just cause should eventually prevail'. It acknowledged, though, that it was essentially the work of one man. For ten years he had sustained an eloquent battle for personal liberty and for the rights of his constituents. Frequently repulsed, wrote the leader writer, he had declined to abandon what at times seemed a hopeless struggle. He never became bitter. With each successive disappointment his strength and stature appeared to grow.

Looking back on the achievement now does not diminish it. Others had tried before and failed. Many who felt he was an attractive champion then might not feel quite such attraction in some of the causes he champions nowadays. Perhaps that fight was one more likely to get support. But there had been other attractive champions, as well-liked by politicians and public, with reputations as parliamentarians and lawyers as high or higher, who had failed.

Benn succeeded. One might fairly call his victory over peerage renunciation the greatest single achievement by an individual MP this century. He established what the law was, when it was uncertain. He determined what the Constitution would have the position of a peer, when that was uncertain. Having done that he changed the Constitution and overturned three hundred years of law. There are not many of whom that can be said, and certainly no others working then as a young, back-bench MP and, for a while, a disenfranchised one.

CHAPTER NINE

'A Very Good Postmaster-General'

In after years, asked for his opinion of Tony Benn, Harold Wilson would say, after a moment's reflection, sucking at his pipe, 'Tony made a very good Postmaster-General.' The second time one heard him say it, going through the same little act, that apparent moment's reflection, for one renowned for his memory, seemed a little contrived. That has led some commentators to consider the remark faintly derogatory, as if to say that being Postmaster-General did not require the same ministerial ability as, say, being President of the Board of Trade, an office in which Wilson took special pride under Attlee. It is likely, though, there was an element of approval behind that superficial sneer, if it was a sneer. After all it was after Benn's performance as a very young Postmaster-General that Wilson gave him the plum post of Technology Secretary in a Government which had its origins and ambitions firmly based in the benefits of technology.

Wilson had set the scene for Labour's campaign in the General Election of October 1964, when speaking at the Trades Union Congress. There were to be a hundred days of decisive action, to break the shackles of twelve years of stop-go, when one year of expansion was followed by the screeching of brakes and three years of stagnation. Later in the campaign he recalculated it to 'thirteen wasted years'. Inspired by a visit to Socialist Sweden, where output per head had grown twice as fast as in Britain, he promised the TUC he would galvanize the economic life of Britain by a spirit of aggressiveness and enterprise. There were to be sweeping reforms, of economic planning, of taxation and, above all, in productivity. A Ministry of Technology would provide the scientific stimulus for a new industrial Britain, for new industries which would recapture Britain's lost exports.

It was a theme which stayed with him even after, successfully installed in Downing Street, he had looked inside the nation's housekeeping books and had his fervour dampened by what he saw.

'We are planning an urgent attack on those sectors of industry where Britain not long ago led the world and where our failure to innovate means not only that we are losing our impact on export markets but that we are rapidly becoming major importers,' he told the belated Labour Party Congress in December.

If he had wanted to illustrate that he might have pointed to the motor-cycle industry where, the previous year, imports had for the first time exceeded not only exports but even home production and which, that current year, were to double the total British output. New technology was certainly operating there, but in Japan not Britain. It was a matter which was to concern Benn intimately, but not until the next Labour Government, in 1974.

After those thirteen 'wasted years' much of Wilson's team was untried. He entrusted his brave new world of technology, his white-hot revolution to two from outside Parliament, Frank Cousins, General Secretary of the Transport and General Workers Union, a dominating figure in the world of labour, with a reputation for sensible solidity, and the academic and writer of academic novels, C P Snow. Benn as a rising parliamentarian, not yet forty years of age, was given a ministry but one outside the Cabinet.

The job of Postmaster-General is not one which usually makes or breaks reputations. Perhaps it is a measure of Benn's drive and determination to achieve what his political principles told him should be achieved — no one is likely to charge him with pragmatism as they might well charge Wilson — that he did make a reputation as PMG. The modernization of the Post Office was long overdue, he told one post office union after he had been eighteen months in the job, and he implied that one modernization should be to cut the number of unions from the twenty at which it then stood, but it must not be rushed. The temptation to act on a hunch must be resisted in an age when scientific management and carefully considered judgments were really needed, he said with words that could have come from Wilson himself and, indeed, might well have done. Modernization surveys, which were to bring about single daily delivery, first and second class postage, postal coding, were under way.

Listing the things done he — like all good democrats — put first those which brought the Post Office under public scrutiny, the creation of the Post Office Users' Council, the calling in of management consultants, the voluntary, indeed enthusiastic submission of Post Office affairs to the House of Commons Select Committee on Nationalized Industries. It was the first time, he said, that the Committee had looked at a Government Department. He had in fact made that possible by his recommendation that the Post Office should become a Public Corporation, thereby, in effect, bringing about his first nationalization. The spirit of his grandfather, with his belief that public monopolies should be publicly owned, must have approved. During his research into the Post Office archives Tony Benn might have recalled John Williams's brush with the Postmaster-General of the day over his belief in a universal need for the telephone and the public need, therefore, that the telephone service be publicly owned. A man named Preece, Tony later said, had told a select committee in 1875 that we had so many messenger boys we would never need telephones. Twenty years later, he said we had so many cheap girl operators we would never need automatic exchanges. Yet, Benn complained, scornful of such un-Benn-like behaviour, Preece had been described as 'the father of the British telephone service'.

One thing Benn did not mention in that union address

was pay. Postmen's pay had been a bone of contention for years but he saw through a three-year programme of increases which, to the outside observer, seemed to go well beyond the pay policies of the day. He had had to make many visits to Jim Callaghan, then Chancellor of the Exchequer, before it went through. The *Financial Times* saw the result as 'remarkably generous'. Militants, of course, claimed it was not enough for a long-term settlement. Benn must often reflect that however far one is, or is said to be, to the left, there is always somebody critical further out. Postmen's pay, however, ceased to be the wrangle it had been.

One continuingly deplorable aspect of the nation's pay, which no amount of increase would ever settle, only worsen — the pay snatch — was behind his proudest achievement at the Post Office, GIRO. In the early 1970's, when Tony allowed a sizeable entry in *Who's Who*, the two achievements he listed — those of which, one can feel confident, he was proudest — were the turning of the Post Office into a Public Corporation and the founding of Giro. Giro and investment accounts for savings banks, he claimed in that union address, were together the biggest development in popular banking since Gladstone founded the Savings Bank in 1865.

In the 1950's and 1960's the pay snatch was even more regularly in the news than the pay claim. Every Thursday and Friday gangs, armed to varying degrees, waylaid cashiers and their guards or even invaded cashier's offices to steal the working man's weekly pay-packet. While a phenomenon not peculiar to Britain, it was one more common and more developed here. Nowhere else did so many people get their pay in negotiable notes and coin, nowhere else did the banks have to pay out so much ready cash for that pay. It had come about because of the Truck Acts. The first, in 1831, was intended to protect the working man against unscrupulous employers. The meagre pay of those days, due fortnightly, not weekly, was virtually

140

certain to run out before the next lot was due. Many companies insisted that any advance, on wages already earned, should be spent in the company shop, the 'tommy' shop, derived it is supposed from 'tummy', it being that complaining part of the worker and his family's anatomy which drove him there. Prices were 10 per cent to 30 per cent higher than in ordinary shops and there were frequent charges of adulteration of goods. Under that Act all wages were to be paid in current coin of the realm. The term 'wages' was made comprehensive. Apart from some laid-down exceptions, such as tools in certain trades, all rewards were held to be wages. This has, on occasion, resulted in some workers being awarded sizeable sums in the courts when they have successfully argued that meals provided were part of their wages and should have been paid in cash, not kind.

The original Act applied to artificers. It was later broadened to cover all manual workers, except domestic servants. That resulted in strange anomalies. A bus conductor is not covered by the Act but his driver is, because if the bus broke down the driver might have to work on the engine to get it going again. A woman cleaning a doctor's home is not covered, but if she extends her work into the surgery she is. The greatest anomaly of all, in the world of the 1950's, was the number of people paid weekly in cash in Britain, compared with other countries, and the consequent lucrativeness of the wages snatch.

The Radcliffe Committee, on the working of the monetary system, meeting in that wage snatch atmosphere, suggested that there should be a simple, safe system for transferring payments, and if the banks did not take steps to provide one then the Government might look at the possibility of a postal Giro system, such as was used in Europe and elsewhere in the world. Workers were notoriously unwilling to accept payment by cheque because bank accounts were likely to cost them money in charges. The Giro system, for credit transfers from one person to

141

another through the post, named after the Greek for ring, *gurus*, was first set up in Austria in 1883. The Conservative Postmaster-General, Mr Reginald Bevins, declared himself 'fascinated' by the idea, went to Paris to inspect the French Giro, operating since 1918, but later instructed his Assistant, Ray Mawby, to declare the advantages were doubtful. The only action taken by his Government was to introduce the Payment of Wages Act, 1960. This allowed payment of wages by cheque, money order or credit transfer, but only at the employee's request and it had little effect.

Almost as soon as he was in the Postmaster-General's chair, Benn ordered another inquiry into the feasibility of a British Giro system. By mid-1965, under such headings as 'Mr Benn has his way', the newspapers were reporting the PMG's parliamentary announcement that Britain was to have a Giro, also the White Paper giving his views on how it was to be done. In the Commons Benn stressed the advantages to the little man. The insurance agent, for example, having collected his money would, with Giro, be able to pop into any post office to pay it in, instead of 'taking it home, hiding it in a sock or under the bed and hoping the burglars did not come to take it away' as he waited for the banks to open next day. Business firms and public utilities, receiving innumerable small payments on a regular basis had already declared their approval of the idea.

The publicity laid stress on the supposedly small number of people who had bank accounts, a total of 13 million, only a quarter of the population. Twenty-three thousand post offices would be available to Giro, open 'all day and every day, including Saturday' as Benn put it. The banks, already open for much shorter hours than post offices, were about to give up Saturday-morning opening. Giro, with one single computerized centre, would be faster than the banks, credits going through in a day instead of the usual three or more. With 1¼ million

142

accounts, averaging £100 to £150, Giro, said Benn, could produce an 8 per cent return on capital. Even the banks seemed fearful of the success Giro might be and rapidly introduced their own Giro system for quick transfers, though admitting it could not achieve anything like the 24-hour service Benn was forecasting.

Admittedly there were sceptics, though not so many as for later Benn projects. Some commentators pointed out that many of those 13 million bank accounts were joint accounts and so covered a larger fraction of the population than a quarter. In fact, Giro was set a stern task in Britain in competing with a banking system which was far more developed than in those other countries where it had become established. Currency in circulation here was only 11 per cent of consumer expenditure, while in France, where Giro was probably most highly developed, it was 21.4 per cent. Even in France only 11 per cent of people used Giro.

Still, even with those reservations visible with hindsight, the arguments for Giro were strong and it went ahead, but without Benn, translated to the White-Hot Seat of Technology after Cousins quarrelled with Wilson over pay policy. What was claimed to be the largest computer centre in Europe was built for it on Merseyside, to be opened by the Prime Minister himself, in October 1968 — in royal fashion, Wilson was found to be without the necessary cash to open an account and promised to send a cheque for £5. Wilson had taken under his wing what was, after all, the most tangible piece of evidence that a new, efficient, science-based Britain was on the way. As it turned out that might have been Giro's death-blow. As one Giro executive put it a year or two later: 'There was a tremendous political pressure on us to achieve in Giro something of the technological miracle that Wilson wanted.' It had been something of a technological miracle to get the complex computer operation functioning in three years from Benn's White Paper but the race to launch

Giro, which should have been a combined operation by a team with other members, such as marketing and publicity, to say nothing of political organization, was won by technology on its own.

For Benn, even then rather more Marxist than Wilson, the 1¼ million target had been the aim of a five-year plan. Before opening day it had, somehow, been cut to a year. There was no pressure on government and public bodies to use the service. Far from the public being urged to pay for car licences and such matters through Giro, it was still impossible to do so five years later, when private enterprise was beginning to value its real advantages.

The result was that the publicity, after the initial surge of Wilsonian words, was all adverse. After six months only 110,000 people had opened accounts. The minimum deposit was cut to £1 but there were still only 200,000 accounts after 16 months. The argument that for the average householder, paying four bills a month and making four withdrawals, Giro was a saving, costing him £4 a year against £6.15s for a bank account, did little to improve things, recruitment was still only 3,500 accounts a week. The public seemed to be thinking that, as with the telephone, it was not much use having a Giro account until most other people had one too. The first six months of Giro showed a loss of £2,000,000 on operations and the losses continued.

One Government department relented. Those losing their jobs found they could collect their dole through Giro — an omen for the 1970's? But the election of Heath's Tories made Giro's survival problematic. In that election year of 1970 Giro offered free facilities for withdrawals and linked with Mercantile Credit to offer a personal loans scheme. Cash balances grew to £50,000,000 and the service was half-way to break-even — but that still meant it was costing £6,000,000 more than its £7,200,000 revenue. The new Postmaster-General, former Olympic runner and world record-holder Christopher Chataway put

144

it into limbo for thirteen months while its future was considered. There were to be no new schemes, advertising stopped and, naturally, businesses held back from using it. For Chataway the renamed office of Minister of Posts and Telecommunications was not to provide starting blocks for a sprint to high office as it did for Benn. The Post Office fought for Giro. The knowledgeable pointed out that despite its current finances it was on course for the original targets, those set by Benn, not by Wilson. At the end of 1971 Chataway announced that the Government had accepted a Post Office recommendation that the service should continue, at least for eighteen months. By then £15,000,000 had been invested in Giro and it provided jobs for 3,500, a factor which, said the cynical, swayed Government thinking towards the reprieve.

With the brake off, Giro introduced new services in 1972, including a cash card and facilities to pay rent, and lengthened the period for repaying loans. It now had over half a million accounts and forecast it would break even by 1977. For the moment, though, losses were still rising, reaching over £7,000,000 a year and careful listeners claimed to hear the sound of knives being sharpened in Chataway's ministry. But the end of the eighteen-month reprieve came without any action and by the next year Wilson and Benn were back again.

Technology was no more, at least as a government department. Unlike Giro it had fallen victim to Tory knives. The plum job now, in a government bursting to remake its scientific, socialist Britain after the ravages of three-day-a-week Heathism, was Industry. Wilson gave that to Benn and, perhaps believing the parent of his favourite god-child, Giro, would make its best nurse, added the position of Posts, just temporarily, said the announcement. That year Giro had a great coup. Woolworths announced it would use its cash deposit service. Paying in branch takings through post offices, it said, would mean head office received the money two days earlier than paying through banks. That two days extra use of money was worth £250,000 a year. That might seem to go against the grain for Benn, with his original emphasis, in 1965, on the value of Giro to the small man, but, in fact, he had then forecast big business would find its quick money transfer attractive. After that breakthrough Giro signed up British Gas and the Co-op. Its financial situation was looking much healthier. Although the number of accounts was still only around half the original Benn target, a year after the original date he fixed for it, the average account was almost twice the £100 he had calculated was needed to get into profit.

The turn-round was under way. That year operating losses were cut by £3,000,000. In July 1975 came the announcement, most welcome for a nationalized service, that it was in profit. The joy over that in its Post Office home, though, was muted somewhat by ponderings whether Giro's earnings did not reflect losses by that older offspring, postal services. Altogether the Post Office lost £300,000,000 that year. Before he left Industry Benn gave his final tonic to what is probably the most successful and best-loved of his ministerial offspring. He prepared a Bill to write off half the accumulated losses, which then amounted to £33,400,000, turning most of the remainder into public dividend capital. The Bill also enabled Giro to compete in more of the orthodox banking services. There were muttered predictions that it was all a move towards the nationalization of the banks, or at least starting a Big Fifth, which might eventually swallow the Big Four, by merging Giro with the National Savings Banks. It was nevertheless good for Benn's reputation that, after his resumption of responsibility, Giro was to prosper.

After a few years of diminishing losses, £7,810,000 announced in 1972, £7,070,000 in 1973 and £5,050,000 in 1974 came years of profits. Break-even in 1975, £64,000 in 1976 and £846,000 in 1977. Then in 1978 it was able proudly to announce that it had not only bettered the 8 .

per cent return on capital which Benn had asked for in 1965 but also the 12½ per cent which Chataway, far less confidently, had said in 1971 was expected. The £2,050,000 operating profit announced in 1978 represented a 15.2 per cent return on capital, £4,600,000 in 1979 was well over double what was asked for and the next year profits doubled again, to £9,500,000.

The turn-round was acknowledged rather grudgingly in some circles. That £9.5 million profit might seem a lot on paper, as a return on invested capital, but it was not much set against turnover. With annual deposits of £14,000 million, in 300,000,000 transactions, it would not take much to swing it around again. The Thatcher Government quickly proved that with its windfall tax on banks the following year. That turned what should have been another good year into a bad one, with a loss of £1,800,000. Aggrieved, Giro joined with the Co-op bank in protest. Giro admitted it was still not fully competitive with the clearing banks. It had not joined in the great money-making spree on high interest rates which they had enjoyed. The Government relented, for Giro, but not for the Co-op. Or, rather, it half relented. It would inject £7,400,000 into Giro as further capital in compensation. Not that that action would cause much of a raised eyebrow by even the most hard-hearted of businessmen or the most monetarist of politicians. Giro, it was said, was paying interest on loan capital roughly in line with long-term gilt yields.

So, after fifteen years, what is the balance sheet for this first and, possibly, favourite ministerial offspring of Benn? Its accumulated profits have offset its written-off losses and it has been giving a better return on state-invested capital than the laid-down figure and, of course, one that is better by far than the normal state industry yield. It provides the quick money transfer service which it was set up to provide, as big business has discovered. The firms using it now include British Home Stores, Ladbroke's,

147

W H Smith and Sainsbury. Anyone who pays his electricity, gas or other bills by handing in the bill and the money over a bank counter, as well as a post office one, so saving himself the cost of a stamp, should look gratefully on the introduction of Giro. (Not that the Post Office appears to be worrying about those unsold stamps. It has its own large profits, nowadays, made in other ways.)

In total Giro does seem to have been an innovation for good rather than bad, unlike some other of the results of that first Wilson government. Some suggest that if Wilson had been in the habit of having money in his pocket, as when he went to open the Giro centre and found he was expected to open an account as well, he might have had a better understanding of the ordinary man and woman's view of the relationship of the penny to the pound, expressed in that old adage 'look after the pennies and the pounds will look after themselves', and would not have made such a hash of decimalization. According to that school of thought he helped spark off the falling value of the pound by reducing it in the eyes of the man in the street to a mere ten shillings or less, a hundred pennies.

In the view of some financial commentators, however, Giro has failed to fulfil its objective. Instead of offering a dynamic alternative to the main street banks it has just become a pale imitation of them. Despite its use of 23,000 post offices it is still small beer, compared to the banks, with its £400,000,000 deposits, and offers no real threat. It is also, they say, very exposed to a drop in interest rates, when its expenses will remain but its income will fall.

As for that original worry, the Friday pay snatch, that seems if not gone at least much reduced, but not through Giro. Those pay snatches provided the stimulus for another, rather more profitable growth industry, the private security business, which sent wage snatchers looking elsewhere. Or is it just that fashions in crime change?

Certainly fashions in pay do not seem to change. Giro

did not bring about the withering away of the Truck Acts. Employers still plead for their repeal. More than three-quarters of Britain's manual workers are still paid in cash, compared with only 5 per cent of West German and 1 per cent of United States employees. According to one bank it costs an employer £32 a year to pay a worker weekly in cash and each worker who changes over to monthly payment by credit transfer saves his boss over £25. Also, it seems, the best stimulus for getting a worker to make that change is to have a wage snatch, of his own or a neighbouring firm's cash.

CHAPTER TEN

Boss of Technology or Bigger is Better

From success at the Post Office, as everyone saw it, Benn was moved by Wilson to what was to have been even greater success. For in the eyes of a confident, optimistic politician — and there was a sense of optimism in the swinging sixties sadly lacking in the eighties — the size of a success depended only on the size of the job. The job Benn was tackling was a big one.

The Ministry of Technology, 'MinTech' as Benn was to call it, was itself big. It was by far the fastest growing of Wilson's babies. In 1964 C. P. Snow had told one inquiring journalist at the press conference to announce its birth that all it then consisted of was the little group of three on the platform. Even their chairs, like the platform, were borrowed. By the time Benn took over, at the end of 1966, the baby was already showing signs of giantism. In early 1967 he told American businessmen in London 'its resources are enormous', with 9,000 qualified scientists and engineers working in its research laboratories. The order of priority in his list of staff, incidentally, ran, first, 'scientists and engineers', then 'those with industrial experience', with 'administrators, economists and politicians' bringing up the rear.

The Ministry's purpose, he told his audience, was simple, to work for industrial success through technology. Its aim was to pick likely winners and back them to the hilt, with everything that was available, including money, a promise on which the Treasury was to prove to have its own views. Its main instrument would be communication, passing vital and profitable information from those who had it to those who could use it.

Britain's mixed economy, a system towards which the rest of the world, capitalist and communist, might well merge, as he was then fond of saying, must be made to work. The key was the rapid application of science. By making the economy successful it would create the wealth needed for Labour's social objectives.

Soon his Ministry had taken over that of Aviation, as later it was to take over Fuel and Power, and the numbers were even larger. The 18 research centres now employed 23,000, with technical and other assistants. Altogether Ministry staff numbered 36,500, with a wage and salary bill of £50,000,000. The total cost of the Ministry was put at about £800,000,000 a year, including about £575,000,000 orders to British industry. Those were days when trade figures had come to dominate Wilson's thinking and Benn was at pains to point out that the best argument for any project was that its implementation would help the balance of payments.

There seemed no doubt in anybody's mind then that 'Bigger' was synonymous with 'Better'. A decade or so later, when a new catchphrase 'small is beautiful' had taken over, a newspaper could republish, with unconcealed scorn, Benn's reply in those days to the actual question 'Does bigger mean better?':

'I think so, actually. Everything's getting bigger, schools are getting bigger, local government's getting bigger, machines are getting bigger. Super-powers are the big powers.'

The idea comes across, less simply but essentially the same, in a speech he made about the same time:

After a century of near neglect industrial reconstruction is now well under way. The managers of British industry are engaged in a massive programme of modernization. The fragmented pattern of industrial organization is beginning to give way to large undertakings that have it within their power to compete successfully against their foreign rivals.

When he included that later in a book of his speeches, he was at pains to point out that 'that managerial view of industrial policy' had been rethought to produce the new policies of the 1974 Labour election manifesto. The way that speech continued, following the words quoted above, shows how history demonstrated the need for a rethink:

British Leyland, to take the most recent example, will be a world giant in automotive manufacture, able to increase productivity and exports dramatically. Rolls-Royce, strengthened by its merger with Bristol-Siddeley, is another such company. Soon we may see similar developments in computers. Shipbuilding is now reorganizing itself into a small number of highly competitive units that can face and beat Japanese competition.' [The first legislation he had introduced as minister was the Bill for the reorganization of the shipbuilding industry.] 'GEC and AEI together will be far stronger than the sum of their component parts. We shall soon have a reorganized nuclear power industry to convert our unrivalled lead in atomic technology into a powerful export effort.'

151

At least the enlarged GEC prospers but, with hindsight, one might cynically comment it would have been hard to have got it more wrong, to have picked more losers. But Benn should not take all the blame. That was the belief of the day. Who would then have thought that the next time, a mere decade later, that Benn would find himself responsible for the nuclear industry the talking point would not be the export of British reactor technology but the import of American. If the blame for that were to be apportioned, scientists and engineers might again be given priority, ahead of the politicians.

On his desk in the giant building, on the site of his childhood home, Benn found two tasks big enough to satisfy the greediest of appetites for technological innovation and industrial reorganization, Concorde and what was to become, under his direction, British Leyland.

To be strictly accurate only one was awaiting him, Concorde, originally acquired, in what now seems almost a fit of absent-mindedness, when all political and business acumen had been put aside, by the Macmillan Government. Benn deliberately took onto his plate the perhaps even more indigestible dish of the native British motor industry, with a gleam in his eye, which, as one of the industrialists concerned, Lord Stokes, says, if it did not hypnotize others seemed to show he had hypnotized himself by his own enthusiasm.

For the British motor industry which, like many other sections of home industry, had been riding high on a post-war wave of exports, with few imports to worry about, the good years were coming to an end. The signs were appearing in company accounts, with falling profits. It could not really be blamed on imports. At the beginning of the decade they amounted to only 6 per cent of home sales and there were hoots of disbelieving laughter when one French manufacturer forecast that British car-makers might one day see foreign competition taking 20 per cent or more of its own market, as the French, German and

Benn with one of his closest supporters, Arthur Scargill, at the scene of a pit disaster at Houghton Main, Barnsley, in 1975, in which five miners died. Benn was then Energy Secretary, Scargill the Yorkshire Area President of the National Union of Mineworkers. *(PRESS ASSOCIATION)*

Benn, a non-believing descendant of Nonconformists, taking part in a political debate held in Southwark Cathedral in June 1978. More recently he has spoken from a church pulpit to advocate the disestablishment of the Church of England. *(DAILY TELEGRAPH)*

Tony and Caroline Benn on the bench on which he proposed to her when she was doing post-graduate research at Oxford. The bench now stands in the garden of their home in Holland Park in London and is, she says, the one spot where he will quietly relax. *(SYNDICATION INTERNATIONAL)*

Benn electioneering in Bristol from his home-made chariot during the 1979 campaign. *(DAILY EXPRESS)*

Italian industries did. By another decade and a half, of course, the laughter had turned to despairing groans, with more than a hint of a death rattle, as imports climbed to over 50 per cent. Perhaps the problem was that there had not been enough imports, the home industry had been feather-bedded. The competition it faced was internal. It fought for shares of a very price-conscious market among customers who were well aware that a car would be the second biggest purchase of their lives, after their homes, the biggest if they had not yet joined the ranks of the property-owners of the Tory Utopia.

Prices were kept low as manufacturers strove for maximum output. Ford, for example, claimed that BMC had kept the price of its advanced, front-wheel-drive small car, the Mini, so low that not only could its competitors, trying to sell older models, not make profits but neither could BMC itself. One result of that was that the level of investment was considerably lower than it was abroad. The British industry was rapidly becoming old-fashioned, in models and factories alike.

The motor industry had helped contemporary politico-industrial thinking to that 'bigger is better' outlook. It was one which had long operated there. Takeovers in the course of empire-building had been commonplace but a new attitude had begun to appear which might be summed up 'When in difficulty or doubt, merge'.

The British Motor Corporation had been born in the merger of the Morris and Austin Motor Companies in 1952. That step was then reported to have been taken in the interests of efficiency. It would enable better use to be made of restricted supplies of materials. The numbers of models would be reduced from the 24 the two companies produced between them. The new group, it was proudly announced, would be the biggest in the world, outside the American big three of General Motors, Ford and Chrysler, and would be well placed for competition with the Americans in export markets 'when it should

153

come'. As an afterthought it was stated it would be better able to cope with import competition at home, if that also should come.

The new group held over half the home market and an even larger share of exports. Its total output was about 400,000 vehicles a year. The 5s (25p) shares in the two companies stood at around £1 15s (£1.75p) giving a yield, in those low-interest-rate days, of 7 per cent — happy days for the shareholders. Output climbed. By the early sixties Sir George Harriman, BMC's chairman, was hopefully forecasting a million cars a year. Those were the days when the Mini and the 1100 series were sweeping all before them. BMC had a designer of genius, Alec Issigonis, but few, if any, as able in the more down-to-earth production and marketing sides of its operation. Or, perhaps, it was that the designer just has to cope with mechanical problems, aside from such matters as fashion, while the production and marketing people have to cope with all the vagaries of human behaviour. Whatever the reason, not only did BMC not reach that million target, neither did its enlarged successor, and the whole British industry now falls short of it.

During those years since 1952 BMC had gone slow on mergers. It had taken over the body-building firms of Fisher Ludlow and Pressed Steel. Two other groups, though, had steadily grown. Jaguar Cars, the pre-war creation of another fine engineer, William Lyons, had absorbed first the old firm of Daimler, then Guy lorries and, finally, the Coventry Climax engine business, which had made a great name with racing engines. In 1966 the enlarged Jaguar company surprised the motoring world by joining BMC to form British Motor Holdings.

Leyland, in pre-war days a relatively little-known Lancashire lorry and bus firm, had embarked on rapid expansion after the war, absorbing many of its native rivals in those two fields. Then, in 1961, it moved into the car-building business by taking over the hard-pressed Coventry firm of Standard Triumph, struggling to keep up with its larger rivals. The belief 'bigger is better' was well established, though it passed under the more academic title of 'economics of scale'.

Perhaps because of that feverish growth by take-over and merger, investment remained small by world standards. All those companies invested only £30,000,000 a year between them, while rivals such as Volkswagen spent more than twice as much and Ford, on its European operation, which it was beginning to rationalize as a single entity, almost three times as much.

Despite that growth BMC, even when transformed by the Jaguar merger into British Motor Holdings, could no longer think itself a giant. Leyland, still regarded by the motoring public as a jumped-up lorry and bus firm which had somehow got a foot in the car world, was considerably smaller, measured by capital employed, output and profits, though by this time BMC's profit record was becoming unsteady. In that 'economics of scale' atmosphere it was natural that there should be some discussion as to how the British industry could close its ranks in face of competition from Europe and Japan. From 1964 talks did go on between Harriman, Donald Stokes, a pre-war apprentice at Leyland's who had made his way to the top as deputy chairman and managing director, and Sir William Black, Leyland's chairman. Black was also merger-conscious. He had found his way into Leyland's by way of one of those lorry groups acquired during post-war expansion.

At first the talks were informal, so informal as to arouse suspicions of industrial spy mania. Apart from meetings under the guise of social evenings at Stokes's bungalow, there was one in Stokes's car, drawn up in a lay-by off the M1. The real fear was that some of Harriman's colleagues might be put out by the terms of any merger. It seemed agreed that in a merger Harriman, from the bigger firm, should have the top job. Stokes was willing to come in as his number two, but superior to other BMH executives. That, it was thought, might stick in the gullet of Joe Edwards. Edwards had had one rags-to-riches story behind him, rising from the tool-room to the boardroom at Austin's. On being fired after the Austin-Morris merger he had returned, as managing director, as a result of the Pressed Steel merger and, it was correctly suspected, would not take kindly to being demoted again.

So things were hanging fire when Benn appeared on the scene. Without Benn there would almost certainly have been no British Leyland. Without the impetus he gave to the negotiations Stokes and the other Leyland chiefs would have realised in time that BMH was likely to prove just a millstone around their necks, a brake on their progress, not a platform for a further advance in the great Leyland climb. Realization did come, but too late for the Leyland board to resist the overpowering urgings of Benn.

During his first winter at MinTech Benn made it quite clear to BMC and Leyland that he would like to see a united British motor industry and their merger was a vital step in that direction. With that impetus the talks livened up to the point where Benn obtained the view of the Monopolies Commission that there would be no objection on monopoly grounds. Competition from American-owned companies, as well as providing the economic spur for the merger, was also to provide the political excuse.

Another creation of the Wilson government, the Industrial Reorganization Corporation, with £150,000,000 to back just such restructuring of British industry, was brought in. Leyland even thought, at one time, of using its services to push forward an outright take-over bid for BMH, as the General Electric Company was then using them to take over its giant but sick rival, Associated Electrical Industries.

There were still doubts, though, particularly among the accountants. Political pressure was increased, at the highest level. In October 1967 Wilson invited Harriman and Stokes to dinner at Chequers. When Benn and he laid their plans beforehand they agreed that the merger was essential, that Stokes might have to be promised control, not Harriman, if the negotiations were to succeed, but that obvious and outright interference would probably prove a brake, not a spur. If the matter came up it would be jollied along. In fact, of course, all four men knew it would come up, a Chequers dinner was not an entirely social occasion and what other reason could there be? Certainly Harriman and Stokes realized the purpose, as clearly as if it had been written into the invitations. The matter came up, it was jollied along, with a friendly hint that the Government would prefer an amicable merger to a bruising take-over. The role of Lord Kearton, head of the IRC, of which Stokes was also a director, was to be that of mediator.

The talks continued on their up-and-down course. On one occasion, in Moscow, where Harriman and Stokes found themselves as joint members of a delegation of industrialists, they were on the point of breakdown. Disagreement in that Communist capital was on the basic Capitalist question, What were the relative shares of each party to be after the marriage? Harriman had assumed that BMH shareholders, with the greater capital assets behind them, would have the larger. Leyland, disagreeing on the true relative worth of the two companies, measured by profits and prospects, had carried out a share-splitting operation which gave it approximately the same number of shares as BMH. The Stock Exchange, it was pointed out, valued them at 16s 6d (82½p), almost 3s (15p) more than those of BMH.

Eventually the terms of a merger were agreed, in January 1968, on an equal basis, one share in British Leyland for each BMH or Leyland share. The Stock Exchange reaction, naturally, was to move them both roughly to the mid-point 15s (75p). Harriman was to be chairman,

Stokes chief executive and deputy chairman. The news was warmly received. An inevitable natural marriage, was one newspaper headline. Once again half the car market was in the hands of a single British firm, in terms of value, 40 per cent in numbers of vehicles sold. Since the Austin-Morris merger BMC had held the largest single share of the market but recently had been closely pressed by Ford. The new group would be the second or third biggest outside America, smaller than Volkswagen but bigger than Renault and on a par with Fiat.

But the marriage knot had not been tied, the shareholders of the two companies had still to approve. At that late stage a Leyland team went to the BMH headquarters at Longbridge, Birmingham, to have its first real look at the BMH books — and its first sight of the ranks of unfinished cars standing outside. What it saw was as upsetting as Wilson's own sight of the national books, which had sent him off seeking dollar aid and pondering the doubtful benefits of devaluation.

It seemed that a loving marriage was off. All that was likely was rape, in the form of a Leyland take-over of BMH (so Stokes told Kearton). But, after all the publicity, after what was known of government involvement, a public dissolution of the engagement would have been too shaming. Persuasion and pressure healed the pre-nuptial rift. Harriman was persuaded to climb down from the chief job under the unconvincing pretext of becoming president. That meant a virtual take-over by Leyland, at least of boardroom power. The Leyland board agreed to recommend the merger to its company meeting and not one shareholder, even those representing banks and insurance companies knowing the background, objected.

What was Benn's role in that period of persuasion and pressure?

Stokes is in no doubt that not only was he a principal nurse, if not the midwife, at the birth, but that he failed to provide the after-birth care the sickly infant needed.

158

Looking back, after a decade and a half, Lord Stokes says, 'We were under pressure, tremendous pressure all the time.' He adds, 'Don't get me wrong. We accepted it in the end, it was our decision. But when you have Government pressing you like that it is difficult to say no.'

On the events of January and February 1968 he says, 'When we found the BMH situation was so bad we tried to withdraw but we were persuaded to go on. If we had not done the merger, BMH would have gone into liquidation.'

Recalling those days he says, 'We were all for the White-Hot Technological Revolution. People in industry wanted it. We wanted a lead from the Government, a strong lead, though we did not want nationalization.'

Benn he describes as 'very persuasive but also very charming.' He added:

'You cannot help but like him, even if you do not agree with his policies. But I think the trouble with him is he does not deliver. He seems hypnotized by his own plans. You get the impression from him he is going to do this, that or the other, but he is so moved by political expediency that it never seems to work out in the way you originally envisaged.'

Benn's plans went further than British Leyland. He wanted the old Rootes Group (now Talbot), then in the hands of Chrysler but still deep in financial trouble, to be included.

'We resisted that,' says Stokes. 'I think his plan for a united British motor industry had a lot of merit but after we had done what we did, after we had formed British Leyland, the support we got from the Government was very poor. They did not even tell their departments to buy British Leyland.'

They had £50,000,000 from the IRC but that was a loan which had to be repaid, not a grant. Stokes commented:

'We had to repay all we got. If they had shown the courage then to put the money into the motor industry which they subsequently put into British Leyland we would not have had a motor industry crisis. The industry could have been saved for far less than has been spent on British Leyland, £1,200,000,000 or whatever the current figure is.'

The Benn connection with British Leyland and Stokes was not over. It still had to reach its traumatic climax and that came when Benn, after four years in Opposition to rethink his industrial policies, was at the Department of Industry.

The target for British Leyland had been a 40 per cent share of car and lorry markets, which it failed to maintain, sales of £1000,000,000, which inflation made more easily realizable, and profits of £50,000,000. The first year of the merger the profit target would have been reached, if £12,000,000 had not been lost through strikes. The next year, recorded profits were £40,000,000 with another £15,000,000 lost through disputes. In 1970, 1971 and 1972 strikes cost the company £27,000,000, £18,000,000 and £12,000,000, according to its figures, bringing profits down to £4,000,000, £32,000,000 and £32,000,000. In 1973 it achieved the full target figure, with £51,000,000 profits despite strikes costing £4,000,000. So for four of those six years it would have met its profit target but for labour problems. The next year, though, 1974, the oil crisis and the three-day week brushed aside all hope of profit.

Investment was desperately needed. The Mini might still be Britain's biggest export-earner but it was fourteen years old and rivals abroad were adopting the Issigonis principle and each putting it into a more modern-looking package. Those rivals were each investing more than British Leyland's total profits. Stokes announced a £500,000,000 investment plan. Money was raised by an issue of stock at 42p but the writing was on the wall for Stokes and his team.

The man who did the writing was Don Ryder, Industrial Adviser to the 1974 Wilson Government, but it was Benn who put the chalk in his hands. In December 1974, Benn told the Commons the Government would provide financial assistance through an equity stake and consider a long-term loan 'as part of a measure of public ownership'. Details would be drawn up by a team headed by Ryder. This was after a row had rumbled on all summer over a supposed list of twenty companies, including British Leyland, thought by Benn to be ripe for nationalization.

Predictably the Ryder report, four months later, was that there had been massive under-investment as well as bad labour relations. The sum needed to make up for past lost investment was now enormous. Allowing for inflation it would come to over £2,000,000,000 over the next decade, plus another £750,000,000 for working capital. There was no hope of British Leyland generating such sums from its own operations. A very large part would have to come from the Government. BL's importance to the national economy was such that the money should be provided. The Government should offer to buy out existing shareholders and then underwrite a rights issue which, Ryder confidently, and correctly, forecast, hardly anyone would take up. That would leave British Leyland effectively in Government hands without the outright nationalization which Leyland shop stewards were then demanding. If that were done, Ryder thought, there might be a positive cash flow, better than break-even, by 1981–82.

Ryder also recommended changes at the top, a smaller headquarters team and a measure of decentralization. The comment which that prompted from Benn — that the key to the report was 'its greater emphasis on industrial democracy' — is a key to the changes that had taken place in Benn's own industrial thinking by that time and to the plans he had for the motor-cycle industry at that time, so different from those applied to the car industry between 1967 and 1969.

The report was accepted. The changes went through.

Stokes received the Harriman treatment, being named president. Shareholders were given the choice of taking 10p for each of their shares or staying in. That choice, they were told by the Queen's Counsel representing the company in the legalization of the ensuing changes, was between a bird in the hand or a ride on a tiger, between accepting the Government's rescue and the money or taking their chance in forcing the company into liquidation.

Ten pence might not have seemed much against the 75p valuation when British Leyland was formed or the 42p of the rights issue a few years earlier, let alone the pre-inflation £1 15s of those heady 1950-ish days of Austin and Morris. But Ryder and Benn were not ungenerous with the taxpayer's money. The stockmarket price had been around 7p a share when dealing stopped at the end of 1974, a price which valued British Leyland at a mere £25,000,000. Those who did stay, accepting new shares for old, were to find them worth effectively only 1½p for each old share by the time the company should, according to Ryder's timetable, have been on its feet again. Needless to say, to watchers of politico-economic timetables, it was not.

Late that summer the Commons Expenditure Committee charged Ryder and his team with having made assumptions that must be subject to huge margins of error. They, and by implication Benn, had thought of money in terms of confetti.

Stokes also thinks the Ryder report was a disaster in the changes it recommended. It was used by Benn to get control — 'he was intent on getting control and had really wanted it all the time.' The main disaster, he says, was that those huge sums of money — £1,200,000,000 — were given too late. Much less, much earlier and it would all have been different. But that is the view of one who was on the inside, not of an impartial outside observer, if such a being exists. All one can say is that if half a million jobs

162

were really at stake, as was accepted at the time, then a thousand million pounds was by no means an outrageous charge for keeping them, even on the most optimistic view of the contemporary costs of job creation. In the era of three million unemployed in the 1980's it would be thought amazingly cheap.

CHAPTER ELEVEN

Brave New Technology, Part Two — Concorde

It is a moot point which has cost the British taxpayer more, British Leyland or Concorde. In actual pounds paid out BL leads with over a thousand million to just under that amount. But quite a few of the Concorde millions were spent in the sixties, when a pound was a pound, or almost, not the debased currency of the inflation-ridden seventies. They were spent before the effects of Wilsonian decimalization and devaluation merged with the external causes of inflation, before Wilson delivered himself of his contender for the most notorious phrase ever coined by a politician — his 'pound in your pocket' (being still worth a pound) must come close on the heels of Chamberlain's 'Peace in our time'.

Benn seems never to have been so strongly motivated in the case of Concorde as in that of British Leyland, never as ready to apply the full pressure of his political personality, except for a time in Opposition. After all, the end product, as far as the average worker was concerned, was to be something just to be admired in the sky, not actually to be travelled in, unlike the BL car he could afford. On the other hand, there were many workers with jobs depending on the project, at the British Aerospace factory at Filton, in his own constituency, something naturally of considerable moment to any MP.

When he took over responsibility for Concorde for the second time, in 1974, he was at pains to tell Labour MPs that he had thought, twelve years before, that Concorde was the wrong aircraft to make. He was certainly right on that. The design of that time was frozen when it was realized the plane could fly at the height and speed promised only if it did not carry passengers. Harold Macmillan and General de Gaulle had agreed on a joint Anglo-French supersonic project after British and French firms had each evolved similar designs for supersonic air transports (SSTs) in the late 1950s. Neither of the elderly statesmen realized what they were letting themselves and their successors in for. Each probably thought it was a fairly innocuous way of securing Anglo-French co-operation. Neither was a fervent apostle of technological advance in the Wilson manner. Macmillan readily, even proudly, confessed it was not really his cup of tea. He much preferred his great-aunt's Daimler which it was possible to enter without removing one's top hat, something one certainly could not do with Concorde. One thing Concorde and top hats appear to have had in common is their escalating costs since those days, for the Macmillan-de Gaulle agreement turned out to be an open-ended commitment to spend, spend, spend.

Originally it was estimated that the cost to the two countries would be £170,000,000, but for that they would have an airliner poised to take a large share of the undoubtedly large market for supersonic planes. Everybody wanted to go faster and faster, and to meet that public appetite for speed at least 200 of the 100-seat passenger planes envisaged would be needed. Almost at once the figures were growing and when a House of Commons Committee looked into the matter it found that Treasury authorization had never been obtained. Still one could hardly demand that an agreement between two such exalted statesmen should be put aside and soon a far more material reason was found why nothing could be done, even though, by that time, it was realized that putting right the deficiencies in design was likely to double the cost.

When Wilson came to power in 1964 and had his depressing look at the nation's financial figures, the estimates had climbed to £275,000,000. Money had to be saved and here was one easy way to save it. Concorde should be killed, despite its value as a symbol of the Wilson era. The Americans disliked it, too, and it was already realized that a large loan would have to be asked of them. It was not just that the Americans feared a competitor for their own projected SST — Boeing had won a competition for an overly ambitious, swing-wing design, so ambitious it was quickly dropped. The US Treasury would like to be relieved of its own SST obligations and did not take kindly to a socialist government pouring out money on their own while coming cap in hand for funds. George Brown, the economic overlord of those days, sounded what was intended to be the death-knell in his paper on the economic and financial crisis. 'The Government have already communicated to the French Government the wish to re-examine urgently the Concorde project,' it stated.

In fact, that was a little premature, when written. The paper was to be published on Monday, 26 October. The Minister of Air, Roy Jenkins, was only hurriedly located, to be told the news, the previous Friday. Urgent calls were put out for the British Ambassador in Paris, Sir Pierson Dixon, who was located on a weekend shoot with, appropriately, the head of the French aero-engine firm, Hispano Suiza. He was summoned back to the Embassy to get his instructions to tell the French premier, Couve de Murville, of the 'wish'.

165

But it proved to be no more than a wish. That Macmillan-de Gaulle contract had one fatal omission. There was no escape clause. Was it just an oversight, as the Commons Estimates Committee thought, or was it done deliberately by Macmillan and Co, to hold the French to the contract, believing the word of a Frenchman was not to be trusted? Whichever was the case it proved to be the French who insisted the British must stand by their word. They pointed out the lack of a break-off clause and then broke off the talks. Elwyn Jones, Wilson's Attorney-General, was told to examine the small print and report what would happen if Britain broke the agreement. He gave his lawyer's opinion that France might collect damages of £100,000,000 and would certainly try to do so. Wilson shuddered. A few months later Jenkins was telling the Commons that 'those concerned, on both sides of the Channel, would press on with a real sense of purpose'. Concorde, though still earthbound, with only the outline of the prototypes visible, had already acquired a momentum which was to prove irresistible. What would have happened if that irresistible momentum had come up against the full force of Benn opposition is a matter of speculation. However, Benn was not responsible then. He was still rearranging the Post Office. When he acquired responsibility, when MinTech took over Jenkins's old ministry, the first Concorde was ready to be rolled out of its hangar at Toulouse. Benn was not visibly enthusiastic. He made a terse speech at the ceremony and afterwards sent his number two, Air Minister John Stonehouse, to see his French counterpart to try to agree a minimum number of orders and a maximum figure for research and development costs below and beyond which it would be pointless going on. The French, though, were all for pressing on.

By spring 1968 the estimate of the costs to be shared had risen to £500 million, with another £30 million for the UK Government on work in its research establishments.

As was to be shown time and again, it would have been cheaper to cancel. By that time, though, there was another powerful factor to be considered, 27,000 workers employed one way or another on Concorde. A year later Concorde took to the air. Benn congratulated the builders, but his Ministry warned of growing costs, narrowing margins of profit, and doubts by airlines whether they would be able to operate the plane profitably.

Benn's ministerial responsibility was soon to be interrupted by the 1970 election but he was able to argue later that when he left office there were 76 options to buy the plane. At £9,500,000 each that would just about cover the latest estimate of total Concorde costs to the two countries, £730,000,000.

Heath's 'Think Tank', the Central Policy Review Unit he set up under Lord Rothschild on taking office, was to go better than that. In one of its first pronouncements it forecast sales of between 120 and 150 planes within five years of its going into production. That forecast might be thought to set the standard of reliability by which to judge later 'think tank' pronouncements, but as a result John Davies, the Industry Secretary, ruled out the possibility of cancellation.

Benn's next appearance on the Concorde stage was in New York and Washington, as a constituency MP representing Concorde workers. In New York he and another Bristol MP, the Conservative Robert Ardley, with the editor of the local paper, Gordon Farnsworth, argued against a State Bill that would effectively ban Concorde from New York's Kennedy Airport by setting stringent noise limits. Tens of thousands of Bristol workers, with their families, depended on Concorde for their livelihood, they declared. If Concorde were cancelled, because it could not land at Kennedy, not only would a quarter of a million people in Britain and France be affected but so would Americans making equipment for it. The Bill was dropped.

He went on to Washington to support the US Secretary for Transportation John Volpe, who was struggling to keep America's own SST going, against reluctance by Congress to fund it. Benn argued that America should stay in the SST business because the Russians were pressing ahead with their own, the TU 144, and planned to enter the world aircraft market at the top by using it as a loss leader. They would probably get the Japanese to buy it by promising flights over Siberia. The Anglo-French had an interest in keeping America in; American interest meant a world market and with Concorde years ahead of the revised Boeing design it would have a chance to clean up on those two hundred possible sales. In Washington, though, Benn did not do as well as in New York. Caution prevailed and the American SST programme eventually became just an assessment of designs for the super-SST of the more distant future.

Back in England Benn was for a while the most outspoken defender of Concorde. If the British Government did not go ahead, it would precipitate a massive Anglo-French crisis which would blow Britain's European entry prospects to smithereens. This was at a time when the 'bigger is better' philosophy had made him a temporary convert to the benefits of the Common Market. American attacks on Concorde, he claimed, were stimulating British interest in it and certainly polls at the time showed widespread support for the project. As for his own intervention on the American SST scene, he claimed that it was the beginning of multinational politics, as distinct from international relations. 'You go wherever the problem is and try to remove it by argument,' he explained. That is one Benn innovation which does not seem to have caught on here, though American Secretaries of State have adopted it, or come to similar conclusions, at least for other people's problems. One might speculate what would have happened if Benn multinational politics had been tried over the Falklands.

Later he wrote to a US Senate committee to counter evidence given to it by the most outspoken attacker of Concorde in Britain, the journalist Andrew Wilson. Benn denied Labour would have cancelled Concorde if it had won the 1970 election and he was able to point out that Labour had given full support to legislation by the Conservative Government to increase funds.

For the projected costs of Concorde were still soaring, to £970 million in May 1972 and £1,065 million in June 1973, shared equally between the UK and France. During a debate in early 1973 on that bill to provide more money, Benn admitted money spent on research and development was unlikely to be recovered but urged that the matter should not be judged on a 'narrow accountancy cost-benefit basis'. If, as he believed, Concorde would be ordered by other countries when it entered into service, production lines must be ready in Britain as well as in France to provide the aircraft.

'It is our wish that the aircraft will get the support it needs, will enter into service and will, in time and in many ways not as yet clear to all of us, reflect great credit on the country that has poured so much skill, workmanship and devotion into its manufacture,' he declared in his capacity as Opposition spokesman.

In June that year, however, came the event which was to set back all SST prospects. Russia's TU 144 crashed while performing what seemed to be unnecessarily ambitious low-level acrobatics at the Paris Air Show. That was regarded by the short-sighted as improving Concorde's prospects. The TU 144 had made its first flight slightly before Concorde, a full production line had been set up and it was thought about to enter regular service. But there must have been an anti-SST faction as well as a pro-SST faction in the Kremlin as well as in other political centres. Enthusiasm for the project seemed to wither in the USSR and its aircraft factories concentrated on supersonic bombers instead. Without that stimulus of keeping up with, or ahead of, the Russians, what interest there was in the USA also waned. Their own project lapsed and their airlines made it known they would not be taking up Concorde options.

With hindsight one can see that the crash of the TU 144 and the consequent loss of enthusiasm by the Russians for supersonic travel ended what hopes there might have been that Concorde would be a commercial success. Some were slow to see it. The manufacturers, a year later, were still imagining Concordes trailing their sonic booms across Siberia on their way to the Far East — a Siberian service to Tokyo was a crucial factor in their accounts of how the plane would operate profitably. Benn saw it sooner than most.

It was not just ministerial responsibility which took the edge off the enthusiasm for Concorde he had shown earlier. As a Bristol MP, as a technology enthusiast, he was still for it. As the responsible minister he was shocked by the figures for Concorde costs he found when he took over the Department of Industry — or so he told MPs to whom he disclosed them almost at once. Immediate cancellation would cost £80,000,000 in contractual and redundancy payments. Another £130,000,000 remained to be spent by the UK as its share of development costs, if the project went on, none of which would be recovered. In addition there would be production losses ranging from £120,000,000 to £300,000,000, depending on the number of planes built and sold. The production total then authorized was sixteen — on which losses were bound to be around £200,000,000.

Michael Heseltine, who had been the responsible minister during the Heath Government, charged Benn with doing the maximum possible harm and the minimum possible good by quoting those figures — unless, he said, Benn intended to cancel the project. (Heseltine, always, perhaps, a little uncritical in his enthusiasms, had even been able to find a measure of 'carping criticism' when given

Benn's support for his bill to increase Concorde funding in 1973.)

Benn retorted that the figures had been available to Heseltine but were never disclosed to the public. The House and the public were entitled to know — a remark which drew the approving comment from one of his fellow Labour MPs that this was a fine example of 'open government', a phrase which Benn was beginning increasingly to use. In a later debate when Chataway charged him with 'rushing out figures damaging to Concorde', he retorted that if the Tories believed a project of that magnitude could only survive by concealment it threw a lot of light on their attitudes to responsibility in office. Reaching decisions on Concorde now involved elements of shock which would not have been present if the facts had been available more generally, as the Public Accounts Committee wished. (The Committee, told the figures during the Heath Government, had urged their publication but the Government had refused.)

Not that Benn was set on cancellation, as Heseltine implied. At a press conference after his statement he pointed out, 'The men who make this aircraft are personal friends of mine . . . if the project, on which half a generation of skill and craft has been employed, were to fail, in my view it would be a national tragedy.'

He went to see those personal friends at the Filton factory, where Concorde was being made, in his capacity as their MP, and advised them that one thing they could do to save their jobs would be to promise to bring Concorde into service earlier than planned, then around spring 1976. Another hint of optimism came when he suggested the Government might be swayed by technological and social considerations.

In the public debate which followed, British Airways were more outspoken than before about the cost of operating the plane. The makers retorted that Britain's balance of payments would benefit by £929 million if 50

Concordes were sold and by £1,839 million or £2,749 million if there were 100 or 150 sales. Almost all the £500 million spent had stayed in this country. The Filton workers added their comment that when Britain was spending hundreds of millions a year keeping the coal industry going, it could afford to carry on with a project which would restore the country's 'tarnished industrial image'.

Benn saw his French opposite number, Achille Fould, who, when asked if Benn wanted to scrap Concorde, replied 'The British do not rule out that possibility'. That arch-critic of Concorde, Andrew Wilson, proclaimed in his paper, the Sunday *Observer,* that Labour was about to scrap Concorde, prompting an immediate Sunday denial by the British Embassy in Paris. Other political commentators hedged their bets. With Denis Healey, Chancellor of the Exchequer, opposed to going on, the odds were against Concorde. But Benn was arguing for it in Cabinet, urged by a massive mail of support. The Budget had allowed for current spending, but no increase for modifications wanted by the French to give the plane a better performance on the sort of route they would operate.

In July Benn told Labour MPs that factors against cancellation were the effect on British relations with the French, Britain's reputation as a partner in international projects and, at home, jobs. Later that month Wilson met the French President, Giscard d'Estaing, and they agreed Concorde should continue. Benn had won that battle with Healey.

In September 1974, after Tory criticism of his revelation of the figures, Benn had his Department produce a full survey of spending. The total cost at that time, to the UK alone, was £880 million at March 1974 prices. The actual amount paid out over the years, ignoring inflation, was £493 million. The French had spent roughly the same. Benn's responsibility for Concorde, as distinct from his responsibility to its makers in the Filton factory, ended when he left the Department of Industry. Eric Varley took over and the politics surrounding it quietened.

Concorde came into service in January 1976, a little earlier than expected in 1974, though years later than originally scheduled in that 1962 agreement. Benn's exhortations to his constituency workers had had an effect. The British Concorde flew first to Bahrain, to headlines such as 'The Magic of Mach Two' and ecstatic descriptions by air correspondents how the champagne bubbled but did not ripple, as the glasses stood steady at 1,320 mph — except, of course, when the journalists were lifting them or the stewardesses refilling. As well as the reporters and officials there were thirty paying passengers on that inaugural flight. Later that year one flight went empty of passengers, but that was extreme. Generally, though, there were many empty seats and the *Daily Express* took oilmen to task for not forking out an extra £88 a trip to fly Concorde, from the profits they were making from North Sea oil.

The trouble was that once again the catchwords had changed. They were no longer 'faster and faster' but 'the cheaper the better' and 'the more the merrier'. The age of the Jumbo and economy tourism had come. Within a month of starting, the Bahrain service was losing £40,000 to £50,000 a week, though British Airways said it was not as much as had been feared. Soon a service was also being flown to Washington, despite a vociferous campaign to have it banned because of the noise. That service did better. British Airways happily announced it had achieved a 90 per cent load factor. That, though, was not quite as good as it sounds for even with a 100 per cent load, twenty seats would stay empty because of restrictions caused by the distance and the heat of the Washington summer. The fact was the plane had been designed for the North Atlantic run to New York and was hard pressed to cover its running costs, let alone capital charges, until that was

173

open to it. In the first year British Airways lost £8½ million on Concorde, and Air France, which was flying it to South America as well as Washington, lost £26 million. Tory MP John Biffen, always a strong Treasury man, dubbed Concorde a 'flying overdraft'. The British public, who had lost money when it was developed, were also losing out when the plane was being built and, even more hurtful, whenever it was flown.

Permission was at last given, at the end of 1977, for the plane to land at New York, to bring some relief to the gloom of the accountants. Even so, Concorde accumulated losses of £25 million for British Airways during its first three years. There were hopes of extending services to new profitable areas, such as Australia. Services were run for a while to Singapore and, subsonically, between Washington and Dallas. Braniff Airways, responsible for that Dallas run, planned to run a Concorde service between North and South America, but that came to naught. Even at the peak of its operations, in 1979, running services to Singapore and Dallas, as well as Washington and New York, British Airways was only using its Concordes for five hours a day, against the seven and a half it needed to break even. The only emotion felt when planes were taken out of operation to provide spares to keep others flying was relief.

In 1979, when accumulated losses on Concorde flight operations stood at £25 million it was realized that the plane would always look bad in the British Airways annual report while its capital cost remained unpaid. The yearly loss, though, might be turned into profit at a stroke of a pen, by writing off that capital investment. That was put at £160 million, despite the production cost of the final planes being £50 million each. In return the Government should receive 80 per cent of those 'stroke of a pen' profits. At last something should come back, revenue on services to New York and Washington were larger than operational costs. It was not enough, though, to cover outgoings, for millions were still being spent by the Governments on support costs. There were again calls for cancellation with, at last, the French on the side of pulling out. Also the cost of cancellation was below that of continuation. In March 1981, the figures were, cancellation £34 million, continuation £57 million. In December, however, after a meeting between Margaret Thatcher and François Mitterand, there was a startling reversal. The cost of continuation suddenly plummeted to £6 million while that of cancellation soared to £47 million. The Commons Trade and Industry Committee frankly did not believe the new figures.

Support operations were still reckoned at £20 million a year. Fatigue testing, though, was ending. After all the plane under test at Farnborough had already covered the equivalent of several lifetimes of flying. There seemed little point in going on, even though Concorde went on flying.

What did it all cost? Was it more or less than British Leyland? In 1979 the Department of Industry put it at £1,960 million at 1979 prices — around the price at which much of the Government support for BL was given. Since then, though, the figures have reverted to pounds as actually paid out. From that view the net cost on research, development and production, less income from operation, comes to around £850 million.

British Leyland undoubtedly saved more jobs than Concorde but in 1975, when Benn was Industry Secretary, his Under-secretary, Michael Meacher said Concorde was costing £1½ million a week, at which figure each Concorde job was costing little more than those to be found under Healey's job creation schemes.

Concorde is undoubtedly a boon for businessmen for whom time is literally money as they speed across the Atlantic. For those of the rest of us who live beneath its flight path it is a beautiful sight, although for those who live too near take-off point, it may be a pain in the ear.

For all those taxpayers who paid out but did not, like Benn's Filton constituents, receive back, it has been a £100 hole in the pocket for each family, at 1979 prices.

But then, as the Duke of Edinburgh once said, no one should knock Concorde by bleating about the cost. It was conceived in an era when the words 'new technology' and their associates 'spin off' justified anything, even sending men to the Moon.

The one thing which is quite certain is that those responsible for the figures got them wrong, time and time again. It was not just that the original estimate was only a quarter or less of the eventual cost, converting that to 1962 prices, but that each time it was argued that it would be cheaper to go on than to stop that proved wrong. But then that is a lesson hard to learn, for politicians will always find it easier to go on than to change course.

In the larger, more intellectual field of political theory, as distinct from political action, Benn has changed course, as any contemplative man must who learns from experience. His time at Technology was an experience which shaped his views into the Popular Democracy, if not People's Democracy, from which has come the great violent reaction against him, even among some members of his own party, in the seventies. 'Tony, instead of mellowing as he gets older, gets even more outrageously Left — and he used to be such a nice, relatively moderate man,' is the common complaint.

Benn, though he acknowledges socialism's debt to Marx, rarely quotes him. One occasion when he did was to use the German philosopher's definition of Technology in a *New Scientist* article in 1973:

'Technology discloses man's mode of dealing with nature, the process of production by which he sustains his life and thereby lays bare the mode of formation of his social relations and the mental conceptions that flow from them.'

Since the time of Marx, he pointed out, there had been

176

a fantastic acceleration in technical change which had polarized society into those with control over technical power and the rest.

'As technical power increases, mankind's apparent conquest of nature may produce new tyrannical organizations to organize that "conquest" and they then extend their domain over their fellow men,' wrote Benn. 'It is never machines that make us slaves. It is the men who own them, and control them, who are creating the new feudalism.'

That is a far cry from the spirit of Wilson's White-hot Revolution, a decade earlier. In our next chapter we will describe how after his time in Opposition, and the time he then spent rethinking, he took quite a different line in his approach to industrial problems than when he reigned in Millbank Tower.

It should not be thought, though, that a sudden change took place in those years in Opposition. The new thinking was already beginning to show in a speech he made at the Royal Society towards the end of his time at Technology, in February 1970, a speech which, he disclosed later, was strongly disapproved of by some of his officials who felt it went too far in urging political control of industrial decision:

As the implications of scientific and technological decisions become more and more the subject of public interest, people will insist on having a greater say in these decisions. If you were to try to shut them out from participation, public dissatisfaction could reach the same explosive proportions as it would have done if the vote had not been given to everyone.

Public education and understanding had been raised enormously in the course of a single generation. People must believe in themselves. They had the knowledge to make judgments on these matters.

One had to be a brilliant surgeon to do a heart transplant but did not need any such qualification to come to a view on whether money was better spent on a few heart transplants or on, say, a better industrial health service to cut down thousands of preventable deaths and disabilities. One had to be a brilliant aerodynamicist to design a space capsule to land on the Moon, but no such qualifications were necessary for saying the money might be better spent on public transport.

But the task was not just one of vetting technological proposals. Ways had to be found of identifying the real needs of society and formulating demands to be met by the use of technology.

Benn then suggested the pressure group might provide the answer. There were many thousands of them and ways must be found for the people in them to have access to those who might solve their problems.

The Parliamentary system of government, by argument, election and accountability, must be extended to cover the whole area of technology which, today, was the source of all new power.

That speech caused consternation among the conservative, with a small 'c', civil servants, he declared later. There are still some who would not accept what he also declared, 'it all seems very mild now'.

CHAPTER TWELVE

Meriden, an Experiment in Workers' Control

Holiday time in the late 1950s, those years when people were beginning to believe they had never had it so good but before the days of package holidays by air, saw the boats to the Isle of Man crowded. For families from the North of England that island, holding in small almost all the scenic delights of larger Britain, was their natural holiday ground. Thousands of others also came, from the South, the Midlands, Scotland, Ireland and even further afield, drawn by one of the most dramatic of sporting spectacles, the TT races. Celebrated by George Formby in film and song, they were an irresistible attraction for devotees of motor-cycle racing. Around thirty-seven miles of ordinary roads, through towns, villages and over moun-tain moorland, the finest motor-cycle racers would test themselves and their machines to the limit — sometimes further as they strayed beyond that last safe half-inch of cornering space into the kerbs and death. A spectacle beyond compare and all free, apart from the boat fare and paying the boarding-house landlady. Even if those years before and immediately after the war, when it seemed only British machines stood a chance of winning, were now over and Italian machines were the favourites, the best riders were still British. Spectators knew, too, that the British machines vying for supremacy with the out and out racing bikes were fundamentally the same Norton, Matchless, AJS, Triumph, BSA road machines they themselves had. It was still a time for feeling proud and happy at being British, particularly if one were in the motor-cycling business.

But into the sunshine of those days, threatening darker

ones to come, among the gaily dressed holidaymakers and old TT hands, appeared a new breed of spectator, smaller, dapper, more formally dressed but politely insistent of getting good viewing points at all the corners, groups of Japanese. Strangely, though they were festooned with cameras in a way which, then, brought smiles from superior Westerners, they seemed more intent on the sound than the sight. Among those cameras slung around their necks were new products of Japanese technology, cassette tape-recorders. As the then champion, John Surtees, and the more expert of his rivals, Geoff Duke, his predecessor, Mike Hailwood, his successor to be, Derek Minter and Bob McIntrye approached, the recorders were started.

Puzzled onlookers even took their eyes off the racing to watch. Some told their friends, the racers and their mechanics, back at the boarding houses. Out came the experts to observe and speculate what these strange Orientals were doing. Some were equally puzzled. Others had a faint twinge of unease as a glimmer of light came into their minds. But they shrugged it off and joined the others in the universal, condescending comment, 'They look like a lot of undertakers.'

Undertakers they might well have been, their tape-recorders tape measures sizing up the British motor-cycle industry for its coffin before the victim knew it was ill, certainly before it knew the cold it was to catch, because of those little yellow men, was to prove fatal. Back in Westminster Tony Benn, pondering the problems of the Viscounty Stansgate, had no inkling that, in due course, he was to be called to the bedside of the already moribund patient to have the industrial medicine of his socialism tested in circumstances that were to prove most unpropitious.

Back home those Japanese fed their recorded sounds into computers for analysis. Engine revolutions, power curves, gear ratios favoured by experts were all worked out, plus the first tentative ideas how to better the machines they had recorded. The Japanese were embarking on the best of all advertising campaigns in the speed-hungry world of motor-cycling, success on the race track.

By 1959 the Japanese had their own noise, the screaming sound of the first racing Honda, in the paddock when the lightweight 125-cc machines warmed up. The pillars of the British motor-cycle industry, on the Isle of Man for their annual jaunt to mix a lot of pleasure with a little business, listened, unmoved. Similar sounds came from the Italian racers but everyone knew the Gileras, MVs, Guzzis the customer could actually buy bore no relation to them and were no threat to sales of British road machines.

Memories of the good days were fresh. In 1954 the industry had had its best year, producing 184,100 machines, exporting 70,300. It had to compete at home with only 3,900 imported bikes. It was a repeat of the situation before the Great Depression of the thirties. In the last years of the 1920's the industry had produced annually on average 150,000 machines, exporting a third, with imports measured only in tens. The 1930's had seen production cut by over half but the post-war years had found an apparently insatiable hunger abroad for British motorbikes.

In 1955 it was almost as good. Production was 182,000, exports 60,700, imports down to 2,900, though increasing numbers of strange objects called scooters and mopeds, which the British industry did not make, were coming in.

By 1959, though, there were misgivings. Production was down to 127,500, having gone below 100,000 the year before. The problem was that motor-cyclists were gravitating to cars. Imports were down, too, to a mere 1,500. Admittedly there was a strong demand for mopeds and scooters by the young and not so well-off. The British industry was now producing them, it was to make 106,000 that year, incidentally the highest figure it reached. Imports of mopeds and scooters were to reach 170,000, also the record, but the industry's concern was over that dwindling market for the more profitable 'real' motorbike. The industry failed to see the course of future events, just as the motorcar industry had been too blasé about the threat of imports. Motor-cycles were to come into fashion again, sales to soar once more, to greater heights than ever, though not of British machines, but Japanese.

That first year, 1959, Honda machines finished sixth, seventh, eighth and eleventh in their class, satisfactory enough a debut to give them the manufacturer's team prize. The next year they improved to sixth, seventh, eighth, ninth and tenth. That year they also entered for the next larger class, for 250-cc machines, and finished fourth, fifth and sixth. More importantly, perhaps, for future sales, they proved their reliability even more than their speed. Not one machine retired on that circuit, notorious for often producing as many retirements as finishers.

In 1961 Honda had it all their own way, taking the first five places in each of those two lightweight races. British enthusiasts, though, were celebrating the fact that a Norton, ridden by Hailwood, had won the main race, the Senior TT, for the first time for seven years, thanks to a breakdown by the one ageing Italian MV.

A sales campaign based on Japanese racing success was having results. For the first time in 1963 motor-cycle imports, at 55,000, exceeded home production, which had slumped to 50,000.

In 1964 Honda took the 350-cc Junior event and imports went up to over 100,000. By 1966 they had taken the one remaining prize, the Senior 500-cc race, and when they faced defeat in the lighter classes it was from new Japanese names. Suzuki and Yamaha were following where Honda had led, into the British showrooms as well as onto the TT circuit.

The British industry was being submerged beneath the

advancing waves of a sea of Japanese imports. With hind-sight we know that attempting to turn back that sea was a task which only a Canute would tackle. It was a task, though, which Tony Benn found awaiting him when he took over at the Department of Industry in the Wilson Government of 1974. Whether he thought of Canute on the seashore he has not revealed. Canute is said to have acted from the best of motives, to show his advisers were wrong when they asserted that his majesty was such that even the ocean would yield before it. Benn was also set on proving his advisers wrong, but they had no illusions about his majesty or the enormity of the task. They were advising against any further interference, not with the ocean of the Japanese industry but with the little pools that were all that was left of the British industry.

Perhaps Benn, though, saw himself not as attempting to turn back the ocean, but just as a seashore engineer, building a groyne to protect just one of those pools.

This time he was to be a lot less grandiose in his ideas than he had been at the Ministry of Technology. The favoured Benn policy of the 1960's, mergers to build up industrial giants, had been tried by the motor-cycle in-dustry itself, with help from the Conservative Govern-ment of Ted Heath. The war had left BSA one of the largest firms in the Midlands. In the fifties it swallowed up the Triumph firm at Meriden, Coventry, where one of the design geniuses who flourished in the British motor world in those days, Edward Turner, had produced the record-breaking Triumph Bonneville. With his colleague John Sangster he had broken into the American market where enthusiasts rapidly saw that the Triumph was not only big, as things had to be to be acceptable in the States, but very good.

BSA dominated the motor-cycle world in those happy days. On its prosperity was based the lavish style of Sir Bernard and Lady Docker, with their gold plated Daimler — Daimler was part of the empire. When that style proved a little too lavish for shareholders Turner and Sangster took over in turn as company chairmen.

The other major company, Associated Motor Cycles, comprising names such as Norton, Matchless, AJS, was in a less happy position at the end of the 1950's. When those Japanese were recording their sound tracks in the Isle of Man the AMC accountants were recording the company's first losses. A few more years and the receiver was called in. On the scene appeared Dennis Poore, an Old Etonian and former racing driver, chairman of Manganese Bronze, who was looking for companies to take over and had already bought Villiers, the two-stroke engine makers. He paid £2,500,000 for AMC.

By 1970 BSA was also in financial trouble. Its bankers made the appointment as chairman of Lord Shawcross, former Labour lawyer and minister but by then a wholehearted capitalist in practice and theory, a condition for continuing a £10,000,000 overdraft.

Neither of the two halves of the industry was thought big enough to survive on its own. They must merge, that was the thinking of the time, and in 1973 the Heath Government, using Section 8 of its 1972 Industry Act, provided £5 million for the marriage. Poore was given the task of consummating that marriage and seeing it was fruitful.

Poore had plans for the future but there was no future for Meriden, home of Triumph, the one successful exporter, in them. He aimed at paring the industry down before building it up again to a target of 120,000 machines a year. Production of a new three-cylinder Triumph would be transferred to Small Heath, but the big twins, the bikes the Americans loved, were to be discontinued. Meriden might produce three out of every four machines sold abroad, exports might be growing by 20 per cent a year, as Meriden workers claimed, but, he said, he might as well stuff a £100 note into the tank of each one of those Triumphs instead of sending them to the States. Meriden was losing £3,000,000 a year. It needed to produce 44,000 machines to break even but had only managed just over 30,000 in the year before the merger.

Poore may, as he said later, have told the Government before the merger that closing Meriden was his condition for taking on the job but he put off finding the half hour to tell the workers there for another three months. He was not well received when he did tell them.

The barricades went up. A sit-in was ordered. A blockade was put on a million pounds' worth of completed bikes and around 10,000 uncompleted ones, to stop Poore selling them. During the winter ahead the factory was festively hung with flags and bunting but only the canteen functioned. There the men and their families kept their spirits up with bingo and discotheques and local Labour MP Leslie Huckfield led carol singing at Christmas.

It was Huckfield and the Transport and General Workers Union's South Midlands organizer, Bill Lapworth, who suggested the Meriden workers should form a co-operative to run the factory. A marvellous idea, was Poore's initial response, provided, of course, the co-op could raise £5,000,000 or so to buy it. He was even prepared to keep the factory open until the following July given the assurance the money would be raised, but that was scuppered by the disappearance, already, of 500 of the 1,750 employees to other jobs. Those were days when Coventry had a thousand-long list of engineering vacancies.

Seven months later, with the money not forthcoming, his patience with 'those hijackers', as he called them, and an 'endless' round of meetings with them, was at an end.

That was where Benn came in, to a situation ready made for his new thinking. At MinTech there had been rationalization and mergers. But the 'bigger is better' fashion had come up for re-examination. He himself was more critical of the idea that mergers actually solved important problems, he said in one interview. In the old days he had talked to industrialists. Now he would be talking to management and trade unions on an equal basis.

His return to Opposition had provided a time for thought and the core of his thinking had been given in 'Thinking about Workers' Control', his title for his address to the foundrymen's union in 1971. Benn was, by this time, the most distinguished member of the Institute of Workers' Control, a left-wing organization whose aims were succinctly expressed in its title, operating from Bertrand Russell House, in Nottingham. In that address he said:

As Minister of Technology, over four years . . . I became convinced that operating at Ministerial level on problems of industrial organization could be a sort of technocratic dead-end. There is a limit to what you can do by mergers and public money and encouraging better management . . .

It isn't only the old family business where the grandson of the founder has inherited power that he is quite unfitted to wield. The new grey flannel brigade with their degrees in business studies, familiar with the language of accountancy and computers, and their shiny offices away from the dirt and noise of the factory floor are still often too remote and claim too much power that they haven't the experience or knowledge to exercise properly . . .

Many industrial disputes are merely triggered off by wage claims and really reflect the deep feelings of workers who are fed up with being treated as if they were half-wits only fit to be told what to do and never asked for their advice or given the power to do things for themselves . . .

Why should the people who own a firm control it. We abandoned that principle years ago in the political arena. For centuries the people who owned the land in Britain ran Parliament. It took a hundred years of struggle to give the people the power to choose and remove their political managers — MPs and Ministers . . .

I have always thought it was a great pity that working people in Britain set their sights so low . . . If the Trade Union Movement were to bargain as strongly for industrial power as it does for higher wages the management would also be ready to concede.

Industrial democracy, if the unions did this, would come, Benn thought, in rather less time than the century taken to win political democracy. 'If the Movement set itself the target of negotiation for the workers' power in each firm, to acquire greater control of that firm, by agreement with the present management, over a five year period — in my opinion it would succeed.'

Meriden presented an irresistible challenge and opportunity, to one who thought like that, with its highly skilled workers, in a business in which they, on the authority of American customers, still led the world, supported by trade union officers, and, as it turned out, a few left-thinking businessmen.

Benn acted fast. Immediately after the election, on 11 March, 1974, he met Jack Jones and Harry Unwin, numbers one and two in the mighty TGWU, and the leaders of the still gestating co-op, Lapworth and Dennis Johnson, the TGWU plant convenor.

Enthusiastic as Benn might be, his powers were limited. An application for help under that 1972 Industry Act had to win the approval of the civil servants in the Industry Department's own Industrial Development Unit and then, having got over that hurdle, mount the even larger one of Treasury support. Also the amount of Governmental finance was limited, without special Parliamentary approval, to £5,000,000. Six previous plans drafted for the co-op had been found wanting. Businessmen were shown the seventh, currently with Benn's number two, Eric Heffer. It had not a hope, they said. It was just a

187

jumbled collection of cost appraisals, market forecasts and work flow charts. One of the brightest rising stars among Labour industrialists, Geoffrey Robinson, was called in. Robinson, chief executive of Jaguar cars and a former Labour Party research worker, had been at the Industrial Reorganization Corporation during those 'bigger is better' years of Mega-Benn industrial politics which had seen the formation of British Leyland. Lord Stokes, Robinson's overall boss, agreed Robinson could work on Meriden's problems in his own time, something which he seemed to be doing for much of the rest of the decade.

At last the application was in a form which it was thought would pass muster with the civil servants. It did not. They doubted if a workforce of 879 could produce the proposed 24,000 machines a year, 500 a week, when Norton-Villiers-Triumph, Poore's merged giant, had employed 1,750 to produce 28,000 the previous year. That showed a failure of imagination, retorted the co-op's presenters. It ignored Meriden's previous labour troubles, when 60 per cent production had rarely been achieved, when, they admitted, there had been 'an entirely uncooperative attitude of labour, maximizing piecework earnings and causing repeated stoppages, overmanning and low productivity because of the "them and us" problem of private industry'. Now all would be different. All demarcation between trades would disappear, craftsmen would cover several trades, production workers would handle materials and do the cleaning. Also there would be an advisory board where workers, through union representatives, would meet monthly to vet the performance of management.

The civil servants were not impressed and it was still no good when glowing forecasts of exports were quoted from American dealers. The submission stayed rejected.

That, according to the terms of the Act, was where it should have stopped, but the normally immovable barrier of the Civil Service was up against the irresistible force of

Bennery, that force which had already overturned centuries of law in getting rid of that Stansgate viscounty and was in the process of upsetting hallowed political principles by securing Britain's first referendum, on the Common Market.

As a first step Benn got Wilson to send in Harold Lever, highly regarded by the Prime Minister as a hard-headed, socialist businessman. At least, while Tories might doubt the first of those adjectives and some Labourites the second, all would agree that Lever had rather more business experience than most politicians. Lever had his doubts too, but rather than doubts about the Meriden workers' capabilities they were that they might find themselves at the mercy of Norton-Villiers-Triumph — events were to show that Lever could not have been more wrong.

That was the first stage in the campaign. The second saw Jack Jones and others lobbying their Cabinet friends for approval. As this lobbying went on Benn called all parties to the Department. Poore agreed to sell and met Robinson the next day to fix the price, £3,100,000 plus a royalty for the use of the Triumph name and of the jigs at the factory.

In due course the Cabinet met and, no great surprise to those who knew the adamantine hardness of Benn beneath the silken exterior of old-world courtesy and good manners, Benn got his way.

When he made his statement to the House of Commons in July he had to report that though the Industrial Development Advisory Board had welcomed the Meriden proposal as a constructive attempt to deal with the deadlock at the factory, a majority had decided it was not commercially viable.

The Government appreciated that, said Benn, and recognized that, like all innovations, this new industrial organization must face problems and risks.

'In the view of the Government, however,' he declared,

189

'these must be weighed against the positive national benefits which would result.'

The world market for motor-cycles was buoyant and the UK share was small. Production at Meriden would help attack that market for most, if not all, would go for export, bringing some £10,000,000 a year export earnings.

Then came words familiar to those following the new Benn thinking. Under the present pattern of industrial organization there had been a failure to recognize the interests of the labour force in running the business. That accounted for much of the friction between management and workers and seriously reduced industrial efficiency. A co-operative in which interests of workers and management were both identified offered a new approach.

'Accordingly, the Government has concluded that notwithstanding the risks involved it is in the national interest that this innovation should be tried.'

The co-operative was to receive a grant of £750,000 and a loan of £4,200,000 for fifteen years. The loan was to carry interest at 10 per cent, the first payment, though, not being due for a year, and repayment of the principal was to begin on 30 June 1980, at the rate of £420,000 a year. That meant the total advance was just within the limit of £5,000,000, above which special Parliamentary approval would be needed. No doubt it was thought that an outright grant of £5,000,000 would be a bit too much for MPs and public to stomach. In fact, though, it might just as well have been a grant. No interest was ever paid and the debt was eventually written off, by that apostle of rigid Toryism, Sir Keith Joseph.

Benn's statement revealed that the co-op had gone beyond even his thinking on workers' control. In his address to the foundrymen he had suggested that the ratio between top and bottom pay in any firm should be no more than 10:1. If the lowest-paid worker received £15 a week then the boss should not get more than £7,500 a year. At Meriden there was to be a flat rate for workers' wages

190

and executive salaries of £50 a week and Benn's consent would be needed for any payment over this. Later, though, it was agreed the chief executive could get up to £8,000 a year, still well within that ten to one ration.

All seemed to be running smoothly. Meriden should be written large in the annals of industrial strife, declared Benn. The brazier which warmed the pickets and the Wigwam, the tent they sheltered in beside it, should be preserved for posterity as an example of human achievement. One worker had, perhaps, a better understanding of the ways of posterity when he told a reporter, 'I only hope when it's all over my children will give me credit for what I did. But I'm not banking on it.' The Lord Mayor of Coventry gave a celebratory dinner, for which he, poor man, was to receive his share of the dirt which was soon to be flying around. For problems still lay ahead before the factory could reopen.

Trouble came not so much from the Opposition in Parliament — their time was to be later — nor from the NVT board — though Poore was calling for more financial backing, from the Export Credit Guarantee Board — as from the NVT workers, particularly those at the Small Heath factory in Birmingham. Benn's Cabinet colleagues, it turned out, had said that the agreement of the other NVT workers had to be obtained to the Meriden proposals. Wolverhampton, producing Nortons, was backing Meriden, Small Heath was not. Benn had said the co-operative would not operate to the detriment of NVT, nor any other plant. But his statement had also referred to the planned Meriden output of 24,000 machines a year. Five hundred Bonnevilles a week, said the Small Heath workers, threatened their jobs producing 230 three-cylinder Tridents a week.

The big guns of the Confederation of Shipbuilding and Engineering Unions were called in in December, when it seemed that the Small Heath objection had delivered a death-blow to the Meriden plan. If there were to be no

191

Meriden, they told the objectors, there would be no Small Heath. Poore needed the balance of his own Government loan and plant from the Meriden factory, to be released when the contracts were signed, not just to expand Small Heath production but to keep it going. Benn wrote a letter of reassurance to the Birmingham workers and it was on the promises in that, they said later, they gave way.

Still, with further haggling over export credits to finance the sale of those blockaded machines, it was not until March 1975 that the contracts were exchanged, the Government cheque handed over, the blockade lifted and the eighteen-month sit-in ended.

In some quarters the cheers were muted.

'In the atmosphere of euphoria which naturally surrounds today's happening I must strike a more sombre note,' said Poore. 'I would be less than honest if I allowed it to be thought that we believe this outcome provides a sound, lasting and sensible solution to the industry's problems unless substantial further investment is provided, at least £15,000,000.'

Immense damage, he said, had been done to the industry and his company by the wrangling. It would have been in an immeasurably stronger position if the original Norton-Villiers-Triumph plan of the 1973 merger, for two factories, had been implemented.

But the Meriden co-op was in business and those who had forecast a new working atmosphere seemed to have been right. There were no tea breaks, the working day lasted up to fifteen hours and everyone was on £50 a week, including Johnson, the chairman. Not that Benn had responsibility for it much longer. In June the Prime Minister, Harold Wilson, made him swap jobs with Eric Varley, the Energy Minister, to a chorus of approval from industry and indignant protests from unions.

For Varley there was trouble ahead. Poore put up his estimate of State aid needed to £30,000,000. Consultants called in to survey the industry listed three possibilities, an industry of much the current size, a very much smaller one, or something in between. The cheapest, smallest course, would need £15,000,000 aid, the largest and most expensive, keeping the current 3,000 workforce, would cost £50,000,000. In all cases production should be concentrated in two factories at most and new models were urgently needed.

In August 1973 Varley announced there was to be no more money for NVT. The Export Credit Guarantee Board would not be justified in guaranteeing further finance to increase stocks unlikely to be sold. This, he declared, was nothing to do with Meriden which had not yet entered the North American market. The £50,000,000 course would work out at £17,000 a man, which was quite unacceptable. There had been a dramatic fall in world demand, unsold stocks of British bikes round the world totalled 13,000 and even if things went well in the future there would be cash flow problems until the end of the 1980's.

The Opposition spokesman, Michael Heseltine, berated Varley, whose statement, he said, was a total repudiation of the commitment given by Benn to the success of the industry, of NVT no less than the co-operative. There had been a major ministerial blunder and there must be a full public inquiry.

Varley retorted that Heseltine was pursuing a vendetta against Benn who had 'fought like a lion to establish the motor-cycle industry'. For Huckfield it was the 'procrastination and failure to sign agreements' by Mr Poore that was to blame.

Then, after Conservative members for the Midlands had charged Benn with wilfully disregarding his advisers in keeping the third factory and with blackmailing and deceiving Small Heath workers, up came his letter to them the previous November. Was it or was it not a commitment to keep their factory and their jobs going?

Varley said Benn had told the workers he would be deceiving them if he gave the guarantee they wanted, five years free of redundancy. He read out one paragraph of Benn's letter: 'I am not today in a position to give you firm undertakings about possible investment on the basis of the long-term plan which is presented by the management of NVT.'

There were cries of 'Read on!' Varley did not. Heseltine did.

'I can, however, give you my firmest assurance that there will be no discrimination by the Government in favour of the co-op to the detriment of the Small Heath or Wolverhampton works,' the Benn letter continued. 'The Government is fully committed to securing the future of the motor-cycle industry in this country and, of course, this involves the success of NVT no less than that of the co-operative.'

What did that 'firm assurance' mean in terms of Wolverhampton and Small Heath jobs? Different things, according to whether one was looking at it from the Government or Opposition front benches. One back-bench Labour MP, Renee Short, from Wolverhampton, reported, however, that her constituents had seen it as something on which to peg their faith in the future. It had been widely circulated in the factories. Did Mr Varley realize the enormity of the situation in the light of his announcement of no more cash? There would be no more British motor-cycle industry. Only foreign bikes would be bought here, adding to the balance of payment problem. With knock-on effects there would be 20,000 unemployed in the West Midlands, where unemployment was already at its highest for half a century.

The very next day Poore announced that the Wolverhampton factory would close. Small Heath would continue with a smaller workforce, from the two factories, producing a new Norton. Plans for new machines, including one powered by a Wankel rotary engine, were postponed. For, he said, NVT was still committed to buying 48,000 Triumphs from Meriden, under the agreement. He castigated Varley for remarks harmful to the industry which would make selling abroad difficult. If Government ministers did not want to support Benn's plan it would cost them nothing to find words to encourage what was left instead of doing their best to destroy it.

The Meriden record after that can be summarized as a succession of crises. Tardiness in the arrival of export credits, during that first year, meant growing stockpiles of bikes, at a time when the factory should have been working steadily up to its 500-a-week output, with no money coming in to pay men and women even the low wages, by local standards, they had accepted. There were moments of optimism when output climbed to the target figure, when Americans were queuing up to buy Triumphs, voted 'Machine of the Year' in 1979, a title it had held in 1965. There were others when the factory was down to a three-day week and one dismal six-week spell in 1977 when all work stopped. During a brief happy period in the mid-1970's the co-operative was receiving £680 for each machine when £600 was the break-even figure, but more often it was the other side of the Micawber equation that prevailed — income twenty shillings, expenditure twenty shillings and sixpence — with its threat of doom.

Lord Stokes, labelled 'Britain's top export salesman' by the Press, was sent to the States to assess the market for the Triumph superbike. He was optimistic. Sales could reach 12,000. At the same time, though, Varley was calling for advice on how Meriden could be made viable and Robinson was seeking the views of friends at the GKN engineering firm on what was wrong. One of their conclusions was that that flat rate of pay was a problem — it was a stumbling block to attracting the right sort of recruit. A managing director was taken on at £10,000 a year, but reports that the principle of equal pay on the shop floor had been dropped were denied. Later, though,

195

some latitude was allowed in productivity arrangements and through overtime, assembling a small bike from parts imported from Moto Guzzi, for workers to boost their earnings.

Interest payments on that £4,200,000 advance had been postponed and the co-operative was asking for more money from a new trunk of £20,000,000 set up for aid to industry. Then in early 1977 all workers were laid off because of a cash crisis. Within four days a rescue operation was announced, financed by £500,000 from the Government and £1,000,000 advanced by GEC against stocks of 2,000 motor-cycles. That million eventually enabled Meriden to cut itself off completely from NVT, buying the rights to the Triumph name and the factory equipment which still, officially, belonged to the parent company.

For a while hopes soared again. Productivity was up, at 22 machines a man-year, a 50 per cent improvement on the best achieved by NVT. The target of 500 machines a week was reached and there were hopes of 750. But then stocks began to pile up again, bringing more short-time working and lay-offs. Accounts in May 1978 showed a trading loss of £687,564 for the 18 months up to September 1977, a period in which there had been six weeks of complete shutdown. Unpaid interest took the deficit to over £1,500,000.

At the end of 1978 Robinson who had been a one-man pressure group for the co-operative, took up the official position of chief executive. He remained unpaid. So did the interest. 'You cannot get blood out of a stone,' Robinson accurately, if unoriginally, commented.

Soon he was telling his 720 workers they had either to accept 150 redundancies, shut down for four months or go on a three-day week for the next eighteen months. A further £700,000 had been lost in the 12 months to September 1978. Despite that there was a good prospect of the company breaking even, he said — provided the interest payments were waived.

196

By this time there had been a change of Government. Mrs Thatcher, her head full of monetarist answers to Britain's problems was at Number Ten and Sir Keith Joseph, devoted Simon Pure to the basic principles of private enterprise with no public help for weaklings, at the Department of Industry. No waiver, he declared. Meriden must do its duty by the capitalist system and pay up, or be bought up. A rather different view came from one Meriden worker:

'Not a buyer around who could save us. We believe we have paid the interest charges by working in the co-operative instead of being on the dole and taking the tax-payer's money. All we wanted to do was to keep a British motor-cycle on the road but, as it turns out, we are no more than political pawns.'

Just as Robinson had said, you cannot get blood out of a stone. Joseph had to accept the inevitable, though he did it only by stages.

First he agreed there should be more time to pay. Then he agreed, in July 1980, when the time for the next interest payments had come and passed, that proposed court action to recover monies advanced — over £11,000,000 was the official estimate — should be held over while a possible take-over was negotiated. But when that take-over was made conditional on the Government waiving interest and writing off loans, Joseph found it too much to stomach.

Yet a month later the total debt was written off because, said Joseph's Minister of State, Lord Trenchard, there was no possibility of its being recovered. A little later another Industry junior minister, David Mitchell, put the amount paid out of public funds to Meriden at £9,877,000.

One sour comment on Benn's brain-child was to come from Mrs Thatcher herself. In May 1981, full of recent experience of Japanese technology, she berated Meriden as a prime example of the perils of British industry failing

197

to use robots and other automatic techniques. Meriden managed only fourteen bikes a man-year — Norton, she admitted, only ten — but Yamaha, using robots, produced about 200. Yamaha employed 5,000 while Meriden had only 150 jobs then.

Whose fault was it that Meriden and the rest of the British motor-cycle industry, when there was a rest, did not get robots? That is one ill which cannot be blamed on the Dockers, there were no such things in their days. The decline of the 1960's was not due to production techniques but to British manufacturers having the wrong range of bikes. They then made frantic efforts to enlarge the range, BSA at one time had thirteen new models, mostly lightweights of the kind youngsters were wanting, but how was it to get the money for the automatic lines to make them and compete with the Japanese? The only chance came with the merger of 1973, under the aegis of the Heath cabinet, in which sat Margaret Thatcher. It would, of course, have taken considerably more than the £5,000,000 which was all Heath and Co, including Thatcher, would allow. Even in 1973 five million was hopelessly inadequate for re-equipping an industry of that size. Five years later a single project for a 125-cc machine, being discussed by Meriden and Moto Guzzi, would have cost £40,000,000.

The head of Moto Guzzi, Alessandro de Tommaso, asked for his explanation of the debacle in the British motor-cycle industry, said, 'It lost its pride of place in the world due to mismanagement.' To others it seems that both Government and industry were slow to recognize the need in the 1960's for reorganization, for re-equipment — and it is worth recalling that those were the days when Harold Wilson was preaching the virtues of new technology and the 'white-hot' revolution it would bring — and the amount it would cost. Poore, who took on the job, found it was far beyond his financial resources.

As for Meriden, perhaps it was just starry-eyed idealism by Benn, who saw an opportunity to put his latest brain-child, workers' control, into practice. Perhaps it would have been better to concentrate more on equipping it to compete technologically and less on making it a showpiece of industrial democracy. Money mattered more than morality.

That said and done, however, the fact remains that Meriden survived. Wolverhampton and Small Heath, the two other large factories, have both gone. NVT has claimed it will come back with a new, advanced machine, one to beat the Japs, probably with the Wankel engine the company has been experimenting with for over a decade. But the failure of the foray into the superbike business of the successful motor racing impresario, Lord Hesketh, which cost him £550,000 and his backers £1,800,000, must raise doubts about the chances of that coming off.

A few small firms turning out specialised racing bikes are all that is left of the once dominant British industry, apart from Meriden. If it had not been for Benn's support of the co-operative would even that survive? On the other hand, if Benn had not ridden roughshod over his civil servants and allowed Poore to go ahead would Britain now have a broader-based, two factory system, producing his planned 120,000 machines in a wider range of models?

Nobody knows. It is just a matter of opinion. One opinion that can be quoted is that of the Public Accounts Commons Committee, reporting in October 1976. That considered three co-operatives born during the Benn reign at Industry, Meriden, the *Scottish Daily News* and the Kirkby Manufacturing and Engineering Company.

All, it said, had paid too much for assets taken over, though it admitted they had probably been unable to negotiate lower prices. All had been given Government money, despite the advice of officials that they were not viable projects. All three had represented a new experiment in industrial organization in manufacturing industry, which, if successful, could have pointed the way to new developments in industrial relations and improved productivity. Those last factors had been considered by Ministers to outweigh doubts about commercial viability.

But, it declared, the outcome of the experiments may well have harmed the cause of workers' co-operatives.

The *Scottish Daily News* and Kirkby both collapsed and Benn's workers' co-operative at Meriden did not save the British motor-cycle industry, nor has it inspired others by its example.

Perhaps it was handicapped by being a decade too late. 'Too little, too late' is the common complaint about government support for industry in Britain. Mrs Thatcher's monetarist policies have tried to make it 'not anything–ever' but in practice events have conspired to change that to 'a little more, but even later', as Keith Joseph found at Meriden.

If earlier action had been successful then it would have saved the country import bills beside which the money put into Meriden, or even the £50,000,000 which Eric Varley jibbed at supplying, is chicken feed.

In 1978 Britain produced 23,900 motor-cycles, all but 4,000 being exported, and 3,300 mopeds and scooters, 1,200 of these being exported. Imports, though, were 56,200 mopeds, 3,300 scooters and 224,800 motor-cycles. An industry which was once a big foreign currency earner is now a heavy trade liability.

But then, perhaps, it was bound to happen unless someone here, politician or industrialist, had analysed the situation and planned his action with the care taken by those Japanese as they planned their appearance at the TT races.

CHAPTER THIRTEEN

Another Constitutional Change

Europe: to go in or not to go in?

That question puzzled minds of politicians and public alike in the post-War years as they balanced the slings and arrows outside with the possible nightmare inside. It was one on which Benn changed his mind. But how many of the rest of us have not? Opinion polls show most people have, from for to against to for again or, more likely, the other way round, as in the case of Benn. As he himself said, during a debate on entry into the Common Market in 1972, 'If flexibility in response to a developing situation is an offence, there is not one man who will be able to claim that he came down the motorway of life without turning the steering wheel to left or right to take account of changing circumstances.'

One man who did not turn his steering wheel, at least on the European road, was Edward Heath. For him there was never any nightmare in prospect inside, only the sweet dreams of shared prosperity. Perhaps significantly, when he and Benn, both fledgling MPs, joined in debate in the early fifties, Heath chose to press the virtue of a wider European community in the Atlantic Alliance, Benn those of democracy and the right of an individual to be wrong.

To Heath goes the honour, or the stigma, of taking Britain into the European Economic Community, to Benn that of giving us the chance of getting out again. Having changed the Constitution once in his battle to renounce his peerage he challenged it again to introduce to Britain the principle of the referendum, a direct approach to the people for their opinion on the burning issue of the day. Some, particularly among his fellow members of the Commons not in danger of being off-loaded against their wills to the Lords, might consider it the greater achievement. After all, it runs counter to the basis of the British parliamentary system, the hallowed contention that an MP is elected to decide what is best for his constituents, that he is not just their delegate but their representative, not their voice but their mind. The electorate provides guidance once every five years by expressing its general view on the way it wants things to go and that is that until the next general election. In between it is up to those who stand in its name.

In 1975, at the time of the referendum, the European Economic Community was eighteen years old, but its birth in 1957 followed a gestation period which had really begun at the end of the War. It is difficult even for those of us who lived through it to recapture the atmosphere then. There is a generation gap which even separates the older generation from their younger selves. They were then aware, with an awareness not diminished by wartime experiences and by victory, of their upbringing. Their childhood had seen Empire Day celebrated annually with heartfelt ceremony in school playgrounds. Maybe some sang ribald words to 'Land of Hope and Glory' but all, singers as well, felt a surge of pride as they went back into their classrooms to look again at the vast expanses coloured red on the maps. We were still citizens of the British Empire, the greatest the world had ever known, and we were unique among the peoples of the world.

Maybe the war should have changed all that. On the surface it may have done but underneath Empire Day still lingered, though it was to be replaced by Commonwealth Day, an infant which proved far too weak to survive. There were the usual post-War reactions, assertions that war must never happen again, though, to tell the truth, deep down many felt it had been a time to savour, a time when they had experienced life more deeply then they ever would again, except, vicariously, when their children and grandchildren set off in another, though much smaller, expeditionary force to the Falklands. There were calls for a United Nations, which it was possible to understand and approve, provided we had our proper place in it as one of the 'Big Three U's', the UK, USA and USSR which had won the war. There were others for a 'United Europe from the Atlantic to the Urals', which we were much less able to understand. The Urals end of it may have sounded a deeper chord than the Atlantic. The returning soldier was pretty left-wing, perhaps because of memories of the thirties, perhaps because of all those current affairs lectures given by left-wing young officers, or deputed to left-wing young NCOs by right-wing officers who could not be bothered — the Army was then very keen on fitting the returning soldier to 'Civvy Street' by means of ABCA, the Army Bureau of Current Affairs. The Army command itself was a shade left-wing by traditional Army standards. The Russians had proved themselves bonny fighters under 'Uncle Joe'. As for the Atlantic side of Europe, that has always been inhabited by Frogs, Wogs and Fritzies. Fritz might be elevated to the more generous term 'Jerry' when we were fighting him — he also was a bonny fighter — but the Frogs and Wogs had not done at all well. Even Jerry-Fritz, or his leaders, had been revealed, with the opening of the concentration camps, to be dirty fighters, not really deserving of the friendly, if condescending, term Fritz.

Anyway, with the war over he was, at best, Fritz again, except to those whose watchword had always been 'Never trust Jerry'.

We were convinced Britain's standing in the world, the superiority of the English — not forgetting the Scots, Welsh and Irish — had come because we had stood away from Europe, off the mainland, and had turned our gaze outwards. For our political leaders there was also a 'special relationship' with the USA, which they cherished as the easier way out of our post-War difficulties.

This was not just the view of the man on the bus but also the man driving it. Churchill may have declared 'We must build a kind of United States of Europe' in a speech at Zurich in 1946, in the opening stages of the 'Cold War' with the Soviet Union, but there was no doubt that he intended that London should play the role of Washington in that European United States. It was Britain's destiny to lead Europe from outside, not to be submerged within. As Harold Macmillan said in 1982, looking back thirty years, the Establishment was united against going into Europe. When the Establishment was united on anything, he added, it was invariably wrong, a comment which might appear just a shade extravagant.

While Britain wanted to maintain its influence from outside, as a separate entity, France, Germany, Belgium, the Netherlands, Luxembourg and Italy were set on achieving a new European unity. General de Gaulle had political reservations but, a French patriot in the old mould, was determined to revive the old glories of France. A realist, he saw that France could no longer stand on her own, if she needed to, against America or Britain. The Cold War meant, of course, that there would never be any question of standing unaided in any form of confrontation with Russia.

Those six countries forged their first links with their coal and steel industries, in the European Coal and Steel Community. In March 1957 came the Treaty of Rome which created the European Economic Community. The Six were progressively to form themselves into one Common Market, with no tariff barriers and with common economic policies. At the same time, with atomic research promising speedy supplies of virtually unlimited power — nuclear-generated electricity, we were promised in those days, would be so cheap it would be hardly worth while charging for it — they joined in Euratom. Somewhat alarmed by the appearance of so large an economic competitor the UK Government tried to negotiate a broad but limited trading arrangement with it but failed. In 1959, after the EEC made its first tariff cuts, the UK sponsored its own Free Trade Area of peripheral countries, with Austria, Denmark, Norway, Portugal, Sweden and Switzerland, in the European Free Trade Assocation.

In 1961 Harold Macmillan, having won an election on the assertion 'You've never had it so good', felt it would be even better inside the Common Market and applied to join. The Establishment unity was showing signs of strain. Heath, then Lord Privy Seal, headed the British negotiating team. Talks went on until January 1961 with seemingly some progress until de Gaulle effectively ended them. At his half-yearly press conference he made it clear he regarded Britain as a Trojan horse for America. Britain had just come to a deal with the USA, at Nassau, to acquire the Polaris submarine-launched nuclear missile, a deal which convinced de Gaulle that Britain was still bound to America and was not sincere in its approaches to Europe. With Britain a member, said the French leader, the Common Market would become a colossal Atlantic Community, depending on and directed by the United States, which would soon absorb Europe. That might be justifiable in certain eyes but it did not suit France. Less than a fortnight later the talks had collapsed.

While the talks were still going on Benn, among others, was canvassed for his views on joining the Common Market. He objected, mainly on political grounds. He objected to the hardening of the division between East and West, to the written constitution, to the fact that, as he saw it, Britain would have less influence inside than outside, to the enshrinement of 'laissez-faire' and bureaucracy in the Treaty of Rome. He also objected to a trading policy which would speed up the widening gulf between rich and poor countries.

That attitude was reflected in the policies of the Wilson Government when it came to power. For the first two years it concentrated on EFTA and the Commonwealth.

But as the harsh economic realities wilted Wilsonian ebullience the policy changed. In November 1966 the Prime Minister announced to the Commons a new high-level approach to the Common Market. The Government was determined to enter 'if our essential British and Commonwealth interests can be safeguarded'. He and George Brown would sound out European heads of Government on the chances. The sounds were mellifluous, even though Brown struck a dischord with Willy Brandt, the West German Chancellor, when he said Willy should help Britain in so the Market could enjoy the natural leadership of Britain. The following May Wilson reported that a formal application would be made. He acknowledged the economic benefits he expected from membership but declared the political argument was stronger. British membership would make Europe stronger, more independent, more decisive in world affairs.

Though both parties put the Whips on for a vote approving the application 64 MPs, half Labour, voted against. There were no ministerial defections though there were 'reservations' in the Cabinet, as Benn reported later. Among the reservationists were Fred Peart, Barbara Castle, Douglas Jay and, later, Peter Shore, but not Benn. The economics of scale were overriding his political objections.

'Technology imposes on us all its inexorable logic of scale,' said the Minister of Technology, lecturing Germans in Bonn on the benefits to Europe of British membership. Britain may have been slow in applying for membership but she was the first to see that technological imposition. The full benefits of European technology could only be achieved if Britain were included in a European Centre of Technology — and whose experience on that could be more helpful than that of the British Minister of Technology.

Economics had temporarily taken precedence over politics in his argument, unless it was that 'bigger is better'

206

also applied to politics. The only political objections he referred to were not those felt in Britain to the submergence of its sovereignty in a wider organization but those among the Six to the admission of Britain. They would be ineffective because founded on nationalism which was becoming increasing irrelevant. Realism must be the foundation of political success.

In talking of a European Technological Community at the heart of an extended EEC he was echoing Wilson. The Prime Minister had emphasized the benefits he saw to Europe of Britain with its great scientific and technological reputation. The Brussels Commission vetting Britain's application was not so sure. British achievements were notable but such matters as the allocation of money on research had not always been well planned. Even with Britain the Community would lag far behind the USA. Still it acknowledged that with Britain the economic base would be larger, potentially approaching America's. A number of points needed to be cleared up but it reported in favour of negotiations.

De Gaulle again concerned himself with those points to be cleared up and made clear his belief they could not. There were food prices, for example. Britain enjoyed cheap food. If prices were raised British wages would have to go up, the balance of payments would collapse. Neither did Britain's economic performance inspire confidence. As soon as it achieved a rate of growth comparable to that of other countries it ran into a balance of payments crisis. There was certainly truth in that. Wilson, who had condemned the 'stop-go' regimes of his predecessors had found himself forced into a 'stop' himself, in 1966 and 1967, after his earlier attempts of the 'go' of his white-hot revolution. Indeed in those years from 1958 to 1967 Britain had the lowest growth rate of all countries in both the EEC and EFTA.

De Gaulle also objected to the threat to European cohesion of Britain's links with the Commonwealth and

207

USA. Britain shared with America strange ideas about new monetary means not linked with gold. How could it join the (then) solid world of the franc, mark, lira and florin? No, he declared. Britain was just regarding Europe as a means to get others to share her problems, to save her substance and to fulfil her hopes of once more achieving a dominant position in the world. He vetoed the application.

The insuperable barrier of de Gaulle's objection was to be removed by the force which overcomes all. He died in November 1970. Before that, though, he had retired from the French presidency, in April 1969, shortly after quashing those talks. With the dominant personality of Europe, one obstinately opposed to British entry, out of office, lesser mortals could try again to change the course of history.

A summit meeting of the Six, in December 1969, approved restarting talks with Britain, also with Ireland, Denmark and Norway, countries which felt their futures should be linked with Britain's. In February 1970 Wilson declared his readiness to start talks 'tomorrow'. Tomorrow turned out to be in June and it was Heath, victor in the election of that month, not Wilson, who was premier during the negotiations, with Geoffrey Rippon leading the British team.

The talks lasted a year and a White Paper at the end promised a new era of prosperity for Britain in an enlarged Common Market. The EEC's 190 millions plus the 100 millions Britain would be taking in with the other three applicants would, seemingly, all be willing customers for British manufactures. Wilson, out of office, was at first sceptical, then hostile. The terms did not go far enough to protect Britain's balance of payments, to control its movement of capital, to soften the blows to its links with the Commonwealth, he said. The Heath view of the world and of Britain's place in it was defeatist. Given the right policies Britain would be at least as prosperous and vigorous outside the Market as it would be if it entered on the wrong terms. When a vote was taken in the House it was the pro-Marketeers who were the Labour rebels this time. They ensured a conclusive majority for entry.

Wilson had responded traditionally, in the fashion of a Leader of the Parliamentary Opposition. Benn, though, was more unorthodox. He had already already launched his campaign for a referendum, in November 1970, by means he had used before, a letter to his constituents, sent also to the Press.

Up to then, he argued, it had been assumed that, like every other treaty, the decision would be reached by the Government after a Parliamentary vote. But this was not the same as any other Treaty. It would be an irreversible decision which would transfer to the EEC certain sovereign powers now exercised by the British Parliament. It was inconceivable that such a decision should be left to a bare majority of the Cabinet, nine men out of 17, who would then put the Whips on, force it through the House and commit the nation for all time. Even if there were a free vote, which the Prime Minister would not accept, this would still leave the matters to MPs, not one of whom was able to commit himself during the election on this issue since the terms were not then known.

Nor would another election fought on the Common Market help very much. It would be wrong to expect a lifelong supporter of one party to vote for the other party, just because he or she agreed with it on the Common Market issue. No general election could allow people to record a separate vote on the Common Market question. The case for a referendum, he declared, was immensely powerful, if not overwhelming.

Those of his constituents with strong feelings on entry, either pro or anti, seeking a sign of a change since 1968 in Benn's own opinion of the advantages and disadvantages would have been hard put to find it. Today, looking back at that letter, it is hard to see it as coming from one who would, in a few years, be leading a fervent campaign to convince the British people that membership was a tragedy.

In the post-War years, he wrote, he had been very hostile to the idea of a Common Market. He did not like the strong anti-Russian cold war bias that lay behind it. Willy Brandt's Eastern Policy and *rapprochement* with the USSR had answered those fears. He confirmed his 'bigger is better' philosophy was influencing his politics. If man, he wrote, did not organize himself into bigger political units the international companies would run the world. We would be like parish councillors in our parliaments, with little say in what happened.

'Of course we can stay out and stand alone, but we will still find that European, American and Russian decisions will set the framework within which we should have to exercise our formal parliamentary sovereignty,' he wrote. 'If that is what the British people want we shall have to live with the consequences of it. It is true that many who are opposed to entry have urged a referendum because they believe that it will reveal a majority against entry. That is a matter for them. Those of us who feel that, given the right terms, the arguments for entry are strong should be the first to see that decision shared.'

Then came the crux of his argument:

'The whole history of British democracy has been about *how* you take decisions and this has always been seen to be more important than what the decisions were.'

That echo from that 1950's debate with Heath was to sound through the 1970's with his growing attachment, in government, to the idea of popular involvement in decision making.

By the following summer he had put down a Private Member's Bill, sent copies of it to every constituency Labour party and to every trade union, and had launched a campaign to convert the Labour Party to adopt the

210

referendum as its policy. That campaign started at a meeting at Transport House at which he pointed out that it was no new gimmick to get the Labour Party off its own hook. He had said, in 1968, when the Labour Government had then applied for entry, 'the five yearly cross on the ballot paper is just not going to be enough' and had called for a re-examination of the objections to referenda.

In the debate on the Heath-Rippon terms of entry Benn concerned himself almost entirely with the question of sovereignty, the right of ministers to dissent on such an issue and the need for an appeal to the people for their opinion — after all, he said, if a poll could not reveal a single supporter for entry even Heath might decide not to press his application.

'If I were a long-standing European, as is the Prime Minister, I would feel that he had killed my European dream, because visions are realized only when men enter a common enterprise freely. They carry the strain. They are rewarded by their effort. One cannot march a nation into a new era and adventure on the scale . . .' With uproar drowning his words he concluded, 'against its will'.

On sovereignty he pointed out that it did not mean we controlled our destiny. Our future could still be decided in the Kremlin, the Pentagon or elsewhere. It did mean that British voters visiting the House could be told, 'This is where your laws are made and your taxes imposed. This is where policies are explained and you can get rid of these men yourselves . . . When the Upper Clyde Shipyard workers take a charter flight to Brussels we shall know where power has really moved.' (The UCS workers had just embarked on one of the first of what was to be a frequent phenomenon of the seventies, a sit-in demonstration against forcible closure and loss of jobs.)

Economic predictions alone were no solid basis for reaching a decision. After commenting on the danger of a new myth, 'Yes for more jobs in Europe', to follow all the other remedies which politicians had promised the public would produce the desired result, he made a general comment on Britain's performance which at least acknowledged the failure of all governments since the War, including the one of which he had been a member. None had succeeded in achieving growth, a balance of payments surplus, stable prices, higher productivity and full employment at the same time. If one had it would have stayed in power for 25 years. A decade on, that comment is still pertinent and looks like remaining so.

The policy of a referendum had not yet been adopted by the Labour Party. The next year, though, the new French president, Pompidou, announced that the French people would be given what Heath was still denying the British public, a vote on British entry. That tipped the scales in the Labour National Executive Committee and Shadow Cabinet and it became officially party policy at the party conference in the autumn of 1972.

Despite his earlier opinion that it would be wrong to expect party supporters to vote for the other party, just because of the Common Market issue, Benn was soon to urge Liberals and Conservatives to vote Labour, not to take Britain out but just to be able to exercise their right to vote on so important a matter. A Labour Government, he said in a speech just before the 1973 Labour conference, would seek to renegotiate the terms on a basis which would entirely safeguard our national interests. They were bound to amend the Act on entry in such a way as to return all the sovereign powers passed to Brussels back to the British people and Parliament.

Another MP to urge a similar line on non-Labour voters was Enoch Powell, a High Tory whose brand of Toryism found him inevitably at loggerheads with Heath. At least it seemed from a series of somewhat tortuous speeches on the matter and from the analyses of them made by editorial writers, that that was what he was urging. Conservatives and Liberals who did so in February 1974 were probably enough to turn the tide of that election which

212

Heath had called on the assumption that popular anger at the strikes of a winter of discontent would sweep him back to power. Labour won. Wilson was back, committed to renegotiation and then a referendum, committed, according to Benn, to a negotiation which would rewrite the whole terms of entry.

With the election over and Wilson so committed Benn stayed quiet for a while on the European issue, applying himself to his job as Industry Secretary. Quiescent, not quiet, should be the word, for he was fused and primed ready to explode when the referendum campaign started, to explode on the anti-side. His antipathy to the Market, put into temporary abeyance by his late 1960's belief in the economics of scale, was reinforced now by his conviction that economics as well as politics argued against membership. He was now part of the hardcore of 'antis' in the Cabinet, along with Michael Foot, Barbara Castle, Peter Shore and John Silkin.

The electorate too seemed fairly quiet on the matter. Polls seemed to indicate that, in early 1975, two years after entry, people did not think much of life inside the EEC but were resigned to it. A majority of people no longer believed, as they did in 1971, that Britain would be better off outside, but there was general decline in support for the view that membership would speed up Britain's economic growth, even strong pro-Marketeers were more sceptical of any real benefits coming.

All was quiet in Government circles, though there was a growing feeling that when it came to the point Wilson would not take the plunge into the now uncertain waters outside the Market, or, at least, not until he had received a hard electoral push. All Governments tend to be conservative, it makes for an easier life, and few supposedly revolutionary governments have lost their initial fervour as rapidly as Wilson's.

Also it had been Wilson who had initiated the negotiations which led to British entry. He had condemned

213

the terms achieved by Heath and Rippon but his reaction was not to withdraw but to improve the conditions. The role he sought was that of the man who consolidated Britain's position inside the Market by securing better terms than Heath. The thought quickly occurred to anti-Marketeers that the Government might try to swing the referendum by making its own recommendation for a vote to stay in. Frank Allaun, on the left of the party, pointed out at a National Executive Committee meeting the fate of the Norwegian Government, which had seen its similar recommendation rejected by its people and had been obliged to resign. Cautious James Callaghan, now Foreign Secretary, was understood to nod agreement. The Government knew, too, that constituency Labour parties and unions were firmly for coming out.

By March 1975 there was less need for caution. An opinion poll found a slight majority in favour of staying in, supposing better terms were negotiated, but a much larger majority believing that, whatever happened, we would stay in. Almost everyone, though, was for holding a referendum, though less than a fifth felt they knew enough to decide.

That same month a Common Market summit on the renegotiations, in Dublin, ended with claims of resounding success, of a victory with no losers. Wilson claimed British objectives had been substantially achieved. A complicated system of budgetary refunds had been worked out which meant that as Britain became poorer, in relation to other EEC members, it should pay less. New Zealand could continue exporting its butter to Britain on favourable terms for a few more years. Some other New Zealand products were left still out in the cold but Wilson felt he could not let the whole negotiations go down the drain for the sake of New Zealand cheese. If he had he would have found himself closing ranks with Benn, something which, day by day, was becoming less congenial as his young Industry Secretary attracted, also day by day, increasingly angry, if frustrated, attacks from the Opposition. The other members at the summit wanted Britain to stay in and were pleased it had been achieved with so little given away. They were now feeling the referendum would be a formality with both Government and Opposition urging a 'Yes' vote. There were smiles all round. Wilson said he and the Foreign Secretary had found the others much more flexible than expected and Callaghan at once announced he would be campaigning for a 'Yes' vote.

The Cabinet split 16 to 7. Only Eric Varley, Energy Secretary, and William Ross, Secretary of State for Scotland, joined Foot, Castle, Benn, Shore and Silkin. Wilson announced the Government would be recommending the electorate to vote to stay in but the doctrine of collective responsibility would be shelved for the referendum. MPs and Ministers who disagreed with the Government were free to state their case and attempt to sway public opinion. With that concession made to his opposition within the party Wilson felt he could safely declare he would not be resigning if the vote went against him.

Ian Mikardo, a strong Benn supporter, got into hot water when he commented on the 'pretty motley, multi-coloured army' Wilson was leading into battle, declaring,

The Prime Minister has behind him two-thirds of his Cabinet, over half of the rest of his Government, a large majority of Conservative MPs, all the Liberal MPs without exception, any other politician or would-be politician who may conceivably be influenced by the Prime Minister's formidable powers of patronage, the Confederation of British Industry, who believe that what is good for General Electric is good for the nation, the City, who do not give a damn what's good for the nation as long as they get some easy pickings out of it, all the Conservative newspapers and most of the other papers and the vast funds of the European Movement, largely contributed for their own interests by the big multi-national combines.

Labour Party headquarters refused to distribute that speech, saying it was an attack on another party member — the Prime Minister's powers of patronage were featuring increasingly in left-wing criticism of Wilson politics. Ignoring the comment, though, it was a fair summary of the situation. The TUC announced it would 'mobilize its resources' behind the withdrawal campaign, it did not consider the new terms good enough. A special Labour Party conference voted almost two to one for withdrawal. When it was suggested in the NEC, however, that the party should be fully committed to campaign for withdrawal Wilson and Callaghan threatened to resign. When that was leaked to political correspondents they saw it as just an astute manoeuvre — they would never resign, said the cynical — designed to ensure the NEC gave the same latitude for the expression of views as the Government had.

But, as Mikardo said, the money bags were in the scales against the withdrawal campaigners. Both sides — 'Yeses', the stay-ins, and 'Noes', the get-outs — received £124,000 in Government grants. All the 'Noes', the National Referendum Campaign, received in addition was £8,630, £1,377.30p of that coming from the Transport and General Workers Union. Little came from other unions. 'Their contributions were disgraceful. They talked only with their mouths,' said Dr Dickson Mabon MP, at the head of the 'No' campaign. Pro-Marketeers received contributions from 229 industrial and commercial concerns. The one industrial concern to contribute to the Antis was a Meriden firm, though not the motor cycle company. Britain in Europe, the umbrella 'Yes' organization received £996,508 from industry and the City and £360,075 from other sources. Its total spending of £1,481,583 was well over ten times that of the 'Noes' and included

£100,000 to American publicity experts for four TV films and six radio programmes. No 'No' campaigner received any travelling expenses. Heath, who made 40 campaign journeys, received £1,306, plus £1,482 for his research staff, and Home Secretary Roy Jenkins, later to become head of the EEC Brussels bureaucracy, £509.

The man who made the headlines, though, was Benn. The time had now come when one was to wonder what newspapers would do about political news if he were to withdraw from the scene. He might be the most charismatic figure in contemporary British politics but his attraction to newspapers lay not in his personality but what he said and what others said of him. The best news is bad news, it is bad news which makes headlines and sells newspapers, and Benn was becoming easier and easier to portray as the man who was bad news incarnate.

His entry into the campaign was relatively sober, though he was giving the bad news, as he saw it, of Britain's position in the Market. In a speech on May 16 he said:

They told us in 1971 the Common Market was our most promising export market. Now, three years later, Britain's trade deficit with the Nine stands at more than £2,000 million. Our industrial investment is falling and unemployment stands at 900,000. We were told that inside the Common Market prospects would open up for Scotland, Wales, Northern Ireland and all the development areas. Now, three years later, many factories and plants in those areas have closed down because they are thought too distant from Europe's industrial heartland, the golden triangle from which they are excluded.

Two days later he exploded the bombshell that was to reverberate throughout the campaign. He declared that about 500,000 jobs had been lost because of Britain's membership, producing government statistics to back his claim. The actual jobs lost in those statistics amounted to 137,000 but also shown, he said, was a loss of trade to the EEC which had had a deflationary effect causing secondary unemployment of 360,000.

It took a day or two for the claim to sink home. Then Denis Healey, Chancellor of the Exchequer, issued a statement, through the Treasury, describing it as a 'cocoon of myth and fantasy' and rejecting it as a 'falsehood'. Asked for his response to the word 'falsehood' Benn refused to be drawn. He did not propose to make personal references. The figures had been attacked but they had not been challenged. In fact, of course, he was pleased by Healey's intervention. It had brought the jobs question into the forefront of the campaign and it was to stay there.

'As our national income suffers, the blight will spread through shops and offices and even into the public services. A weakened Britain within the Common Market will soon be driven to throw teachers, office workers, secretaries, local government officials and other public servants out of work,' he said. It was a view of the future worthy of the highest-quality crystal ball, whether the jobs loss was due to the Common Market or not.

Jenkins was the next to enter the fray. Unlike Healey he named Benn, accusing him of 'deliberately distorting figures to mislead voters'. He then hit the headlines himself when he declared, 'I find it increasingly difficult to take Mr Benn seriously as an economics Minister.'

Wilson was prompted to intervene, telling Ministers they must not wrangle in public.

The normally polite William Whitelaw was moved to reply 'Yes' when, having said Benn had stood facts on their head, he was asked if he was calling Benn a liar.

Benn stuck to the subject. Heath had told us we would sell so many of our manufactures in the Common Market that it would create jobs. Now with Common Market steel, cars, machinery and textiles flooding the country and throwing our people out of work facts showed he was completely wrong.

But no matter whether Heath was wrong and Benn right, or Benn wrong and Heath right, the electoral cards were stacked in favour of the 'Yeses'. Not only did the 'Noes' have less support in finance and publicity, they were handicapped just by being 'Noes', or so they claimed. Voters, after being told by their referendum forms 'The Government has announced the results of the renegotiation of the United Kingdom's terms of membership of the European Community', were asked, 'Do you think the United Kingdom should stay in the European Community, Yes or No?'

It was a form of question which attracted the answer 'Yes' said psychologists, just as the alternative 'Do you want to come out?' would have done.

The opinion polls forecast an overwhelming 'Yes' vote. No politician can risk further dwindling of his support by admitting polls against him may be right. They were wildly wrong, Benn told the Press Association, a week before the vote.

'A pro-Market campaign by the Press lords, the mass media and big business has been so biased that it has offended the sense of fair play of the people. Mr Heath's threat that Britain is so poor that we cannot leave the Common Market and that beggars can't be choosers has touched our sense of national pride.'

If it was a matter of national pride then unfortunately, by those Empire Day standards, it had not been touched. As the vote was being counted Benn refused to speculate. 'When the great democratic processes of our society are working their way through a respectful silence is appropriate,' he said. After the result, 67 per cent voting to stay in, 33 per cent to come out, he expressed the view the referendum had had a healing effect. 'It has bound the wounds. When the people have spoken in a referendum which we gave them we must accept it.'

219

Most anti-Marketeers accepted, except for Powell who declared the question could never be considered settled until Britain withdrew from Europe.

What the referendum campaign did reveal was the power of the Press when linked with the big battalions of politics. It is probably true that newspapers do not shape people's opinions, at least not directly. Readers read the news columns and do not automatically adopt the opinions of the leader columns. But when the news is opinion, as during the campaign, opinion on which is the better of two courses, with no facts to go on, and the emphasis is in one direction then readers are swayed in that direction. At no other time would there have been so definite an approval of membership of the Common Market. One might almost say that at no other time, left to their own judgment — possibly not even at that time, left to their own judgment — would electors have voted for it.

In 1969 only one in three approved of Wilson's application to join. In August 1971, at the conclusion of the Heath negotiations, 35 per cent were for entry, 44 per cent against, though claims of a bright future ahead had made the prospect more alluring, the previous month it had been only 25 per cent for, 57 per cent against. By January 1977 the EEC's own survey found a re-run of the referendum would produce only the tiniest majority for membership compared with the massive 'Yes' vote eighteen months before, with 45 per cent in favour, 44 per cent against, though even before that British polls were finding a majority against membership. By August 1977 only 35 per cent were for membership, 53 per cent against in a NOP poll which questioned 2,056 adults in 120 parliamentary constituencies.

Looking back it is obvious that the foundations for British membership laid by Heath and Rippon were far too shaky. Cracks started appearing in the structure at once and all the Wilson negotiations did was to paper over them. Further renegotiations have gone on virtually continuously. Instead of the bright, prosperous future promised in the Market there has been the economic decline which Benn forecast. The half million lost jobs of which he spoke, to arouse such anger, are now lost in a greater pool of unemployed. To what extent the British decline was due to membership, or would have been worse were we not members, it is impossible to say. As Benn said before the referendum you cannot put all the economic factors into a computer to see how it will work out. Neither can one set a computer to look back and diagnose all that went wrong. All one can say is that the forebodings about what would have happened outside the Market appear to have been pessimistic. Britain has continued to grow more slowly — lately to decline more rapidly — not only compared with other Common Market countries but also with those EFTA countries we left in the supposedly cold world outside. Nor are they cut off from trade with the Common Market as it was feared we would be. Finland, for example, does a quarter of its trade with Common Market countries, as much as it does with the Soviet Union, on which it is supposedly dependent, and almost as much as the one-third share with other members of EFTA.

It is fairly certain that the two areas which voted 'No', the Shetlands and Western Islands got it right, for areas dependent on fishing. British fishermen no longer enjoy the rights they did in British waters, protected by British gunboats. In ports like Hull the fleets are now one-tenth the size they were a decade ago, in others fishing boats have vanished altogether. Over half the fish we eat now is imported, caught by fishermen of other nationalities, often in waters which once were British. That can be laid directly at the door of Market membership.

It is small satisfaction to be told that our leaders are still striving to improve matters, to negotiate smaller contributions to the Common Market budget, to which we felt we were bamboozled into paying too much, on the grounds that we are now a 'poor' country. We who once looked on all others as 'lesser breeds' to be classified as among the poor!

One person did come out of those campaigning days of 1975 with an enhanced reputation, Anthony Neil Wedgwood Benn, now beginning to insist that he should be referred to only as Tony, the man of the people.

As the *Daily Telegraph* said in its summing up of the campaign, he was the man who made the biggest personal gain. Not only did he bring about the referendum itself but he made all the running on the anti-Market side. The left-wing of the party now regarded him as their champion, despite certain continuing suspicions of his non-working-class origin.

The holding of a referendum, he admitted at the start of the campaign for one, would be a major constitutional change. It was and, like the Peerage Bill, it was his achievement.

CHAPTER FOURTEEN

A Sideways Kick

'The Conservative party is a primitive party. It has to have a bogeyman and its present bogeyman is the Secretary of State for Industry.'

Edward Short is not one of the most quoted of politicians but that comment is worth recording. He was speaking as Leader of the House of Commons in the late spring of 1975, at the height of a newspaper and political furore over the activities of Tony Benn, both at the Industry

Department and in leading the 'No' campaign in the Common Market referendum.

Nowadays any child psychologist hearing someone telling children 'the bogeyman will get you if you don't watch out' is likely to be as horrified as if he had seen the bogeyman himself. In fact, of course, no child needs to be told. We all, adults as well as children, believe it instinctively. It is a primeval human belief rooted in some sense of a malign purpose always at work. Adults may be more vulnerable than children to what, in more contemplative moments we would dismiss as bogeyman irrationality but which, when we are moved by our imaginations, as after reading one of M. R. James's deliciously horrifying stories, will find us glancing uncertainly over one shoulder as our pace speeds up when walking alone on a dark and stormy night.

Certainly in politics adults are particularly vulnerable. Some of us regret, even though it would mean less exciting debates and less readable newspapers, that politics are not conducted purely as an intellectual exercise, in which arguments for and against particular actions or beliefs are assessed solely on their logical basis or logical development. Listening to Parliamentary debates convinces one it is not always so in Parliament, one suspects it is not always so in the Cabinet and knows it is rarely so in everyday life. Politicians believe that there is little, if anything, so good as strong 'Mr Bogeyman' propaganda for keeping the voters in line. Loathing is the longest-lasting of emotions, far longer-lived than love, if only because it is an appetite which, in civilized circumstances, grows without ever being satisfied.

Give the people something to loathe is good advice. That is the way revolutions are won, even how elections are run, with greater emphasis on the iniquities of the other side than the virtues of one's own. To find a good bogeyman is the easiest way to run a political campaign and, regrettably, perhaps the best way to win one.

Almost certainly the young Tony Benn was not kept in order by his Norland nanny with bogeyman stories but quite certainly today he is the prime victim of them — at one and the same time he is victim and Mr Bogeyman himself. Enoch Powell may have run him close at one time as Bogeyman-in-Chief but lately Benn has been out on his own. First Britain was told 'Bogeyman Benn will get you if you don't watch out', then the same message was given to the Labour Party and it was not only on the second occasion that some of his colleagues listened, observed and acted as if convinced themselves. That is, of course, not to say that the title of Bogeyman was not deserved. That should still be a matter for careful thought and logical decision. What is to be deplored is that his case has been taken out of the region of careful thought and logical decision.

The Labour Party fought each of the two elections of 1974 with a manifesto which promised intervention in industry, through a National Enterprise Board. It promised, or threatened, according to one's point of view, take-overs of branches of industry where investment remained unsatisfactory. The February manifesto put it bluntly: 'Whenever we give direct aid to a company out of public funds we shall in return reserve the right to take a share of the ownership of the company.'

With Benn as responsible minister it was unlikely there would be any soft-pedalling on that policy but it was a policy bound to meet entrenched opposition. Benn's aides have told how, when he reported on his first day, he was greeted by his Permanent Secretary stating, rather than asking, 'I presume, Secretary of State, that you don't intend to implement the industrial strategy in Labour's programme.'

By the late summer, as industry became more and more aware that he did so intend, a whispering campaign had begun, according to Joe Haines, Wilson's press secretary at the time. Commercial circles were telling the Treasury

224

that something would have to be done about the Secretary of State if confidence was to be restored, the confidence needed to bring an investment drive which would lift Britain out of its post-Opec, post-three-day-week despond.

Benn is fond of saying that he is a bogeyman only in the eyes of the Press. That is not so. The whispering campaign against him, if Haines is right, was well under way before the Press joined in and at its height, during the following spring and early summer, the main role of the Press was to report the clamour among industrialists and politicians. Sometimes it may have appeared the Press was leading the way, when it claimed opposition to Benn among his own Cabinet colleagues, but on those occasions, too, it was to transpire, it was not imaginatively speculating but reporting factually, through leak and innuendo.

On the first such occasion the leaks were on both sides, pro- and anti-Benn, and the issue not his ministerial responsibility but one which was to loom ever larger for the rest of the seventies, his growing power in the party. At the 1974 party conference Benn had, for the first time, headed the local parties' poll for national executive places, taking over from Michael Foot as the darling of the constituencies. Following that he was elected Chairman of the Home Policy Committee. This was to prove, in Benn's hands, a position of profound, perhaps paramount, importance. Pronouncements on policy came continually and frequently — with bewildering frequency for his less mentally agile opponents in the party — to be taken up, campaigned for and, usually, adopted. Doubtless Benn would say that often the committee was responding to ideas coming up from rank and file party workers. If that were so the proponents of those ideas found an unusually receptive ear. When Benn was proposed for the position that was to prove so important, objections were raised by Denis Healey and Shirley Wil-

225

liams. Such a post, they argued, might conflict with his responsibilities as a Cabinet Minister. Their argument was sound. On many occasions Benn, as an exceptionally active chairman of the Home Policy Committee, did find himself in conflict with the prime ministerial view of the obligations of a cabinet minister under the doctrine of 'collective responsibility'.

Sound though their argument might be it failed. They had not prepared their case. Benn had prepared his answer, almost as if he had had foreknowledge. He was able to point to other occasions when a cabinet minister had sat in that Home Policy chair. Herbert Morrison, not just a cabinet minister but second only to Attlee, had done so from 1945 to 1952. Another deputy leader, George Brown, had done so as recently as 1962 to 1970. The Healey-Williams opposition collapsed. It may have been the examples quoted that led James Margach, the *Sunday Times* political journalist reporting the incident, to describe Benn as 'Wilson's effective number two'. It was, wrote Margach, nothing to do with the pecking order around the Cabinet table for Wilson kept him at a distance there. It was because of his overall standing in the party. The more he was attacked from outside, also, indeed, from inside by his Cabinet colleagues, the stronger he became. He grew on criticism. Criticism was building him into a terrifying, larger-than-life figure. Benn was now the hero of the constituencies. He had shown remarkable organization ability and was the key minister regularly going in and out of Transport House, the Labour Party headquarters. Apart from Michael Foot he was the minister most in rapport with the trade unions. His influence was expanding fearsomely and none should savour it better than Wilson, for, recalled Margach, when Wilson resigned from the Attlee government it was the Bevanite movement and the militant constituencies which kept him afloat in politics and enabled him to capture the party leadership on the death of Gaitskell.

226

In January 1975 the Industry Bill, which was to give effect to Labour's manifesto promises, was published. Benn was at pains, on its second reading, to stress the powers it provided for take-overs if industry did not invest more in new equipment and plant. In February the National Enterprise Board was formed with a bank of a thousand million pounds for industrial development and the extension of nationalization, under the terms of the Bill. Ripples from the alarm in sections of industry reached Brussels where Common Market officials were quoted as pointing to powers in the Treaty of Rome which could prevent widespread take-overs of British industry by a socialist British Government. From Downing Street and the Treasury came soothing messages that Benn would not be able to use powers given by the Bill without prior approval from the Cabinet. In the end the decision would be Wilson's — who could be relied on to behave in a far less hot-headed manner than Benn.

In March, though, Benn sought powers to take over 45 firms in the shipbuilding and aircraft industries. Shares in the companies fell, some by a quarter to a third, as stockbrokers described the proposals as a 'kick in the teeth' — for Benn had said compensation would be based on average Stock Exchange prices in a period ending in February the year before, when industry was in the doldrums of the three-day week. From the reaction of Ralph Bateman, President of the Confederation of British Industry, it went beyond their worst fears. The scope of the proposed nationalization was wider than had been expected, the terms of compensation lower. Even worse was Benn's proposal that the new Shipbuilding Corporation should be able to diversify into other industries and buy up other companies, at home and abroad. The Government, declared Bateman, was clearly set on bringing about the end of private industry. The City and Industry must combine forces to preserve the private sector and the market economy.

Not that these and similar comments from industry, charges that it was all based on dogma, that Benn's interest in industrial democracy had now become an obsession, diverted Benn from his own attack on industry. He warned that two million jobs were at risk because of industry's poor performance. He proposed doubling the rate of investment in the manufacturing industry to £5,000,000,000 a year. It would impose a heavy strain but the alternative was disaster. Manufacturing plants had to be re-equipped and expanded to restore Britain to a competitive position, not just in world markets but even here at home.

His answer to the industrial crisis was to go for growth. Not for him the defensive action of monetarist policies. Every closure involving a thousand workers, he said, cost the Government £2,000,000 a year in reduced tax revenue and extra social security payments, apart from the cost to the worker of his lost job and to society of lost output. In a passage which might qualify him for the role of Cassandra, as a truthful prophet of doom, he said, 'If trends are allowed to continue we will have closed down nearly 15 per cent of our entire manufacturing capacity and nearly 2,000,000 workers will have been made redundant between 1970 and 1980.' He was to be proved if anything too cheerful for a Cassandra.

Much of what Benn said on the need for investment could be approved by industry. It was the message which the CBI had been trying to put to the Government, commented the *Daily Telegraph*. His next suggestion on investment was not so well received. In April, in a paper before the Labour Party's Industrial Policy Sub-committee, he proposed that insurance companies, pension funds and other financial institutions should be required to channel some of their new money to government-approved investment schemes.

The chairman of the British Insurance Association and the Life Offices Association joined in protest to the Prime

Minister. In his reply Wilson wrote: 'I have not seen the document to which you refer. It does not in any way represent government thinking. The proposals contained therein have not been put to the Government and I see no likelihood that if they were they would be adopted as official policy by the Government.'

The following day Benn made it clear that if those proposals did not represent government thinking they certainly represented his and were what he believed Labour Party policy should be. It was essential that those funds be invested for the good of the country, he declared.

Soon after that Wilson was off to the Caribbean, for a Commonwealth Premiers Conference in Jamaica, and then to Washington for talks on yet another of the recurrent sterling crises. Back home the papers were still full of the iniquities of Benn — or, alternatively, his determination to carry through Labour Party policy in his Department, though that interpretation of his activities was not so commonly expressed. Then, as Wilson was returning from Washington, the *Daily Telegraph* had a scoop. Splashed on its front page was a piece from its highly-regarded political correspondent H. B. Boyne, stating the Prime Minister would be 'cutting Benn down to size'.

It was to be made clear to MPs and the country, wrote Boyne, that it was the Prime Minister, not the Secretary of State for Industry, who was in charge of the Government and its policies, including the policy on State participation in private industry. It would be the Prime Minister who would make appointments to the National Enterprise Board. Benn would be consulted, but only alongside the Chancellor of the Exchequer and the Board's chairman, Ryder. It would be the Prime Minister who would be responsible for general direction of the Board on matters on which it consulted the Government. Finally, all financial arrangements connected with the Board's activities would have to be approved by the Prime Minister as First Lord of the Treasury.

Boyne's reputation and the confident tone of the article convinced most that Boyne's source was very near, if not actually at, the top and that the story accurately represented Wilson's thinking. Any doubts there might be were swept away two days later when Harold Lever, Chancellor of the Duchy of Lancaster and generally regarded as Wilson's confidant and inspiration on business matters, confirmed that Wilson was to be in overall control of the Industry Act.

It was only after he had left office that Wilson confirmed what many believed, that he himself had been Boyne's informant. In the last volume of his memoirs, 'Final Term', he told how he planted the word that Benn was to be sacked from his job at Industry. Wilson was in a quandary. After his promises of a free hand and free speech for ministers opposed to the Common Market during the referendum campaign it would have been 'difficult, provocative indeed' for him to raise publicly the moving of Benn, while Benn was leading the 'No' campaign. On the other hand it was vital that Washington, Bonn and the International Monetary Fund, all those whose help was being sought over the sterling crisis, should be reassured that British industry would not be reshaped as Benn appeared to be proposing. So he decided to plant a story, the only time, he declared, he took such action. Boyne was a paragon of discretion who would not disclose his source, so he took him on one side during a reception in Jamaica and did the planting. Six months later Boyne retired, his long and distinguished career marked by a knighthood.

When Wilson got back from Washington the question 'Are you going to sack Benn,' was put to him directly by television interviewer Peter Jay, son of his old-time, left-wing colleague Douglas Jay and son-in-law of James Callaghan. (Jay, under the Callaghan regime, was to become Britain's ambassador in Washington.) While avoiding a direct reply, in orthodox prime-ministerial fashion,

230

Wilson made it clear to viewers that he intended to put Benn in his place. Then, in less orthodox prime-ministerial terms when talking of a Cabinet colleague, he described him as 'an Old Testament prophet without a beard'.

On radio as well as television Wilson reiterated the message that the Government's policy was for a mixed economy, decisions on the National Enterprise Board and public ownership were for the Cabinet and that Benn's ideas on the investment of pension funds were not the Government's and had no prospect of becoming Government policy. Two days later Benn was in relatively conciliatory mood in the Commons, denying any deep divisions within the Cabinet and declaring there would be consultations with both sides, unions and employers, on industrial matters.

None of this, of course, stopped the baying for Benn blood. When winning step up the attack is a maxim dear to politicians as well as to generals. Peter Walker, Benn's predecessor at Industry during the Heath government, devoted a speech to Birmingham Conservatives to the threat posed by Benn and had the satisfaction of seeing it repeated as a feature-page article in the *Daily Mail* under the heading 'The Most Dangerous Man in Britain Today':

Mr Anthony Wedgwood Benn has become the dominant voice in British politics. If his progress continues unchecked it will become Mr Benn's Britain, a Socialist Britain, abhorrent to the majority of British people.

Walker was speaking under the stress of conflicting emotions. Alongside his horror at the prospect of a Bennite Britain there was obvious admiration for the way it was being achieved and for the man whose progress was 'remarkable and unparalleled in British politics this century'.

231

Working with a Ministry, which, Walker could not help but admit, was only a third the size of the Department of Trade and Industry which he himself had presided over and vastly smaller than the great Technology Empire which had been Benn's in the previous government, he would, within two years, the way things were going, 'have achieved more in making Britain a Socialist State than the Labour Party has achieved throughout its history'. On that point, while eschewing any personal claim of overall responsibility, Benn was to tell a union meeting, a little later, that he was proud to be a member of a Government that, in fourteen months, had made legislative provision for taking 195 companies, including subsidiaries, into public ownership.

Asking how it was that Benn had been able to do that, Mr Walker said cartoonists, politicians and others had combined to treat him as a joke, an advantage for a dangerous politician in itself, but Benn also enjoyed other advantages, immense energy, dedication and ability. Leading moderates in the Labour Party might have ability but they lacked the other qualities.

Benn, claimed Walker, was daily, in private and in public, condoning and encouraging the wage inflation which Wilson and Healey so earnestly deplored, because it would send firms, seeking taxpayers' money, into the embrace of public control.

To support his claim that Wilson had lost his own control over Benn and Benn had obtained control over the Prime Minister, Walker listed a number of points, including the pension-fund proposal and Europe, on which Benn had defied and spoke out against Wilson. Any Prime Minister with power would have displaced a Minister who spoke so openly against his own authority, declared Walker, but with each of those deliberate public slaps in the face Wilson had remained totally silent.

Not totally silent, we know. He had spoken to Mr Boyne. He had also written to Mr Benn. Benn was to tell a National Executive meeting of the Labour Party, two years later, that he had preserved six letters from Wilson threatening, at various times, to dismiss him. That was a revelation which James Callaghan, Wilson's successor, allowed to pass without comment.

In his twenty years in politics, declared Walker, there had been no senior minister whose objectives had been more remote from the aspirations of the great majority of British people but, at the same time, no senior minister with greater success in obtaining his objectives.

'Can the forces of moderation in Parliament check a man whose views are held by less than 20 per cent of Parliament and 10 per cent of the country?' he asked with a note of despair in his voice which now seems more than a little assumed.

In the Lords Lord Watkinson, a former Conservative minister and then chairman of the CBI's companies' committee, threatened that the private sector of industry would use its muscle power in the same way as unions were using theirs to achieve their aims if it were driven into a policy of confrontation and non-cooperation with the Government.

He deplored what he called 'double-talk' from Cabinet ministers, praising Healey for his analysis of the economic crisis but condemning 'violent political dogma irrelevant to the present critical state of the nation' which was coming between businessmen and their sponsoring department of state. To make his point clearer he added that Benn's activities were 'incomprehensible, extremely frightening and discouraging'.

Sir Keith Joseph, frustrated in his hope of becoming Leader of the Conservative Party but making his name as the party's economic guru, expressed himself in remarkably colourful terms for one usually regarded as rather grey. He called Benn the 'Dracula sucking the blood of British Industry', a phrase which the Speaker would probably have ruled as unparliamentary language if used in

233

the House. Apparently not too confident of the literary
knowledge of his businessmen audience, though television's late-night horror movies should have informed
them on the subject, Sir Keith explained the vampire
legend. 'The vampires suck their victims' blood. When
the victims die they in turn become vampires and repeat
the process on others.' The Vampire of Industry, 1975,
Count Benn Dracula, having sucked the life blood,
money, from some firms by wage inflation, in the manner
already described by Walker, would send them sucking
the same life blood from other companies by accepting
subsidies. Benn would rush to save those imperilled firms
which had strong union backing with taxpayers' money,
but that, in turn, would place still heavier burdens on
other firms. Every job saved by subsidy destroyed a job
somewhere else, he succinctly observed in an early expression of the monetarist theme which he was to find so
difficult to apply when he himself was in charge.

It was about this time that Edward Short spoke up for
Benn. For the rest — of the Cabinet — it was silence.
Not for all back-bench MPs, though. It was the duty of
Benn's colleagues, including the Prime Minister, to defend him against the charges being made, James Sillar,
MP for South Ayrshire, told a Parliamentary Labour
Party meeting. All Benn was doing was implementing
policy laid down in the party manifesto. Wilson must have
permitted himself a wry, if inward, smile when Sillar criticized the PM for not denying those Press 'rumours' of
the sacking of Benn which, we now know, Wilson himself
started.

The Wilson sense of humour must also have responded
to the urgings of Ray Fletcher, MP for Ilkeston, that no
'hack journalist' should dictate the composition of the
Cabinet. Dennis Skinner, the noted left-winger representing Bolsover, took the opportunity to air a Bennite
view which was to be stressed more and more by its main
protagonist during the coming years, that the changing

234

character of the office of Prime Minister, the increasing powers it gave its holder and the way those powers were used were matters needing investigation — a view even taken up by some Conservatives when Margaret Thatcher provided her own interpretation of what should be the role of a Prime Minister and the size of staff needed by him, or her, to carry out that role.

Skinner's express concern was that the Cabinet was 'selected' by the party leader when he was Prime Minister, instead of being 'elected' by MPs, as when the party was in Opposition. Some ministers, he stated, were sacked because they were too old, others because they were incompetent, others, and here he gave the words an emphasis to denote that was what was concerning him, because they were too brilliant. Such ministers, those too brilliant, should be promoted not sacked. If, of course, Benn was effectively number two in the eyes of the country, Wilson might have mused, there was only one position to which he could be promoted.

The Liberals, effectively holding the balance in Parliament, mostly remained quiet, though their future leader, David Steel, then Chief Whip, made his contribution to the headlines with his description of Benn as representative of the 'extreme Phoney Left' — 'phoney', it seems, because of his origins. Steel said he could understand and respect working-class radicals but he had no respect for 'upper-class public school and Oxford-educated sons of the peerage who seek to exploit class grievances as the only means of obtaining political power for themselves — power which their own ability or political record would deny them'. Steel was being considerably less generous than Walker in his estimate of Benn's abilities and record but, apart from that, such comments, implying that it is all right for the working class to try to grab a bit extra for themselves but not for the more privileged to help them do so, conflicted with what might be called the 'ultraliberal' view of the Young Liberals, let alone what many older Liberals might think the Christian view.

Steel also seems to have fallen for the view commonly expressed in the less well-researched sections of the Press that Benn is just a renegade aristocrat. Though the son of a (political) viscount and himself, temporarily, a viscount, his origins a generation further back were by no means aristocratic. As we have seen his grandfather, the founder of the family reputation, helped push his younger siblings in a pram along a muddy, rutted country lane to the temporary shelter of an empty cottage, provided by a charitable neighbour, when the Benn family was evicted from its own home.

The unions sprang to Benn's defence, or, rather, made defensive noises. Clive Jenkins, General Secretary of the Association of Scientific, Technical and Managerial Staffs, moved an emergency resolution at his union's spring conference, noting with concern and resentment attacks on the Secretary of State for Industry. A motion asserting that Benn's actions had demonstrated a new and progressive policy essential for the health of industry was carried. South Wales miners unanimously gave their conference support for Benn's 'determination to implement Labour Party policy.'

As the 'sack Benn' campaign hotted up so did union words. Lawrence Daly of the mineworkers described the attacks on Benn as 'the most violent and vicious campaign against any politician in this country since Nye Bevan'. Ray Buckton, of the locomotive men's union said, after the referendum result, it would be a negation of democracy and of Wilson's pledge on referendum freedom of speech if a minister were to be removed or transferred to another post. If there were any signs of such a happening the whole trade union movement should register the strongest possible protest.

On 8 June Jack Jones of the Transport and General Workers Union, probably the most influential of all trade union leaders of the time, said the removal of Benn would be felt as a grave affront to the trade union movement.

Two days later Benn failed to turn up at a meeting of the Commons Committee on the Industry Bill and it was obvious from the comments of some members that they thought they had suffered a grave affront, that Benn was high-handedly ignoring them.

But it was not so. Benn had not fallen from his usual standards of courtesy. He had been summoned to 10 Downing Street to be told that he was no longer the responsible minister. He was to switch jobs with Eric Varley and go to the Department of Energy.

Out came the champagne in more than one company executives' dining room. Now industry will be able to invest, rashly promised the right-wing pressure group Aims of Industry. The CBI hoped the change of face would mean a change of the 'destructive policies that have so endangered industry'.

In the view of Tory MPs Wilson had not done enough. He should have sacked Benn outright. While he remained in the Cabinet, they advised the Prime Minister, Benn could still embarrass Government efforts to get on a better footing with industry. Teddy Taylor, a Front-bench spokesman, saw Benn's appointment as 'utter madness'. Wilson had made a major blunder.

The threat of a union revolt proved to be just words, to be soothed away by more words. Clive Jenkins claimed Wilson had reacted to 'immense pressure from the CBI and individual employers'. Buckton exclaimed, 'What a tragedy — what foolishness — and what a time to do it.' A few more union leaders declared it was just a sop to big business and the Right, but most decided, on reflection, that there was no reason to kick up a fuss. As Tom Jackson, of the Post Office Workers, put it, 'It's a sideways kick for Benn but I think the Prime Minister knows what he's doing.'

Jack Jones decided there had been no grave affront

after all. Varley and Benn each had the confidence of the unions. The miners, indeed, seemed to have more confidence in Benn. Lawrence Daly said he positively welcomed the change. Benn would be good for the nation and for the coal industry — one new complaint to come was that he was too good to the miners.

Though Benn may have seemed, momentarily, to members of the Industry Bill Committee to have slipped from his own standards of good manners in failing to apologize for his non-appearance, he was apologetic courtesy itself to the Committee on the Petroleum and Submarine Pipelines Bill two days later, though some might think there was a sting, a polite sting, naturally, in the tail of his remarks.

'I must apologize for the disappearance of my predecessor and, maybe, apologize for my own appearance,' he said. 'Whether it is right to describe this as an act of God or not is a matter for argument. At any rate it was not an act of mine.'

CHAPTER FIFTEEN

An Energetic Interlude?

Let Mr Benn himself set the scene for the next act. It is his office in the Ministry of Energy, just along the Embankment from his childhood home and his previous headquarters at MinTech, on the second floor, overlooking the Thames. One wall is covered by a National Union of Mineworkers banner. On his desk stands a statue of a miner, carved from a generous lump of coal, alongside a miner's lamp. On one side of his desk sits Benn, beside his papers a pint mug of tea. Opposite are his visitors, a group of journalists perhaps, trade union officials, experts from the coal, oil or other energy industries, taking their tea from the superior elegance of ministerial cups and saucers. As well as plying them with refreshment Benn plies them with questions. 'What do you think of this?', 'Give me your opinion on that?', 'What do you think is the best way of doing this?', and so on. He seems to be genuinely searching for information, for what he feels to be the democratic view. Every so often, though, the questioning ceases. Instead of asking he is propounding. As one of his journalist visitors put it afterwards, 'The Jehovah look came into his eyes.' The latest Benn idea for further advance towards the goal of democratic socialism in a land brimming with the fruits of an adequate energy supply of its own — the only one in the industrial west, as he was fond of saying — is being tried out.

Energy, according to the text books, is the power of doing work. Work is movement against, or with the aid of, a force. For the nearly four years Benn was at the Department of Energy his own energy was as great as ever, as much as ever to be admired and envied by other politicians. Work done, though, might appear less, certainly in terms of commotion caused. That, of course, was Wilson's intention. The opposing forces would be less and so headlines, if not the achievement, correspondingly reduced. At Energy there would be far less clamour about nationalization, it was a field in which nationalization already held sway, in coal and nuclear power, in electricity generation, gas distribution. Even half of British Petroleum was Government-owned. There was another reason. Overt interference with people's affairs fitted in less and less with Benn's ideas on democratic control. More and more the words of the Chinese philosopher Lao-Tzu, quoted, as quoted by Benn, at the beginning of this book, were providing the standard by which political leadership should be judged — 'when the best leader's work is done the people say "We did it ourselves" '.

Benn had been fond of saying that the Meriden and other co-operatives grew up from the workers' own wishes, that it was no use imposing a co-operative on an industry or firm where a profitable future was more likely if the workers had not reached the stage of demanding it themselves. So it was to be with energy. The development of Britain's vast energy resources should not just be with popular consent but by popular initiative, with all sections of the community consulting together on the best way forward. Indeed in the Benn years at the Department a great deal was done. Those were the years when oil and gas began coming ashore in ever increasing quantities, when important decisions were made on the role of nuclear power, when emphasis was returned to the coal industry as the guardian of energy reserves that would still be there when the oil and gas had run out.

His first step towards the formulation of energy policy through general discussion came with a forum in February 1976. The most notable event then, from contemporary reports, was a stand-up row between Sir Derek Ezra, Chairman of the National Coal Board, and Sir Arthur Hawkins, of the Central Electricity Generating Board, on the pricing of power-station coal. Benn said afterwards that he had wanted to open up that conference to the public and the Press but the participants had refused and he had backed down. When the reports of the row appeared he regretted his weakness in agreeing. Reporters had had to get their accounts at second-hand and 'what survives are people's memories of their moments of triumph'. Moments of triumph, he gave the impression, however delightful at the moment for those who triumph, should be forgotten in the general interest.

The public and the Press had their chance to see open government and policy-making by consent at work at a public conference the following June. With one notable exception the 56 speakers generally welcomed the Benn initiative. To Enoch Powell, though, the concept of energy policy through public discussion was 'ill conceived, pernicious and the prescription of frustration'. Many of the participants gave point to Powell's comments by airing their own pet grievances rather than approaching the subject of policy-making on the exalted intellectual level which the Energy Secretary was hoping for, if not expecting. Lord Ryder, this time wearing his hat as a member of the British Gas Corporation, referred to talk of raising the price of gas to help the competitive position of gas's rivals, saying he had to pinch himself to confirm he was in the real world and not at a 1976 version of the Mad Hatter's Tea Party. Perhaps later he awoke to the realization that Lewis Carroll's was the real world and it was the Mad Hatter's Tea Party, as gas prices soared and gas board profits were seized by the ever-hungry Treasury.

Still, a happy Benn, in his summing up, gave the broadest of hints that this was only a beginning. There would be a high-powered policy committee on the lines that many of the 470 delegates apparently wanted. But much as Benn wanted his Energy Commission, the name he eventually settled on, he found insurmountable difficulties in getting people to agree on its form, who should serve on it and such preliminary matters as that. A year later he was telling the National Economic Development Council that he was pressing ahead and that the Commission would play a key role in revising Britain's energy policies. Once again, though, he was meeting opposition from the CBI. Benn had made it clear that one of his main priorities was seeing that the poor and needy received adequate supplies of fuel and were not in danger of having electricity and gas cut off for being unable to meet the rapidly rising costs of heating and lighting. The CBI considered the main task was to get supplies and prices right first — for industry — and only then consider the social aspects.

Benn's plans for an Energy Commission were doomed

to gather dust in a ministry pigeon-hole, but not while he was in office. Continually he tried to give the impetus needed for take-off. There were regular consultations with experts, regular press conferences to report on progress, followed by just as regular verbatim reports of lengthy proceedings. 'It was like having the Sunday edition of the *New York Times* coming through your door,' said one just-as-regular attender.

Many people thought he was being a bit too democratic. It was a minister's job to take decisions. The CEGB's Hawkins, who was to have many tussles with his ministerial master, pointed out that democracy had existed in this country for many years but it had never meant that all decisions were made by mass meetings in the market place. George Tyler, General Secretary of the British Association of Colliery Management, thought it was 'a load of nonsense' when Benn, that same year, 1976, canvassed unions for their views on appointments to the National Coal Board. There was then speculation about the future of the chairman, Sir Derek Ezra, who wanted to carry on, and strong pressure that, if a change was made, the job should go to a politician. Benn circulated lists of board members with details of their salaries and how long their terms of office had to run.

'The minister is entitled to take soundings on who ought to get the job but he should also accept the responsibility of taking a decision,' declared Tyler. 'Unions should do no more than offer suggestions. They are not sufficiently competent or well informed to say "This is the man for the job".'

Despite that Tyler did comment that he thought the top job should not go to a politician but to an engineer, such as Norman Siddall, then deputy chairman. It was Siddall who, eventually, succeeded Ezra.

On some other matters Benn was much more definite, assertive indeed. There was the question who ran the negotiations with oil companies over participation rights in the North Sea. When Benn was moved to Energy, newspapers reporting the reshuffle claimed he had been warned off taking part in negotiations or having direct contact with oil companies. What was the situation? asked Patrick Jenkin, the Opposition spokesman, when Benn attended that first committee meeting as Energy Secretary.

Benn said there had been no change, his powers were the same as those of Varley. These, he would have had to admit if pressed, amounted to a watching brief. The Energy Secretary was chairman of a committee that observed the negotiations. The actual negotiations were carried out by a panel of three, his own Minister of State, Lord Balogh, Edmund Dell, the Paymaster General, and Harold Lever. Lever, everyone knew, was the real power in the negotiations. Explaining the situation Benn pointed out that there was another Cabinet committee, on which he sat, to which the 'observing' committee reported. Above that was the Cabinet itself. 'There is a great hierarchy of ministerial involvement here,' said Benn, though he went on to say that, given the magnitude of the issues involved, that was right.

Still, as in other matters of Cabinet unanimity, the private opinion can differ from the public face. A battle went on behind the scenes over who should have the prime responsibility for negotiating a major government stake in North Sea oil. Just under a year later Benn had won. Wilson had gone and Callaghan agreed that Benn should take over from Lever as head of the ministerial negotiating team.

There was no change in Government policy, said Callaghan, but at once Benn made it clear there was to be an increasing state control. The British National Oil Corporation was to have a 51 per cent stake in new exploration blocks, to obtain greater influence over development. Benn was not satisfied with present arrangements for State participation. The next licensing round, he said, would be used as a lever to secure State participation in fields found under existing licenses. Some companies were proving reluctant to relinquish part of their share voluntarily and the next round would see an extra effort to persuade those 'laggards' to hand something over. The prospect of licenses for future exploration would also be used to further the unionization of offshore rigs and platforms, companies would be expected to recognize the trade union right of access to offshore employees.

In 1978, after the sixth round of licensing had been completed, he was able to put his claims for success into figures. Sixty per cent of that round's licenses had gone to the public sector while between 65 and 70 per cent of successful applicants were British companies. The public sector's stake in North Sea oil had been doubled, from 12½ to 25 per cent. He promised to continue the same robust line. Some of his critics argued that some companies had been frightened away by that robustness. Could anyone really think that oil companies could be frightened away from the North Sea after what had happened in Iran? he asked. Accepting a motion at the 1978 Labour Party Conference, calling for the public ownership of North Sea oil, Benn said that the multi-national oil companies would have to accept a move from being concessionaries to being contractors.

Lord Kearton, Chairman of the British National Oil Corporation, acknowledged the role of Benn in winning that State interest in oil. Speaking after the 1979 General Election which removed Labour, and Benn, from office, he said Benn had been 'an absolutely first-class minister'. Oil had previously been in the absolute possession of private interests. They had developed it very well and efficiently but Governmental control was minimal. All that had changed. When the first participation agreements were negotiated some people had mocked. But now oil

244

had become one of the single most important assets the country had, politically as well as economically.

'That would never have happened without the steadfastness of Mr Benn and his brilliance in discussions with the very top brass of the world's major oil companies,' Kearton declared.

How should that oil wealth be spent? or, rather, how should it be used for the national good?

Benn was in no doubt, it should be invested, used to rebuild Britain's outworn manufacturing base. When newspapers were full of stories of 'the British disease', of the wrecking influence of trade unions, lazy workers, incompetent managers, Benn argued that the workers — and managers — should blame their tools. Britain's problem was that highly qualified men and women who went to work in industry found their products were inefficient because they were working with the tools of yesteryear, he told the 1976 Welsh TUC. Germans, Japanese, French, Americans and others were working in well-equipped factories. If investment did not come from private means it must come from public sources — and, returning to the theme which caused so much upset when he was at Industry, 'when there is investment on the public account there must be public accountability and public ownership to go with it.'

Comments like that probably sent shivers up and down the spine of some of his Cabinet colleagues, including Healey, the Chancellor of the Exchequer. Healey had been a Communist in his student days, the days, also, of Stalin's Five-Year Plans for the forced industrialization of the Soviet Union. Presumably he had believed then in forced investment by the State. Not any longer. It was common knowledge in political circles that while Benn was pressing for a special investment fund, using oil revenue, Healey was putting the Treasury view that first call on the money should be to pay Britain's financial debts and that what was left would encourage investment and provide production incentives better i used for tax cuts rather than invested directly in industry.

In December 1977, when a White Paper was being drafted on the subject, Benn used the opportunity of a meeting with the London Chamber of Commerce to press publicly his case. Unless North Sea oil revenue was used on an ambitious programme of public investment Britain could face an economic crisis with 1930 consequences, he said. As it was, oil revenue was more than offset by the wasted productive capacity of 1½ million unemployed. Unless Britain followed the example of other major oil producers and used the money to re-equip industry the country could eventually find its manufacturing base was uncompetitive. British people might be forced to emigrate in search of jobs.

Two months later, when the White Paper appeared, Benn's proposals for an oil fund were missing. The doctrine of collective responsibility did not stop him telling the 1978 party conference, six months later, that he was not prepared to see the process of de-industrialization and strategic withdrawal taking place masked by the temporary bonus of North Sea oil revenue. Manufacturing industry would remain the foundation of Britain's economic strength long after the oil had run out.

Four years on, if he had been so minded, he could have pointed out that imports of manufactured goods were on the point of exceeding exports for the first time for over a century and asked what connection there might be between that and the decision not to invest oil revenue in new, more efficient industry, as he had proposed.

Benn also found insurmountable opposition to his plans for changes in the electricity supply industry, this time from the Liberals. Shortly after Benn took over the Energy Department a committee under Lord Plowden reported on a proposed reorganization. The crux of their proposal was that there should be one controlling authority, instead of the industry being split between the production body, the CEGB, and the supply body, the Electricity Council, with, in practice, area boards performing the supply function with little reference to the Council. Nine months later the CEGB's Hawkins thought the gestation period had gone on long enough, that Benn should now be producing the baby, a Bill. There were no contentious issues, declared Hawkins, everybody agreed that the unsuitable existing structure urgently needed changing. By the time the Bill was drawn up, though, plenty of contentious issues had appeared. The basis was straightforward. There should be a single body, the Electricity Corporation, replacing the two existing bodies. But the Bill also had to deal with a number of issues vexing the minister which he believed should be part of any reorganization. Apart from the matter of charges which would not place light and heat beyond the reach of the pensioners and the poor, apart from the place of coal and the miner in Britain's energy set-up, there were such fundamental Bennite matters as industrial democracy, investment and, above all, accountability.

The Corporation would be able to supply by-products of electricity generation of which the most obvious was heat. This would have opened the way to district heating projects, which the CEGB had always claimed were ruled out by the charge laid upon it to produce electricity as efficiently as possible. It would also be able to diversify into the manufacture of equipment and spare parts and search for and extract minerals, apart from coal and oil, used in generating electricity.

To ensure the Corporation and twelve subsidiary boards, roughly replacing the CEGB and the area boards, were accountable to Parliament, Benn proposed the minister should have power to make appointments. The minister would also be empowered to direct the Corporation to carry out projects considered to be in the national interest and, if necessary, compensate it for so doing.

The support of the Liberals was needed to get the bill

247

through and this support was not forthcoming. It would centralize control of the industry and give miners too much power, they said — and give Benn too much power too. They also saw the proposal that the Corporation should take part in manufacture as 'back-door nationalization'. As for one clause empowering the charging of bills according to the customer's ability to pay, the Liberal view was that an inability to pay should remain a matter for social-security machinery.

Benn retorted that the time had come for a serious reassessment of how nationalized industries could make the maximum contribution to the development of Britain's resources, what best they could do in the national interest. Maximum managerial responsibility should be devolved to operating units consistent with the proper discharge of their functions, providing energy as cheaply as possible, cooperating with the national energy policy, promoting industrial democracy, preserving the productive capacity of their suppliers, undertaking research and disclosing information.

The Liberal leader, David Steel, pursued the argument at a lower philosophical level. It had been suggested that the Liberals were irresponsible and cantankerous in their opposition to the Bill. 'I am the least cantankerous of men,' he declared. 'Mr Benn, on the other hand, is the most obstinate and doctrinaire.'

The Plowden Committee, though it felt it would be better to push through with the Benn scheme as a second-best to its own proposals, was also critical, especially of the powers of patronage Benn would have. Lord Plowden thought the Energy Secretary had sufficient powers to intervene without seeking more. A trade union member of the committee, Frank Chapple, leader of the electricians union, said the appointment of civil servants to the new body would 'add bureaucratic nonsense to bureaucratic nonsense'. He also objected to giving the industry manufacturing rights. He thought that would lead to boards coming under pressure to sell expensive State-made equipment.

Criticism also came from another of the electricity industry's union leaders. In the view of John Lyons, General Secretary of the Electrical Power Engineers Association, Benn wanted to use nationalized industries as instruments of social change. By subsidizing the electricity supply industry (through, for example, compensation for building coal-fired stations) he would gain control over it and ensure it behaved in ways congenial to him.

'He looks on the electricity supply industry as, in essence, a giant outdoor relief organization,' declared Lyons. 'On the one hand he has brought great pressure to bear on the industry to do away with or else greatly curb its power of disconnection for those who do not pay their bills. On the other hand he has brought pressure to bear on the industry to assist its supplying industries when they themselves have got into difficulties.'

It all reflected a political theory, claimed Lyons, that nationalized industry's primary purpose was to serve as an instrument of social engineering. It was because the industry resisted that approach, believing its function was to produce electricity as cheaply and as efficiently as possible, that Benn felt it was necessary to break its powers somehow and take control himself.

The Bill failed. The only change there has been since from the Lyons approach is that the interpretation of the CEGB's function, to provide electricity 'as efficiently as possible', has been relaxed to allow experiments with district heating. Income from heat diverted from the turbines, it is now agreed, might be used to offset extra costs of generation caused by diverting that heat. Britain is testing with a toe the financial temperature of a pool in which not only electricity companies in other countries but some of its own larger industrial companies, with their own generating facilities, have been happily basking for years.

Something still had to be done about those two matters on which Lyons expressed concern and opposition, compensating or subsidizing the industry for preferential treatment of coal and the threat of disconnections hanging over poorer people facing rising charges for heat and light. On the second Benn managed to negotiate a £45,000,000 winter fuel bonus, in the autumn of 1978, for pensioners and others on low incomes, to help meet electricity bills. The CEGB itself received £50,000,000, under a short Bill replacing the failed Bill, as compensation for the early ordering of the Drax 'B' coal-fired station in Yorkshire.

That Yorkshire power station was to typify the sour relations between the Coal Board and the CEGB during Benn's time at Energy, just as it was the outward cause of the sour relations between Benn and the CEGB. What Britain needed to get full value from its coal riches, according to the Coal Board, was more coal-burning power stations. Hawkins and his successor as CEGB chairman, Glyn England, saw it differently. What would prevent the CEGB giving value for money was pressure on it to build coal-fired stations when it was by no means certain that coal was the cheapest source of power and, certainly, before there was any foreseeable need for extra capacity.

The matter was bedevilled by conflicting views on what was the cheapest form of energy when capital and running costs differed so much for different forms of station, certainly when no one could forecast, confidently, running costs when a new station came on stream. Who would have tho ght at the end of the sixties that power stations then being built to run on cheap oil would prove so much more expensive to run than coal or nuclear stations a decade later, so that, what with the expense and the reduced demand, they faced shut-down?

The Benn approach, though, rightly or wrongly, took into account other things than accountants' uncertain figures. It was not just a matter of providing work for miners but for other essential workers also. There was a severe crisis in the heavy electrical engineering industry, he told the 1976 party conference. CEGB orders fluctuated wildly and there was then a downturn in forecasts of future needs. The Government was looking urgently at the industry's problems. Not only did fuel and energy require long-term planning but their supply industries as well.

The CEGB was told to press on with Drax 'B', two years before it really needed to do so declared an indignant Hawkins, in May 1978, a fortnight before he was due to retire. It made no sense to spend hard-earned money on unnecessary new plant. Their job, he said, at one with his union counterpart Lyons, was to produce electricity as cheaply as possible, not to fork out consumers' money to support the social costs of other businesses. 'It is a cheek even to expect us to do so and monstrous to try to screw us down.'

A little later Benn received a standing ovation from the miners' union conference when he said he was carrying out an urgent examination to see how power stations could burn more coal — home-produced coal, he emphasized, for he was telling the generating and steel industries to cut imports of cheap foreign coal.

That aroused the indignation of England, who had now succeeded Hawkins. He intended to raise a number of points with the Energy Secretary, he said. Three-quarters of British electricity came from British coal but the right to import foreign coal must be kept in case the price of domestic fuel soared. After all the Board was contracted to buy the million tons of Australian coal imported, under an agreement reached during the fuel crisis of 1974.

The cheapness argument did not cut much ice with Benn. He was in favour of using indigenous fuel, not only coal but nuclear fuel, he declared in a Commons debate shortly afterwards. It did not make sense to stockpile coal while importing coal and oil. Two years before he had told the Scottish TUC that the Government would act alongside the miners' union to counter the threat to Scottish jobs by Scottish power stations burning less coal.

After all, as he was fond of saying, the coal would still be there when the oil ran out, enough to meet Britain's needs for another 300 years. For a politician that is a very long time. He was lucky, he said once, to be in a job where the major problems were those of growth, unlike his colleagues.

Miners had reason to be grateful to Benn for the support he gave them while Energy Secretary, reason to show their gratitude in supporting him, politically, in return. A confidential discussion paper he prepared for the Cabinet in early 1978 would have ensured their place at the top of the earnings league, through an agreement guaranteeing generous future rises, on the lines of one that brought an end to a firemen's strike. 'Outrageous' was the comment of some of his Cabinet colleagues. A scheme for compensating miners suffering from pneumoconiosis, dust on the lung, was introduced in his time, another for early retirement.

Only once did he find miners slow in responding to a Benn initiative, when he offered the union an effective veto over future pit closures. Executive members have told of their fears that that would put responsibility for unwelcome closures on them, opening up divisions between union headquarters and the areas. Thank you, they said in effect, they would rather stay with the devil they knew, the Coal Board's right to decide — after, of course, due consultation. That was a decision the union's next president, Arthur Scargill, a keen political supporter of Benn, publicly regretted before a Parliamentary Committee in late 1982, after the Board had presented him with a list of 60 pits which might be closed. The union should have the power of veto which Benn had offered, he told MPs.

Not that the Coal Board had no reason to feel grateful to Mr. Benn. Though not Energy Secretary he had played a part in the Labour Government's 1974 'Plan for Coal' which had set up a Tri-partite Committee of unions, management and ministers to push forward planning. That produced, in 1976, 'Coal for the Future', which set a production target of 170,000,000 tons a year by the year 2000, involving an annual expenditure on new pits of £475,000,000 to produce new capacity of 4,000,000 tons a year. Four times as much coal was being found in new reserves as was being mined and coal's future appeared rosy, rosier by far than when that list of 60 possible closures was produced. By then estimates of future needs had shrunk alarmingly along with the capacity of steel and other industries to use it and in the face of foreign competition. Europe, as a whole, might be short of coal, British coal might be as cheap as any in Europe, but it was not as cheap as supplies from outside.

Trying to please not everybody but anybody on that vexing question of the burden of rising fuel bills proved more difficult. The winters of the mid-seventies, after Opec oil increases, brought harrowing accounts of pensioners and other poor people having their electricity and gas cut off because they could not pay their bills. As a first step Benn authorized more time to pay. He then set up a committee under his Parliamentary Under-Secretary Gordon Oakes, with Jack Ashley, Labour MP for Stoke-on-Trent South, noted for battling on behalf of the 'under-privileged', the seventies' word for that class we are told will always be with us, and Mrs Frances Morrell, Benn's own policy adviser. It reported in June 1976, that electricity and gas boards should lose the power to disconnect defaulting customers. The Electricity Council immediately declared that charges would have to be raised by a tenth if that happened. The only people who would benefit were 'dodgers, scroungers and brinkmanship budgeteers who could afford to pay but did not want to'. Their benefit would be at the expense of those who paid promptly, including the vast majority of pensioners and those on limited incomes. British Gas also claimed such a step would put up prices by a tenth. Age Concern, the pensioners' pressure group, was delighted with the report, but regretted that Benn had not given it full endorsement. For Benn had said the Government would consider it but that publication did not imply Government endorsement.

At the party conference that autumn Benn found himself having to resist demands for the ending of the power to disconnect. The policy of disconnection 'as it had existed for a hundred years' needed to be re-examined but the most he could promise was that a code of practice would be published.

Two years later, just before his final winter at the Department, Benn found himself in the unfamiliar position of being heckled by pensioners and parents as he explained various measures taken by the Government to try to stop disconnections. He was having to admit that none of the methods of helping people pay fuel bills had proved totally successful.

The problem was really beyond the powers of an Energy Minister to solve. It was outside his province, properly. The trouble was that so many poorer people had to put up with the most expensive systems of heating. While the well-to-do queued up, at least on the phone, to have their homes converted to heating by cheap natural gas — before the price of that was artificially raised to stop such goings on — council tenants were stuck with the all-electric homes, complete with such architects' delights but heating engineers' horrors as ceiling heating. The old woman in a single room, perhaps not even receiving a State pension, had to rely on a paraffin stove or an electric fire, both hit by the oil price rise, and she switched off when she could and sometimes when she should not — papers of the seventies also had shocking stories of deaths from hypothermia.

If only, Benn might have wished, the atomic prophets had been right and abundant nuclear energy was pouring warmth and light into even the poorest homes. But nuclear power itself was a bit of a headache.

Opposition was growing apace to nuclear power or, rather, to its accompanying dangers, radioactive waste, the possible proliferation of nuclear weapons. Benn's published view, naturally, was that the public should be given all the facts to come to its own conclusions. The minister would still have to make his decision, in the light of his responsibility to Parliament and to the electors.

But not all the facts were known and those that were were not all brought to public notice. After one mishap to a British reactor, when he was Minister of Technology, Benn had given instructions that any incident, however minor, was to be reported to him at once. When, however, he was responsible minister again, at Energy, there were delays of several weeks before details of two major leaks of radioactivity at the Windscale plant were given him. 'Major' was Benn's description of a spillage of highly radioactive liquid from a sump into the ground. 'Just a few tens of thousands of curies' was the assessment of Sir John Hill, then Chairman of the Atomic Energy Authority, in words meaningless to lay protestors. Benn ordered a full inquiry but the operating company, British Nuclear Fuels, showed little concern.

However, Benn considered nuclear energy was an essential part of the energy mix. On safety he pointed out that it was not just nuclear power that could prove dangerous. Coal mining had its thousands of victims and the motor car its millions. If there had been an inquiry into the new technology of the motor car, with convincing predictions of the casualties likely to follow, would it ever have been allowed, he asked.

Acknowledging safety problems and the dangers of weapon proliferation he pointed out one way to reduce them — to rely on Britain's political stability and nuclear skills. They made Britain a better place than most others for processing waste fuel. That was a view with which many on the left violently disagreed when he expressed it publicly in 1976. Why should Britons run increased risks from the waste from foreign power stations brought here for processing?

What was in dispute was a reprocessing plant at Windscale to take Japanese and other waste as well as British. The proposal came before Benn soon after he took over at Energy. He went to Tokyo to follow it up. There followed several Cabinet meetings, public meetings in Cumbria and London to explain the policy, a commission of inquiry, a parliamentary debate and innumerable newspaper articles and letters before the decision was taken in May 1978 to go ahead. 'Hardly a charade' was his comment on the public debate which, he admitted, had delayed the decision by two years.

By then responsibility for waste processing had been removed from his office to the Department of the Environment. Reactors, though, were still his province. A few months before the Windscale decision was made he announced orders for two more, both British AGRs, Advanced Gas-Cooled Reactors. This followed another wide discussion, over the future of Britain's nuclear power industry. After the success of the earlier gas-cooled design, Magnox, used in Calder Hall, the world's first commercial-sized nuclear station, the 'advanced' model had run into trouble. Construction times and costs were proving much higher than hoped and the current programme was running years late.

There were three alternatives, to use another British design, the SGHW, or Steam-Generating Heavy Water reactor, to switch to the PWR, Pressurized Water Reactor, by far the most widely used design in the rest of the world, or stay with the AGR. Also under development at Dounreay in Scotland was the fast neutron or breeder reactor. This should make it possible to use a much greater proportion of the restricted supplies of uranium and also the plutonium produced by ordinary reactors, which were behind the worries of weapon proliferation. Breeder reactors, though, were primarily a longer-term answer for a world demanding vastly greater quantities of electricity. Economic difficulties had taken the urgency off a decision on that subject, Benn had, almost thankfully, told an inquiry into the Atomic Energy Authority's proposals for it.

It came down to a two-horse race, between AGR and PWR. The SGHW, though attractive in its promises, particularly to those working on it, was lagging too far behind, or so it seemed then. It certainly was untried and hopes in the AGR were raised by the first four reaching the commissioning stage, albeit belatedly, in 1976 and 1977. Benn announced that after eighteen months of taking stock and advice on the SGHW he was discontinuing work on it. There were doubts about the safety of PWR. Though the most widely used system it had also suffered the most widely publicized accidents. Benn decided that AGRs, the two newly ordered and others already being built, would have priority in Britain's nuclear programme but it would be wrong to be dependent on just one system. There should be an insurance in the PWR. Provided a suitable design, one suitably safe, was produced, a PWR would be ordered, though a start on it could not be made before 1982.

No start had been made by the end of 1982 though one was in prospect at Sizewell in Suffolk, alongside an older Magnox station. On the other hand none of the AGRs still being built when Benn made his statement, let alone those for which he gave the go-ahead, was working satisfactorily. On such matters, of course, a minister is dependent on specialist advice. Those nuclear industry employees who, towards the end of his time at Energy, protested against his apparent preference for coal, have not found history on their side.

Other nuclear workers had some reason to feel pleased with him, those engaged on the most ambitious research of all, into fusion — 'taming the H-bomb' as newspapers were quick to dub it when early, premature success was claimed by a British team at Harwell in the late 1950's. The task of obtaining power from the fusion of light atoms, the various isotopes of hydrogen, instead of by the splitting of heavy ones, uranium and plutonium, was proving so enormous that the only way ahead seemed through international co-operation. The countries in Euratom had combined in the early 1970's to produce a design for a machine based on principles worked out by Soviet scientists, the design being done at Culham, near Harwell. It was to be called JET, acronym for JOINT EUROPEAN TORUS. The question was where should it be built? Benn was determined it should stay at Culham and Culham should stay a world centre of excellence. There was also the question of jobs. Apart from the British scientists in the original design team who would prefer to stay in Britain, some, indeed, were hinting they might take their knowledge to the USA if JET was to go elsewhere; British engineers and technicians and contracting companies would be employed on it if it were built at Culham. The other Euratom countries, though, were each producing convincing claims for JET. During years of indecisive negotiations, during which, at times, it seemed JET might never be built at all, Benn went to the USA to discuss fusion co-operation there, making it clear to his Euratom partners that Britain had other options. The matter was still unresolved when he left Energy but by then there was little doubt that Culham would eventually be selected, as it was.

That was not the only brush Benn had with Common Market colleagues or with Brussels bureaucrats while at Energy. These came to a head in 1978. In February there was the matter of EEC policy requiring Britain to close oil refineries. Questioned in the House about it Benn replied tersely, 'There is no question of the Government encouraging refineries to close in the United Kingdom.'

He was not prepared to see a decision on our refineries taken elsewhere. Pressed by Tory MP John Biffen to leave the Brussels Commissioner concerned under no illusion that the responsibility properly belonged here, despite the Treaty of Rome, Benn said he had already telephoned the Commissioner to indicate the gravity with which the UK regarded the matter and to invite him to London to be told so more directly.

A little later, asked why he had not ordered more nuclear power stations, he said that only the previous week the EEC had prevented his signing an agreement with Australia to buy uranium.

Soon after that he called union leaders together to tell them of threats to British energy policies from the Common Market, the two already mentioned and four more. The EEC wanted to end British Gas's monopoly position as a buyer of North Sea gas, so other member countries could compete in buying it from oil companies. The British Government's insistence that North Sea oil should be landed in Britain and up to two-thirds refined here was also regarded as a breach of Community rules on fair competition. The EEC further wanted an end to what the Commissioner considered a 'Buy British' policy on offshore supplies and also the running down of a system of interest relief grants to British companies competing for North Sea orders against foreign competition.

The 'shock and anger' the union leaders felt at such an account of EEC perfidy was duly reported, in Brussels as well as in London. The matters were not pursued and any outstanding disagreements with Brussels remained to vex Benn's successor unless, as in the case of refinery closures, they were solved by declining demand in the growing economic recession.

During his years at Energy that coal sculpture of a miner on his desk had been ever present to remind him not only of the importance of Coal but also of his belief in the democratic need to consult workers and others.

One official complained 'he never made up his mind on anything without going out into the street to ask somebody about it.' In retrospect he did make up his mind on quite a lot of things, though he did not always get his way. All in all, perhaps, the lady sculptress who produced another carving, of him astride a turtle, to depict his performance — slow-moving, nothing done without interminable seeking of other views — was being a shade harsh.

CHAPTER SIXTEEN

Ministerial Irresponsibility?

When Wilson forced Tony Benn to castle with that sideways move from Industry to Energy he may have checked him but certainly did not mate him. At the Department of Industry Benn had been putting into effect that part of Labour's policy dearest to him, its industrial strategy, at least as he saw it. At the Department of Energy the same opportunities were not open to him and his efforts within the Cabinet to influence industrial policy came to little. Still neither Wilson nor Callaghan should have been surprised to find that their younger, thrusting colleague was not to be held down so easily. Often with a castling move in chess the main thrust of the thrusting player's game moves elsewhere on the board. So it was with Benn. The Department of Energy not being able to absorb all of Benn's political energy he started to direct more to political work within the party itself, as a member of the National Executive, or so it appeared to outside observers. Certainly work achieved there by his energy became much more apparent, expanding to fill the headlines to such an extent that readers might be pardoned for believing that he was the only politician in Britain of any originality of thought, even if, from the newspaper view, it were an originality to be deplored.

Not that membership of the NEC was new to Benn, nor that he had been a quiescent member before. He was first elected, not only the newest but the youngest member, in 1959, at the age of 34. The following year he resigned, on the eve of the 1960 conference. That was at another of those times of inner-party conflict and clamour to which the Labour Party is prone. The main issues then, as so often since, were unilateral disarmament and the extent to which MPs were bound to policy decisions by the annual conference.

Interestingly, in the light of what has happened more recently, he did not resign over either of those matters but on the one of party unity. A motion from the Transport and General Workers Union, then led by Frank Cousins, on nuclear disarmament was felt to be obscure. Benn proposed that representatives of the NEC and TGWU should meet to clear up those obscurities.

When his proposal was rejected he promptly resigned because, he said, it was the only way he could 'warn the conference of the great danger in which the party stands'. If the meeting had been held, he said, it would have given a chance of avoiding a showdown and a split in the party, but mutual distrust had reached the point where some leaders would not even agree to meet each other — divisions in the party, one might reflect today, are nothing new. For some people, Benn then said, a split in the party seemed inevitable, for others desirable, for a few urgent, but for the overwhelming majority of delegates it would be a ghastly tragedy.

As a sacrifice the Benn resignation achieved nothing in averting a split, as a demonstration it was lost in the conference confusion. That was the year when the party voted for unilateral disarmament, on a motion from the

Engineers, not the TGWU proposal, and Gaitskell proclaimed his determination to 'fight, fight and fight again' to reverse it.

The trade-unionist chairman of the conference arrangements committee condemned the Benn action with words which were to become very familiar. It was 'completely irresponsible' and would only damage the party. It was an 'act of vanity' in the later judgment of one of Benn's Cabinet colleagues, when Labour was in power, the 35-year-old just did not carry enough weight in the party to make such a gesture meaningful. Benn himself later admitted he had made a mistake in resigning but not in his assessment of the situation, the party was set for a clash which had nothing to do with the Bomb. Benn was already a member of the Campaign for Nuclear Disarmament and was about to see his views accepted as party policy so there is no call to doubt the reason he gave for his action.

Benn was re-elected to the NEC at the 1962 conference and has stayed there. Membership of the NEC has been essential in the struggle to make his policies, and the policies of those on the Left who think with him, Labour party policies — a struggle which has won considerable success — and the still inconclusive struggle to make those policies binding on Labour MPs.

However, it was his chairmanship of the Home Policy Committee which proved the most effective position in that struggle. Under no other chairman has that committee produced so continuous a flow of policy statements and seen so many of them accepted. It was a position of influence which at times seemed to make prime ministers powerless to treat him as they would other recalcitrant ministers and sack him, but one which has led to very strained relations with prime ministers.

Not that Benn limited himself to pronouncements on Labour Party policy nor did he stay on the defensive in his disagreements with prime ministers. His political pronouncements ranged over the whole field of government

and included direct attacks on the power of prime ministers, greater, he has said, than those of medieval monarchs or American presidents. Through these has run one
thread, there should be open government, with a much
wider release of the information on which decisions are
based. It is a principle which he claims to have brought
to his chairmanship of the Policy Committee. After meetings he has briefed political journalists on the proceedings. Some of those briefed, though, have sometimes
claimed that Benn's openness was not complete. 'He tells
what was discussed, what was decided, a general account
of what went on. If you ask him, though, for details of a
vote, for example, or what objections were raised and by
whom, he often just says "Oh, we needn't go into that"
and that is the end of it as far as he is concerned,' one
journalist complained.

Whatever some of the journalists thought — and most
were happy at what they thought was a much better than
usual flow of information — prime ministers did not like
it. In March 1976, Wilson sent a minute to Benn telling
him not to brief political correspondents after meetings of
the Committee, that this could conflict with the collective
ministerial responsibility of Cabinet Ministers. This was
after the Committee was reported to have endorsed a
document calling for the nationalization of four banks and
six insurance companies. Benn, it transpired, had not
been present and had not done the briefing.

The minute sent to Benn, copied to other Cabinet Ministers, reminded him that the principle of collective responsibility applied to discussions within the NEC or its
committees, indeed applied especially to such discussions,
requiring ministers not to take an active part on policy
matters which fell within other ministerial departments.
It stated they should not advocate policies not those of
the Government nor those which had not been collectively
considered.

That happened shortly before Wilson resigned the premiership. After Jim Callaghan had taken over he rebuked Benn for abstaining in the NEC on a vote on a left-wing resolution criticizing proposed spending cuts. As a Cabinet Minister he should have supported Cabinet policy and voted against the resolution. Conservative MPs had been trying for some time to get a debate on collective responsibility, to raise publicly Benn's position, and one, Peter Blaker, asked a question about the incident. Callaghan stated bluntly, 'The doctrine of collective responsibility includes all ministers who must be willing to defend the Government's policies at all times.'

Benn took no part in the exchange but Eric Heffer, his former junior at Industry, now on the back benches, declared there was nothing laid down in the constitution about collective responsibility, the principle had just grown up. Conciliatory statements from Callaghan and Benn were read out at the next meeting of the NEC. Possibly as an expression of conciliation but more likely because of the absence of six members on the Left, left-wing proposals on import controls were well watered down before being passed.

A month or so later Benn might have been thought to have been raising policy matters that properly belonged to another department, his old one of Industry. Nationalization of basic industries had been a disappointment to those who saw it as an opportunity to increase workers' control, he said. More industrial democracy was required with no unilateral application of executive action by management. About the same time, however, Benn played the part of a neutral chairman at a meeting of the Home Policy Committee which decided to circulate a document, opposing Government plans on spending cuts, to MPs and trade union leaders.

Callaghan was reported to be upset when Benn failed to turn up at a NEC meeting that same month, July 1976, which passed another motion attacking the cuts. Some of Benn's own colleagues on the Left, though, thought he should have stood up for his convictions, voted for the motion and resigned from the Cabinet. That, in Benn's view, would be just a demonstration, he could still do better work as a minister. In September it was leaked that he had come to an understanding with Callaghan and would not vote for the Home Policy document on cuts when it came before the NEC before the autumn conference. Without Benn's support it would not get a majority, *The Times* correctly predicted.

Benn was still arguing for the right to speak his mind and advocate left-wing policies. In early 1977 people were avidly following reminiscences of Cabinet manoeuvring in the late Richard Crossman's diaries, serialized in the Sunday press, and accounts of life in Wilson's 'political kitchen' at Number Ten from Joe Haines. The orthodox politician's response was to deplore such information being made available to ordinary taxpayers and voters before the Record Office was prepared to disgorge the relevant papers, thirty or more years later. Benn's complaint, though, was that the revelations should come more quickly. There should be open disclosure of all Cabinet discussions while they were going on. He asked:

If Parliament, public and press have now braced themselves to accept the plain and obvious truth that Cabinet discussions are interesting, vigorous and sometimes revolve around alternate policies, why should even the disclosure of an outline of the points at issue — while these discussions are in progress — be guarded against so relentlessly and so ineffectively from any risk of publicity?

The adverb 'ineffectively' recognized the fact of leaks from participants disguised as 'think pieces' by political journalists. No think piece, he added, was a satisfactory substitute for the right of Parliament and the public to know what were the choices before decisions were made.
He went on:

265

Secrecy in decision-making does not occur by accident or default. It is because knowledge is power and no government willingly gives up power to the Commons, the public or anyone else. Open government would disclose more about the processes of decision-making, including the workings of officials and advisers, and involve both admitting and encouraging pressure upon ministers . . . Collective Cabinet responsibility, under which all ministers describe, explain and defend majority Cabinet decisions no longer extends to the maintenance of the fiction that members of Cabinet minorities all experience an immediate conversion to the majority view at the very moment when the Prime Minister records it in his summing up.

Practical and public expression of that came eighteen months later when there was strong disagreement in the Government about whether Britain should join the European Monetary System, the 'snake' which would link the exchange rates of currencies.

Benn, with his strong anti-Europe views, could be expected to oppose and some of those leaky think-pieces reported that he did. Joining the snake would mean that Britain would not be allowed to devalue the pound without making comparable cuts in public spending and would rule out his ideas for getting out of the economic depression by investment and growth — ideas which were being enshrined in party if not government policy. A sizeable group of ministers went with him but Callaghan and Healey, though not committed to joining the snake by the time of a joint meeting of the Cabinet and NEC, in September 1978, were obviously feeling their way towards it.

After Benn had spoken at length on European matters Callaghan said, 'Tony has advanced his own point of view', somewhat to the surprise of other NEC members who had thought he had advanced the declared NEC view. The premier continued to state the Cabinet had not yet reached a decision but when it had 'collective responsibility will then be operative and any member of the Cabinet coming out against the decision would face the consequences'.

Benn appeared to dismiss the subject with the comment, 'That is entirely a matter for you, Prime Minister, and nothing to do with me.' His ally, Heffer, though, broke in to declare an important principle was at stake. Callaghan's comment could cover a number of ministers thinking like Benn, also members of the NEC. It meant that pressure would be brought to bear on NEC members who had been elected to represent sections of the party and not the Government. The party secretary, Ron Hayward, saw the point of that argument and thought he should submit a paper to the NEC on it. Frank Allaun, then chairman, suggested it should be referred to the party's organization committee.

In December that committee voted 8–4, on a motion from Benn, to set up a sub-committee to review the situation. It had been told by Heffer it would be 'intolerable' if ministers on the NEC could be threatened with the sack if they opposed Government policy at NEC meetings. It would mean the block of eight ministers on the NEC would have their votes pre-determined by Cabinet decisions, even though some of them were not members of the Cabinet and had little influence on its decisions. It meant that no one who wanted to express his own view inside the party could now accept ministerial office.

But the whole matter proceeded to fade away, as did the suggestion that Britain should join the EMS. Perhaps that could be accounted another success for Benn.

The premier's powers of patronage was a related subject often on Benn's lips or the point of his pen in the later seventies and one on which he had the House of Commons librarians working hard. One unsung benefit of being an MP, particularly one of a literary bent or one

267

intent on accumulating information, is having available a staff of experienced researchers, ready and able to dig up any fact likely to be of use in his duties as he sees them. Some of the work done by that library team on Benn's behalf was revealed when he reviewed Wilson's book *The Governance of Britain* for his local Bristol paper, in October 1976.

In a fashion not unknown to professional reviewers he used a text from the book for his own sermon on the subject, covering ground he felt not adequately cultivated by the author. The sermon was on patronage, the text Wilson's claim that Britain was governed not by the Prime Minister but by the Cabinet:

'The Cabinet bears his stamp, it is true, on each and every policy issue but it is the Cabinet, not the Prime Minister, who decides.'

An indisputable proposition, on the face of it, commented Benn, but the source of Prime Ministerial power must be sought elsewhere, in patronage. With acknowledgments to those Commons librarians, he gave the figures. During his two periods at Number Ten Wilson personally appointed, or reshuffled, 100 Cabinet ministers and 403 non-Cabinet ministers. He created 243 peers, appointed 24 chairmen of nationalized industries, controlling 20 per cent of the nation's gross production, and 16 chairmen of Royal Commissions to administer various policies or make recommendations for future policy, controlled all top-line appointments within the civil service and the Honours List. For not one of those appointments was a Prime Minister constitutionally required to consult Cabinet, Parliament, public or party.

The premiership was, in effect, an elected monarchy, wrote Benn. No medieval monarch in British history had such power as had every modern British prime minister. No American president had power approaching the British premier's — 'Congress would not allow it.'

No weapon was so effective in securing compliance as

the hint of possible preferment or possible dismissal. That weapon, however, was not so easily deployed against the trade unions, the Labour conference or the NEC. Pressure on the NEC could only be brought through ministers who were elected to it. Here, with perhaps some prescience of what was to happen two years later on the NEC over the EMS, Benn recalled that in 1969 Wilson had dismissed Callaghan from his Inner Cabinet for his opposition, on the NEC, to Wilson's industrial relations policy. Wilson had reproduced, in an annex to his book, his statement to Cabinet Ministers warning them it might be necessary to rule they could not stand for election to the NEC.

The conclusion Benn drew was that Britain's difficulties stemmed from too little democracy, not too much, and that the personal power of the Prime Minister was a major factor in preventing those difficulties being overcome.

It was a subject which Benn felt should be steadily updated. He had the research extended to cover all post-War premiers, from Attlee onwards. After the 1979 election he was able to inform one audience that they had, between them, produced nearly 700 Members of Parliament, in the persons of newly elevated peers, 'more than forty million did last month'. Fuller details appeared in a lecture on 'The Case for a Constitutional Premier' which he was to have delivered at Bristol University. The University's Vice-chancellor banned it when he heard how Benn's subject had grown from the original proposal of education and democracy, deciding it was much too partisan for a 'family occasion' such as the University's Open Day. The essence of the lecture, however, was printed in the *Observer* newspaper.

Those seven premiers, Benn had found, had appointed 1,484 ministers, 309 of them to the Cabinet, 85 chairmen of nationalized undertakings and 35 heads of royal commissions. Apart from new peers those prime ministers had created 118 baronetcies and 264 knighthoods. Top civil servants, ambassadors, chiefs of staffs, heads of security services, MI5 and MI6, swelled the list further. On the not unreasonable assumption there were two or three hopefuls for each job, prime-ministerial influence was brought to bear on 5,000 to 7,000 people. Benn neglected to add in archbishops, bishops and judges, presumably because they must be considered beyond such human frailties as responding to influence.

History showed not even good kings could make absolute monarchy acceptable. Not even good prime ministers made such concentration of power acceptable either.

This time Benn went on to give his suggestions how to control such power, to produce a constitutional premiership more in keeping with the tenets of democracy. They were abolition of the House of Lords, the election of Cabinet Ministers, an extension of the select committee system as a means of increasing the accountability of ministers, and a Freedom of Information Act.

All these matters had been aired in the Home Policy Committee under his chairmanship, some, such as the abolition of the Lords and the reform of the Honours System, regularly. A critical analysis of the Honours System that he wrote in the mid-sixties, resurrected by the Home Policy Committee, had been the basis of a Labour Party inquiry into the system in 1976, chaired by himself. This had been provoked by unwelcome Tory recommendations for peerages approved by Wilson. On the abolition of the Lords, after he had expressed himself forcefully on the matter on several occasions that same year, a congenial American interviewer had said he was surprised it was not in the Labour programme. So am I, replied Benn. It was one of the controversial points he succeeded in getting endorsed later, against the opposition of many of his fellow MPs. Callaghan's own resignation honours list, with ten more names than even a controversial list produced by Wilson on his resignation, proved the last straw for a majority of delegates at the

1979 conference as they confirmed party policy on the matter.

In 1977, in a talk to Press Gallery journalists in which Benn referred to the Labour system of electing the Shadow Cabinet when in Opposition, he said: 'Many Labour MPs would argue, and I agree with them, that nothing would do more to strengthen the influence of MPs than by maintaining that election system for the Cabinet when Labour is in power.'

Even that was not enough. Having elected the ministers MPs should be able to keep a firm check on them. The following year, in a lecture at London's Imperial College of Science and Technology, he called for a major shift of power between government and governed by strengthening the role of Parliament, through extending the select committee system which had proved its worth in science and technology. An NEC study group, of which he was the moving spirit, the same group which put forward the proposal to abolish the Lords which party conference accepted, reported on just those lines. The committees should shadow the work of individual ministries but the group saw no benefit in having the committees organized on bi-partisan lines as was the current Westminster practice. There was no future in 'consensus government by all-party committees', the department committees should be staffed and advised by specialists on party political lines.

Effectively this would 'dispense power in Parliament and out of it to the political parties and to those groups and individuals who support political parties'.

Such a radical revision of the political power structure would inevitably meet the opposition of the Civil Service, the group acknowledged, so legislation compelling-disclosure of government information would be indispensable.

Benn developed the information theme when addressing a British Association meeting later in the year. Secrecy

271

was the enemy of democracy, he said. People in high places were able to hide behind the blanket of the Official Secrets Act. Instead there should be a 'Freedom of Information Act' which would confer statutory rights to information on both Parliament and electorate.

Science, previously the liberator of mankind, he told his audience of scientists, could be used to enslave it if those in charge of big organizations, governmental, industrial or financial, were able to shroud themselves in secrecy, using national security as the excuse.

After that it was no surprise when, a few months later, in a paper to the Home Policy Committee, Benn floated the idea that the espionage and counterespionage services should also be accountable to a select committee, proceedings being in secret when necessary, the committee reporting annually in a form that could be published.

The suggestion of some sort of committee examination of the security services has come since, from other MPs, on those recurrent occasions when spy trials and newspaper speculation give the impression that Soviet agents are everywhere. Benn has also had the satisfaction of seeing the extension of the committee system to individual government departments recommended, in bi-partisan form, by the Select Committee on Procedure and, watered down to deny the committees the right to summon ministers, proposed by Norman St John Stevas, Tory Leader of the House, and accepted, in 1980.

The approach became wider, particularly as an election neared. In February 1978 the Home Policy Committee had before it what was called the Benn Budget. It proposed £2,700 million reflation, raising growth to 4½ per cent a year, creating 1½ million new jobs, and halving unemployment, by 1981. The hundred largest companies would be forced into planning agreements with the government. To prevent unwelcome foreign constraints on such expansionist policies $5,000 million of International Monetary Fund loans would be paid off. Pensions, child benefits and tax allowances would be raised and spending on housing, education and health increased. Petrol prices would be raised but vehicle excise duty phased out — a measure he had previously said would stimulate manufacturers to produce smaller, more efficient cars. Apart from the contentious issues such as planning agreements and ending vehicle excise duty, the actual budget announced by Chancellor Healey was broadly on those lines.

In Benn's budget, though, North Sea oil would be playing a more direct part in financing growth. He had already effectively thrown down the gauntlet to Callaghan with a call for a campaign for a full-blooded socialist programme, leading up to the next election, in a speech in which he reaffirmed that industry and the public sector should have the first call on oil revenue. That policy, not unexpectedly, received the backing of the Home Policy Committee in the summer.

The election manifesto, it said, should properly reflect decisions of the NEC and annual conference and state the party's socialist objectives clearly, without any blurring. There should be further nationalization, bringing a leading company in each main branch of industry into the public sector, with the National Enterprise Board's budget increased to at least £1,000 million a year.

Benn, of course, realized that although there was a requirement that the manifesto should be considered by both NEC and Government Callaghan had an advantage. Only he knew the date of the coming election and could make his preparations accordingly.

All this talk of nationalization would prove an electoral liability for the Labour Party, proclaimed Tory propagandists. They hoped Benn would carry on on those lines. He did.

A report from the Industrial Policy Committee, chaired by a fellow thinker of the Left, Judith Hart, then Minister of Overseas Development, raised the number of companies in which the Government should intervene from

273

100 to 500. There should be legislation compelling each company with a turnover above £50,000,000 to sign a planning agreement with the Government. The Home Policy Committee approved.

In December a draft manifesto for the coming election, though still no one outside Callaghan's confidence had any idea when it would be, drawn up for Benn's committee, was leaked to the Communist newspaper, the *Morning Star*. It was rapidly reproduced in other papers. Though drawn up by Transport House staff in consultation with ministers and political advisers, to minimize areas of disagreement, it acknowledged objection might be found to some points when Government and NEC got down together to consider it. It was an attempt to secure agreement on a thorough-going programme in line with party conference decisions — it claimed to 'draw deeply upon the principles of socialism and democracy'.

It repeated the Benn proposal to use North Sea wealth for investment in industry, conservation and the Welfare State by the establishment of a revenue fund administered by the National Enterprise Board and for planning agreements with major companies. The NEB, it said, should have funds of at least £1,000 million a year. As well as the merging of Giro and the National Savings Bank into a new State Bank, as urged by Benn, ways would be considered how to create a further substantial public stake in the finance sector. Other points which Callaghan would not have found to his liking included commitments on job creation — 'something like a million' — a strengthened price control policy, while glossing over the vexed question of wages control, and a wealth tax on net amounts over £150,000.

A pledge to abolish the 'undemocratic and unelected' House of Lords was followed by a sentence which some commentators seized on as indicating Benn's determination to hold on, dictator-like, to power should he achieve it, despite his democratic stance. It read: 'To safeguard electors' rights any extension of the life of a Parliament should be subject to approval by a two-thirds majority in the Commons.'

The objections were due to misreading of the sentence, declared Benn, but it was changed to make it clear that Parliament would have to be dissolved at the end of five years.

Benn may have started the manifesto battle on ground of his own choosing, or almost of his choosing, but Callaghan still had the superior guns. The manifesto on which the election was fought differed materially. Benn was allowed a relatively small part in the election campaign, confined, almost, to his home constituency. At least the Tories who claimed that Benn nationalizing talk would win the election for them could not be proved right — interestingly, Benn later commented approvingly on the forthright way Mrs Thatcher fought the election. On the other hand his other post-election comment, a repeat of his pre-election comments, that socialist policies would have won, also went untested.

CHAPTER SEVENTEEN

Principle or Expediency?

Benn's emotion as the result of the 1979 election was declared may not have been unrelieved gloom. The loyal party member and hard-working minister must weep at the interruption to the task of applying party principles and policy to the British way of life. But the party reformer might manage a smile at the thought that the task of making sure those party principles and policies were those of true democratic socialism could now go ahead without the constraints of ministerial responsibility and Cabinet unanimity.

'I shall be able to speak my mind,' he declared in an early morning telephone call to the Press Association, shortly after the election, announcing he would leave Callaghan's Front Bench. Benn's explanation was that he wanted to study and analyze the experience of the last five years, to examine the relationship between the Labour Government, the Parliamentary Labour Party, the NEC and the annual conference. It was a task all Labour MPs should undertake 'so we can apply the lessons learned to the future work of the party'. While not directly attacking Callaghan's conduct of the election, neither in that announcement nor in a speech in Birmingham a few days earlier, his message came over clearly — Labour had lost because it had cold-shouldered policies of the annual conference and the NEC.

'We must defend, explain and advocate in Parliament those policies which have been decided at our annual party conference,' he declared in that Birmingham speech. 'The Labour Party, including the Parliamentary Labour Party, must be made more democratic, responsive and accountable to its rank-and-file members and supporters, so that the party becomes an effective instrument for those it was set up to serve.'

'He is just windy' was the comment of one Cabinet colleague on learning Benn was not standing in the Shadow Cabinet election. Relations between Benn and some of those colleagues had not been good for some time. One of the hazards, or pleasures, of being a Lobby correspondent in those days, particularly one called upon to write political profiles or regale backchat garnered in the bars, was to be taken aside by one of them and given the latest Benn story. How he had whipped out an instamatic camera to record moments of interest for posterity, the jokes scored off him, the latest *bons mots* in his defence of the pure milk of socialism. How, after breaking

276

away from what busy ministers, anxious to get off, regarded as the real business on the agenda, to go into long philosophical dissertations, he would take the Prime Minister by the arm and ask 'You do understand me, don't you, Prime Minister?'

'If he had answered honestly he would have said "no",' said the retailer of that story who, perhaps, had as little regard for Callaghan's philosophical side as he had for Benn's.

If his aristocratic, or natural, breeding had permitted it, Benn might have retorted that the man who headed the Labour Shadow Cabinet poll a decade earlier, Reg Prentice, had not only been returned as a Conservative MP but installed as a minister in Mrs Thatcher's Cabinet. He might also have forecast that some of those who would be returned in the coming election to Labour's Front Bench would also have left the party, long before another decade was up.

Some of those moderates saw the Benn announcement as a declaration of war against Callaghan, and political commentators read it as a move to extend his power base further among the unions and rank-and-file workers.

The battle was already joined, on a far larger scale than a joust between rival politicians, Benn might have said. He told a group of American Republicans in 1978 that in Britain a struggle was going on between monetarism, corporatism and democratic socialism. He did not identify candidates for those labels but left his audience to suspect that he meant the Conservatives by monetarism, the Callaghan faction by corporatism and identified himself and those fighting with him to transform Labour conference decisions into government policy as democratic socialists.

Achieving that would mean changing the attitudes of those MPs compliant to Callaghan corporatism. That could only be done by making them properly accountable to the rank and file of local constituency parties who, he had reminded his colleagues the previous year, would

277

soon be 'working their hearts out, tramping the streets, knocking on doors' to get them elected.

He had already had brushes with Callaghan over where the loyalties of some of those party activists lay. At a 1977 NEC discussion on a report on Trotskyists Callaghan said he had five in his constituency party and quoted, approvingly, the view of Max Morris, a teachers' leader who had recently left the Communist Party, on their disruptive role. Benn did not think too much notice should be taken of the views of a lapsed Communist and reported he had a number of members of the Militant Tendency in his and found them very helpful.

Before that, at the end of 1976 there had been another row over the appointment of Andy Bevan to be the party's youth officer. There was a double objection to him. First, the Labour Party workers' own union criticized the method of his selection and said the job should have gone to one of its own members. The second objection was on the grounds that Militant Tendency, with which Bevan was associated, was a Marxist group. The row prompted a full-page article in the *Guardian* by Benn on the debt owed by such eminent Labour leaders as Andy's namesake Aneurin to Marx. Marxism has, from the earliest days, been accepted as one of many sources of our inspiration, wrote Benn, along with, though less influential than, Christian socialism, Fabianism, Owenism, trade unionism, even radical Liberalism (with a nod to his own father and grandfather).

To be a Marxist was not necessarily to be a Communist. Communists were disqualified but to ban Marxists who accepted the Labour Party programme and committed themselves to socialism through parliamentary democracy would have grave implications.

After a two and a half hour wrangle at a NEC meeting Benn was the only minister to vote for Bevan. Ranged against him were Callaghan, Foot and Shirley Williams but alongside him were enough of the other NEC members to carry the day by 15 votes to 12.

All that was symptomatic of the divisions springing up in the party.

On one side were those who saw themselves as the workers doing the hard graft in party branches and trade unions, spreading the party gospel among the people, who regarded the NEC as the custodians of party policy reached at conference and the Parliamentary Party as the paid professionals whose duty it was to apply that policy — and, of course, those MPs who thought likewise.

On the other side were the MPs who also regarded themselves as professionals, but members of a profession skilled in deciding how far voters could be carried in accepting that policy — plus those at trade union and branch level who went with them.

By the 1979 conference the two components of the mixture had crystallized visibly to all. One was determined to push through reforms which would make party policies binding upon MPs as party representatives in Parliament, the Left. The other was concerned with the need to temper the fervency of party activists, to shape and represent policy in the understanding of what would appeal to voters — the moderates. On that view the party, looked at from Left to Right, was like its squabbles, it had a beginning, a middle but no end, the 'moderates' ranged out to the furthermost point of the spectrum.

There was bitterness and rancour on both sides. After all, said activists, the House of Commons was not called the best man's club in London for nothing. So-called Labour MPs swallowed Tory views with the gins and tonics they shared with Tory MPs in the bars. On the other hand it was mixing with 'Commies' and 'Trots' in demonstrations, doorstepping with them, sharing pints in the pub afterwards, or, worse, instant coffee or teabag tea in committee rooms, which blinded well-meaning Labourites to the realities of electoral life. Perhaps it was the teabags. After all, didn't Tony take a pocketful of teabags and his pint mug with him when he went out into the wilds away from Westminster?

At times, from the 1979 conference onwards, one felt the battle was being fought at that level. For there was a battle, with Benn versus Callaghan, a battle which there can now be little dispute Benn won.

Before battle was joined at that 1979 conference there was the minor skirmish of the European elections. What honours there were in that went to Benn. He asserted himself early by having 6½ million copies of the Labour campaign document, 'Labour for Europe', scrapped on the grounds that 'for' was the opposite of party policy. It was retitled 'Labour in Europe'. Then Callaghan objected when he found he was to be the only one of four speakers opening the campaign who was 'for', the others being Benn, Heffer and Barbara Castle (who, as a Euro-MP was eventually to decide she was 'for' after all).

'I am not a wheelhorse to be wheeled on to a platform whenever I am needed,' Callaghan declared. But he was pacified and went onto the platform, still in a minority of one.

That summer the lines of battle for the autumn conference were drawn — mostly by Benn and his adherents. A 'Labour Coordinating Committee' was set up to coordinate the fight for constitutional change as well as changes in economic policy. Arthur Scargill, then president of the Yorkshire area of the National Union of Mineworkers, a member of the Committee, called for the procedure for the election of the party leader to be changed to one that 'truly reflects the grass roots' — 'If this is done I am certain the next leader will be Tony Benn,' he declared. A rival 'Campaign for Labour Victory' included Shirley Williams, Roy Hattersley, David Owen and Roy Mason. Callaghan, they declared, had the firm support of the whole Shadow Cabinet and a majority of Labour supporters in his resistance to constitutional changes which would turn the party into a 'narrow, sectarian and intolerant organization'.

Benn and his supporters secured NEC approval for constitutional changes, first for the wider election of the party leader and automatic reselection of MPs by their constituency organization, with the necessary waiving of the three-year rule prohibiting discussion of the same subject more than once in that time, then for the NEC having the final say in drawing up the election manifesto.

That last NEC decision brought Wilson to the radio to give his view on Benn — 'philosopher, theorist, almost a theologian . . . Tony wants the pure milk of the doctrine to be accepted by the Labour Party and I think he will give up any chance of the leadership to get that done.'

He saw Benn's inspiration coming from nonconformism, rather than Marxism: 'He's certainly not a Communist, he wouldn't last two minutes in Moscow, he'd be sent out to Siberia or somewhere.'

Elsewhere Wilson modified his description of Benn as 'philosopher', declaring that when he got into the philosophical stratosphere he was woolly and occasionally boring.

A philosophical politician, whether woolly or not, is a rarity in Britain today, which might account for the interest in him. Reports of trade union conferences centred on their response to the Benn philosophy. The TGWU supported him unanimously on reselection. Aslef urged stricter control on MPs. When the engineers' conference appeared likely to call for radical reforms in the party the chairman closed the proceedings abruptly. The agenda for the party conference showed that left-wingers had succeeded in making the methods of selecting parliamentary candidates and the party leader the main issues. Sixty-six of 380 resolutions were on those matters.

Callaghan appeared in desperate mood on the eve of conference, threatening, Gaitskell fashion, though before the battle, not after, to 'fight, fight, fight again'. This surprised some observers because an inquiry into the inner workings of the party, urged by trade unions, had already been agreed and any constitutional changes proposed were bound to be reviewed in the light of its report. An attempt to have debates on those contentious issues postponed until after the inquiry was defeated, however, and Callaghan probably saw better than those commentators the likely composition of that inquiry. There was bad news for him when the AUEW delegates decided to support reselection and NEC responsibility for the manifesto.

On the first day of the conference there was considerable criticism of the way Callaghan had fought the election and of the manifesto. The party chairman, Allaun, and the party secretary, Hayward, both attacked the previous Cabinet for ignoring decisions of party and TUC on such crucial issues as the Healey 5 per cent pay policy which had led to the 'winter of discontent'. Healey retorted that Callaghan had been the party's main asset in the election, polls putting his popularity ahead of that of Mrs Thatcher and the Labour Party itself. Foot, once the darling of the Left, also sprang to Callaghan's defence but only aroused ribald laughter when he claimed the Cabinet had not ignored TUC and party opposition to pay policy. Angrily and in an obvious reference to Benn, he declared if he had not agreed with the pay policy he would have got out of the Government.

The next day the motion for mandatory reselection of MPs was carried, after a ruling that it was disqualified because it had been discussed the previous year had been set aside

'Hundreds of delegates rose to their feet as one yesterday in joyful celebration of their famous victory,' the Communist *Morning Star* reported in satisfaction.

The motion to set up an electoral college with trade union and rank-and-file representation for the election of party leader was defeated but any relief Callaghan had in that was tempered by the poor reception he received from conference when he appealed for differences to be sunk in the cause of unity. He had excused conference in advance from giving him a standing ovation and conference took him at his word, though Benn was among those who stood to clap.

The manifesto vote was put off to the next day and it proved the second major blow for Callaghan. After a short but acrimonious debate in which a number of constituency workers spoke of the demoralizing effect of finding party commitments for which thay had fought watered down if not just left out, the conference voted that the NEC should have the final say and instructed it to draw up proposals for the change for the 1980 conference. Heffer, winding up for the NEC had declared that Callaghan had personally vetoed inclusion of the abolition of the House of Lords and nationalization of the construction industry when the manifesto was drawn up.

The conference also called for the renationalization without compensation of parts of nationalized industries sold off by the present government.

Benn had rapturous receptions from fringe meetings but in the conference hall limited himself to forecasting the next Labour Government would have a tremendous battle with financial and banking institutions. He did dissuade conference, however, from passing a motion demanding the nationalization of 200 companies and of banks and insurance companies. Delegates, he warned, must take resolutions seriously if they wanted the leadership to do the same and such a far-ranging commitment could only be worked out line by line with the trade unions concerned.

Callaghan's forebodings about the make-up of the inquiry were proved justified later that month when the NEC rejected his appeal for special representation for the Parliamentary Labour Party. All five members of the NEC voted onto the inquiry were left-wing MPs, Benn,

Heffer, Allaun, Joan Lestor and Jo Richardson. In addition there were five trade union leaders, Callaghan, as party leader, Foot as deputy leader, Norman Atkinson, another left-wing MP, as party treasurer, and Alex Kitson, of the TGWU, as party vice-chairman — preferred, on the motion of Benn and Heffer, to the party chairman, Baroness Jeger, whose acceptance of a peerage, in the eyes of some, outweighed her left-wing past.

The following summer, though, the inquiry reported it had been unable to come to an agreement on the constitutional issues, despite six months' hard work trying to reach a 'consensus'. So, said David Basnett of the General and Municipal Workers, former chairman of the TUC and the prime force behind the demand for the inquiry, they said 'sod it, let us put them to the conference'.

Some months before there had been a meeting between party and trade union leaders at Bishops Stortford to iron out misunderstandings, at which there had been apparent agreement on an electoral college to decide future leadership elections. But, on examination, it proved too complex to be workable. Was it a dead duck, Michael Foot was asked, when the inquiry reported. A true politician he replied, 'I am not saying that but it is not exactly alive.'

The inquiry had also been unable to agree who should have the last word on the content of election manifestos. This was due to come up again at the autumn conference but Benn and his fellow chairmen of major sub-committees of the NEC, Heffer and Lestor, pre-empted that discussion during the summer, in what may well have been a tactical blunder. They called a press conference to announce a new draft manifesto, approved by the NEC, containing all the controversial policy commitments approved by conference of the various committees.

Callaghan and his supporters on the Shadow Cabinet were bound to object on the grounds that under Clause V of the party constitution they had a duty to shape the manifesto to ensure the maximum appeal to the electorate. They doubted the electoral appeal, taken individually, of such matters as a large-scale extension of public ownership, including nationalization of North Sea oil, renunciation of a new generation of nuclear weapons, abolition of the House of Lords, withdrawal from the EEC, and were in no doubt that together they would add up to an insuperable hurdle. Foot was sent to demand that the party secretary should cancel the press conference. Hayward had no choice but to do so. The result was to publicize further the split over the control of the manifesto.

When the matter came up at the conference the motion the NEC had been instructed, the previous year, to prepare on the transfer to it of responsibility for the manifesto, was narrowly defeated. Benn, for the NEC, told union leaders who had shifted their ground that it was no good their coming to the conference with big block votes and demanding policies of their liking if they were to use the same block votes to permit those policies being vetoed.

There was little else to please Callaghan, whose speech to the conference pleading for unity sounded more like one from an elder statesman than from a party leader fighting for his views. It convinced observers that he was about to announce his withdrawal from the fray.

In contrast Benn urged passionately those leftward moves which, he had told an enthusiastic fringe meeting, were needed to enable the people to regain their independence. A Labour Government, he instructed conference, should introduce Bills to extend nationalization, to restore EEC powers to Westminster and to abolish the House of Lords — creating a thousand peers, if necessary — within a month.

'I am surprised that Tony was so unambitious. After all it took God only six days to make the world,' said Shirley Williams.

The conference proceeded to vote for leaving the Common Market, a commitment which, by this time, in the

285

light of opinion polls, might be considered good electoral fodder but one which Shirley Williams had said in advance would make her leave the party.

The NEC proposal for compulsory reselection was re-affirmed by a sizeable majority. The vote in favour of a widening of the franchise for the selection of the party leader, however, had a margin of little over 1 per cent, and the conference failed to agree on how the vote was to be shared between constituency parties, trade unions and other affiliated organizations and MPs. It was decided to hold a special conference in January 1981 to settle this.

The party also firmly committed itself to unilateral nuclear disarmament, declaring the election manifesto must be equally firm on this. That went through on a show of hands but a call for withdrawal from Nato was heavily defeated on a card vote.

A sidelight on conference backstage procedure was given by the affair of the engineering union delegate. The moderates had realized that they had been out-man-oeuvred when Benn had left the Shadow Cabinet to concentrate on building his position on the NEC. They now had to reduce that power base by electoral campaigns against his supporters there. In this the votes of the Amalgamated Union of Engineering Workers could be vital. The union's leadership, president Terence Duffy, secretary Sir John Boyd and the six-man executive, was firmly for Callaghan but the delegates had a nasty habit of making up their own minds on voting matters, showing no reluctance to go against the 'instructions' of Duffy and Boyd. This year the leadership was quite confident that it would be different. They had taken soundings and they assured politicians and journalists beforehand that the near million votes the union wielded would be cast for moderates and against the Left. To their dismay, though, when the delegates decided how to use that block vote an extra hand went up to join the known Left, that of Dorset engineer John Knott.

286

'He did not know how he was voting,' declared Duffy. 'His excuse for not voting the way I told him was that he did not know who to vote for,' was Boyd's own excuse. But those apparent aspersions on Mr Knott's intelligence and understanding proved unjustified. Nor was the explanation by Jack McPherson Quinn, convenor of left-wing delegates — 'We out-smarted Duffy and Boyd and got to this chap first' — the full truth. Mr Knott made it clear he was neither right nor left, just a conscientious member of the Labour Party who had voted for an executive which had done justice to those who elected them.

The outcome of those elections was that the Left was strengthened in its representation on the NEC, not weakened.

'We've hit rock bottom,' said one moderate, estimating they could only count on seven votes on the 29-strong committee. Rock bottom it was, the opposition to Benn had its campaign better organized the following year.

A fortnight after the conference Callaghan stood down from the leadership. Benn appealed to the Parliamentary Party to accept that the party had decided future elections should be by electoral college, even if it were undecided just how this should be done, and to let Callaghan's deputy, Foot, take over as caretaker. The PLP, though, decided to carry on with its own election. Benn was dissuaded by the Labour Coordinating Committee from standing, on the grounds that this would legitimize the contest. At first Foot said he would not stand, leaving the contest between Healey and Peter Shore, with John Silkin as a possible third choice. Neither Shore nor Silkin were thought strong enough candidates to defeat Healey and Shore further distanced himself from the Left by failing to acknowledge the electoral college. Eventually, in response to a 'Stop Healey' campaign Foot agreed to stand. To his surprise, he stated afterwards, he won, on the second ballot. This victory by Foot, with his old left-wing reputation, took the impetus out of a drive to have the

287

election declared invalid and even Benn, who had previously said he would challenge the leader under the new rules, accepted the result.

Perhaps, in the end, that was a victory for Callaghan and his view of what was best for the party. He knew full well that an electoral college gave Benn his best, perhaps his only, chance of becoming leader. By retiring when he did he pre-empted the college and left the choice of his successor to the PLP. From the point of view of keeping Benn out the result was probably better than if Healey, closer to Callaghan's own thinking, had won. For Benn almost certainly would have challenged him and, as we now know, the result of that battle would have hinged on a number of obscurities impossible to make clear even in retrospect today.

Of vastly more interest to the Press and public at large was the election which followed nearly a year later, for the deputy leadership, which Benn did contest against Healey.

The January conference on the electoral college was held amidst predictions that confusion would continue. Even Benn seemed to think that a possibility — 'We will go on until we win, however long it takes,' he told his supporters beforehand. He condemned those Labour MPs talking of joining a centre party as people who wanted to see Labour defeated at the next election. Naturally, they had the full backing of the media.

'We must brace ourselves for leading articles in the old "Thunderer", *The Times*, reminding us of our moral duty, signed by Rupert Murdoch,' a comment which had those of his audience more familiar with Murdoch's role as purveyor of sex and sensation in the *Sun*, along with those who read *The Times*, rapturous with applause. Those who spoke of forming a new centre party, said Benn, were unanimous in supporting the EEC, the over-riding influence of the International Monetary Fund, the maintenance of American bases, the continuance of Britain's nuclear weapons programme and, as far as he could make out, the continuation of the House of Lords, 'into which most of them hope to go'. The day after the conference had decided how the votes were to be shared. Shirley Williams, Roy Jenkins, William Rodgers and Dr David Own, labelled by the Press the 'Gang of Four', announced at a Sunday lunchtime meeting at Owen's Limehouse home that they had taken the first step towards forming the Social Democratic Party.

If there was to be an extended franchise for electing the leader then it should be one member, one vote, in a secret ballot, Mrs Williams had earlier said, but she and her colleagues would probably have accepted a college in which the PLP still had a majority. A motion from Duffy's engineering union which would have given the PLP 75 per cent of the votes fell at the first hurdle but another, from the General and Municipal Workers, allotting the PLP 50 per cent, with the rest going half to the constituencies and half to trade unions and other affiliated societies, led the way for the first two votes. Experienced conference watchers, though, could see that everything hinged on which of two other motions would be left to challenge the GMWU motion on the final vote. The NEC proposal was for equal shares for the three major sections, 33 per cent each to PLP, constituencies and trade unions, the remaining 1 per cent going to other societies, such as the Co-op. The shopworkers union, USDAW, proposed that 40 per cent should go to the unions and societies and 30 per cent each to the PLP and constituencies. Some delegates who preferred the NEC equal shares formula were persuaded that the USDAW motion would go down better with the unions and so voted for it as the one more likely to win in the end. The result was that, against some expectations, the USDAW motion came second on the second ballot, narrowly ahead of the NEC motion, which was eliminated. In the run-off between GMWU and US-DAW motions the shopworkers' came home comfortably.

The second ballot turned out, in the end, to be crucial to Benn's chances in the election to come.

Foot, though he had wanted the larger role for the PLP, accepted the result. Some trade union leaders suggested they might try to overturn the result, though party secretary Hayward publicly stated that could not be done. Just in case of trouble, though, the Labour Coordinating Committee brought eleven left-wing organizations together under the banner of the 'Rank and File Mobilizing Committee for Labour Party Democracy' to fight off any threat to their college.

Foot was not challenged for the leadership but Benn announced he would stand against Healey for the deputy post. There had never been a deputy-leadership election comparable to the one which followed in the autumn. Newspapers covered the build-up to the voting almost as if it were a general election. The banner of unity was raised on behalf of Healey, for rumours had begun to circulate that there would be more defections by MPs to the SDP, which the Gang of Four had now formed, if the ructions continued. Others had already gone, none following the example of Benn's father of resigning his seat and fighting a by-election to win a mandate for his changed views.

The Times, giving biographies of the candidates — Silkin joined Healey and Benn in the lists — ascribed to Benn ownership of a farm, linked him with a family tax-haven trust in Bermuda and told of 'several million dollars' in other trusts associated with his wife Caroline. It had to retract when Benn denied the first two and declared the third grossly exaggerated.

Another retraction came when Healey, provoked by hecklers at a rally in Birmingham, where Foot had had to come to his help, declared it had been engineered by Benn's principle aide and charged that aide with leading another demonstration against him. The aide proved he had been many miles away on each occasion.

The early confidence of Healey supporters ebbed as the conference neared and doubts grew on which way some vital trade union votes might be cast. Healey was confident of an overwhelming majority of the PLP vote but knew that would be countered by Benn's support in the constituencies. The decision rested on how that 40 per cent for the unions was shared. A debate by the three candidates before a TUC audience was considered to have boosted Benn's chances. The TUC had already shown it favoured such Benn-inspired policies as withdrawal from the EEC, unilateralism and no pay restraint. Unions canvassed their members' views in different ways. The TGWU took soundings in its districts and then its executives staggered the Healey camp by recommending its delegation to back Benn. Their own soundings, they said, showed a majority of TGWU districts supported Healey. As newspapers got themselves, if not all their readers, into quite a fever over it the TGWU delegates voted to support Silkin in the first ballot. Even though everyone knew that Silkin would be out after that, whatever the TGWU did, no decision was taken on how to vote on the second count. A hurried consultation, when Silkin had been eliminated, switched the union's vote to Benn.

On that first count Healey had taken 45.369 per cent of the votes, Benn 36.627 per cent and Silkin 18.004 per cent — someone at Labour headquarters had evidently thought the outcome might be so close that three places of decimals would be required. It did not need so careful a mathematical approach to deduce that all depended on what share of the Silkin vote would be transferred to Benn. As delegates returned to their seats after the second vote the word went round that Benn had won, not enough of the Silkin vote had gone to Healey. But proper allowance had not been made for abstentions, which turned out to be considerable, particularly among MPs.

As the chairman announced the figures for the different sections those of a calculating mind could see Healey had 'won by a whisker' as the headlines were to put it. He obtained 50.426 per cent to Benn's 49.574 per cent. The constituencies had voted almost five to one for Benn, the MPs two to one for Healey and the unions had split three to two for Healey.

A straight transfer of the voting pattern shows that under the 'equal shares' formula proposed by the NEC Benn would have won by 2 per cent. As it was, abstentions had decided the issue. The Tribune group of MPs had been almost equally divided between Silkin and Benn on the first ballot. Almost all those who had voted for Silkin on that ballot abstained on the second and a few voted for Healey. If those supposed Left MPs had voted for the Left candidate, declared the Benn campaigners, Benn would have been home. Arithmetic supports that. Twenty more MP votes, the number of the Tribune group said to have deserted Benn, would have produced a 1½ per cent swing to him, also giving him victory by 2 per cent. Joan Lestor was one of those who abstained and the outraged constituency workers voted her off the NEC the following year. Neil Kinnock, another abstainer, found himself involved in angry arguments outside the conference hall with Benn supporters who could not understand why their hero was not the unanimous choice of the Left. The abstaining MPs counter-attacked, declaring that Benn, by standing, had deprived the Left of the deputy leadership. Benn was 'divisive', they said, Silkin would have been a 'consensus' candidate, able to bring together all Left sections. But Benn supporters did not attempt to disguise their belief that, in the end, Silkin could not be relied on to fight for Left policies as Benn could.

Those on the 'Hard Left' of the Tribune group felt those suspicions confirmed in December 1982 when Silkin turned up at a shareholders' meeting of the *Tribune* newspaper as a proxy armed with the shares bequeathed by Aneurin Bevan to his widow, Jennie Lee, in company with others of similar views, to launch a take-over. Their complaint was that *Tribune* had moved too far to the Left under its editor Chris Mullins, a close associate of Benn. Mullins was voted off the board, Silkin and his colleague Lord Bruce of Donnington were voted on. It was regarded at the time as a clever move, beating the Bennites at their own organizational game. Shares in left-wing journals are usually regarded as valueless, expressive only of the support of the shareholders for the paper's aims, not of any hope of pecuniary gain (though the new harder-line *Tribune* was proving popular enough among party activists to begin to draw in advertising) nor, usually, of any desire for control.

Later that month, though, it seemed that the Silkin group had neither been comprehensive enough in their take-over nor had they studied the rules as carefully as their Bennite opponents. At the take-over meeting they had allowed themselves to be persuaded by Jack Jones, the veteran trade union leader and party conciliator, to allow two staff members to remain on the board. They also neglected to turn up for the next board meeting, two days before Christmas when MPs were launching themselves into the festive season away from London — though Silkin afterwards explained he had gone to the dentist.

It transpired that although the Silkin consortium could count on a working majority of the issued shares there remained, unissued, a greater majority. Only 423 of *Tribune*'s authorized 1,000 £1-shares were subscribed when it was incorporated in 1937. The board, minus Silkin and Bruce, proceeded to authorize an employees' share system, giving each worker the right to a 5 per cent holding, and then to issue fifty shares each to nine of the ten employees. It also gave Mullins a three-year contract. Foot, with sixty shares, could probably have stopped the power-struggle, gleefully reported in the Press, before it got out of hand but he, characteristically, had remained aloof.

293

That was a full year ahead.

In the reaction after the leadership election Healey declared it had been a victory not for him nor for his ideas but for the broad base of the Labour movement.

Benn was observed to wipe a tear from his eye as, acknowledging the sympathy of a far more enthusiastic audience than Healey's, he declared they had won the argument.

He and his supporters were not to win all the arguments that conference. A move to introduce a black-list against ultra-Left organizations was defeated, unilateralist policies were reconfirmed but the motion to leave Nato was defeated again and confusion again prevailed over the question of final responsibility for the manifesto. After a motion giving it to the NEC had been approved, with Benn vigorously applauding, a second vote was called to incorporate the change into the constitution, with the reverse result. As the conference had also decided, against Benn's wishes, to resurrect the three-year rule it meant that that contentious issue had been put into cold storage until 1984.

The NEC elections saw the unions far better organized in their drive to cut Benn's support. The engineering union leaders were able to use the union's vote as they wished and they joined with the General and Municipal Workers to organize the defeat of four left-wingers. One victim was Renee Short who was thus deprived of succession to the vice-chair and then, the following year, to the chair. The engineers also ditched Norman Atkinson, Treasurer since 1975, though he was an AUEW-sponsored MP, securing the election of Eric Varley in his place. Foot was now in control. With the rest of the executive split 14–14 his voice would be decisive. He chose to use that control in conciliatory fashion, using his influence to keep Benn and Heffer in the chairs of their committees.

Atkinson described the NEC changes as a major defeat

and a remarkable change in British politics. A good beginning, was Duffy's verdict, with a promise of better to
come. But with the power of the Left trimmed in the
NEC the emphasis switched to reducing the power of
the ultra-Left, mainly the Militant Tendency in the
constituencies.

Benn, however, managed to extract some advantage
even from a Foot NEC victory when the party leader
secured backing for an inquiry into their activities. He
emerged from the meeting to declare to astonished reporters, 'Speaking as deputy-leader, because, of course,
Denis Healey's entire majority has now defected to the
SDP, I would like to say to Labour Party people at home
not to be discouraged but to go on campaigning for peace
and justice.'

'He's talking through his hat,' commented Foot. To
John Golding, Benn's most active opponent on the Home
Policy Committee, it was 'typical of the looney Left'.

Eleven further MPs had defected to the SDP, Benn's
supporters in the House explained. Nine of them had
voted for Healey. If, knowing they were about to leave,
they had done the decent thing, by Benn standards, and
abstained, it would have been Benn, not Healey, who
would have won by that whisker.

Some wondered if it was a serious Benn claim to the
deputy leader's place in the Shadow Cabinet, if he would
ask for a ruling on the validity of the defectors' votes. It
proved, though, to be no more than a demonstration of
what Benn felt was the weak moral position of those who
opposed him, the lengths to which they would go to secure
the defeat of principle by expediency.

He soon made it clear his way was to be the way of
principle, as he saw it, not expediency. Foot urged him
to stand in the Shadow Cabinet election, promising his
support if he did, which was tantamount to an offer to
see he was elected. Benn, though, would have to toe the
line. Which line was Benn to toe, the party line or the

Shadow Cabinet line? After several telephone calls to Benn the exasperated Foot issued a 1,200-word statement declaring he could get no clear answer so he answered it himself — 'No'. Benn claimed that what had upset Foot was a statement that he would advocate Labour conference policies inside and outside Parliament. The Foot statement was interpreted as an instruction to MPs not to vote for Benn and he finished seventeenth in a poll for fifteen places.

About this time, as if to disprove the assumption that he and his policies were an electoral liability, Benn was drawing by far the most enthusiastic audiences in public meetings during a by-election, contested by Shirley Williams, in Crosby, Lancashire. Which, of course, may only show the irrelevance of public meetings to election results in an era of campaigning by press conference, radio and television.

Preparations for the 1982 conference began with a bargaining session in January at Bishop's Stortford. Benn agreed not to reopen the deputy-leadership battle provided Foot exerted his influence to moderate action against the Hard-Left in the constituencies. Some of Benn's associates considered he had been too trusting, that Foot would not be able to restrain the Right when the time came. After the time had come, after the conference, they were to claim their misgivings had proved right.

While Tory ministers and Press were belabouring the Labour Party over the Marxism of the Hard-Left, of Militant Tendency, Benn was invited to give the annual Marx Memorial Lecture. He would not describe himself as a Marxist, he said, but he recognized that Marx had inspired millions, giving them hope and courage in face of persecution and oppression. He likened 'negative propaganda' against Marx today with the way Christianity was treated in its early days.

On the use of force to secure social change he said, 'If

the Labour movement and the Left were ever to resort to force it would not be to overthrow the elected government, it would be to defend that elected government. It would be in defence, not in defiance of the elected government.'

He went on, however, to declare, 'There is clearly an inherent right to take up arms against tyranny or dictatorship, to establish or uphold democracy, on exactly the same basis and for the same reasons that the nation will respond to a call to defeat a foreign invasion.'

That was to be quoted against him after Argentina had invaded the Falklands. From the beginning of the Falklands campaign he and Judith Hart, then party chairman, had resisted the use of force to regain the islands, urging a United Nations administration for them while the dispute between Britain and Argentina was resolved. He remained unswervingly of that view throughout, not just while the party leadership seemed beset by uncertainty but when Mrs Thatcher's despatch of the Task Force saw only 33 Labour MPs, plus two Welsh nationalists, in the lobby against her.

When the matter was debated in the NEC Foot and Healey declared that Labour's stance had changed Mrs Thatcher's attitude and forced concessions on her on negotiations. Disputing this Benn called for an immediate and unconditional ceasefire and condemned the Prime Minister's decision to veto any Security Council call for a ceasefire. His motion was rejected in favour of a Foot call for a ceasefire linked to Argentinian withdrawal. Labour should not go beyond calling for Britain to go back to the United Nations, said Foot, and the Shadow Cabinet, as well as the NEC, backed him on this.

Benn then suffered a home policy set-back. Word started to go around in the spring that moves were afoot to water down the pledge to abolish the House of Lords. It appeared that Benn had had his calculations right when, at the 1980 conference, he had called for the creation of a thousand peers to achieve it. There were a shade over that number already eligible to sit or, more pertinently, vote. With convention decreeing that only two new Lords could be introduced at once and that only twice a week, it would take the whole lifetime of a Parliament to prepare the groundwork to carry out that pledge, one MP worked out. There would be no time for other controversial legislation. That was why, said Benn, it was necessary to put it into the election manifesto. The monarch might assert her constitutional position and call for another general election if a prime minister demanded the wholesale creation of new peers without a mandate for it. If the electorate had approved this in advance then, he believed, the action would be constitutional. Nevertheless the moderate view prevailed, the party should only ask for enough peers to ensure no great hold-up in its legislation.

Experience like that led to one more attempt to influence the contents of the next manifesto. A policy document, 'Labour's Programme '82,' was drawn up for consideration at a joint meeting of the Shadow Cabinet and NEC. This compendium of conference-approved policies — sometimes, said the critics, exaggerated developments of those policies — should be considered as a whole, said Benn. Foot was heard to comment, acidly, that it would take 40 years of Labour Government to get it through. Foot had his way and the next election manifesto remained uncommitted.

That was to be Benn's last chance, for a while at least, to attempt to pre-empt consideration of the next election manifesto from his position as Chairman of the Home Policy Committee. The drive to break his support on the NEC was being intensified by his opponents. If 1980 had been the year of rock-bottom for the moderates then 1982 was to be one of soaring success. A coalition of politicians and union leaders, drawn together under the banner 'Forward Labour', prepared a list of preferred candidates to be circulated among voting sections, with an accompany-

298

ing 'hit list' of Left-wingers it was hoped to see off. It accepted it had little hope of influencing the constituency parties but it urged the rejection of Eric Clarke, of the mineworkers, and Douglas Hoyle MP, in the trade union section, of Joan Maynard MP in the women's section and Leslie Huckfield MP in the societies' section. All four went in a mass purge which left Benn and his supporters in a minority of nine to twenty.

The removal of Clarke staggered some conference watchers who had thought that 'Forward Labour' had been a little ambitious in putting him on their hit list. Behind him lay the triple alliance of mineworkers, steel-workers and railwaymen, all pledged to support their nominated candidates. How it had been achieved was revealed by chance. When arrangements were made on the electoral college it was decided that votes should be recorded for publication. People should be able to see how individuals and bodies had voted. It had been suggested that this practice should be extended to NEC voting but this was not done. An objection during the 1982 NEC voting, however, resulted in the lists being studied. Whereupon it was found that Sid Weighell, the moderate leader of the railwaymen, who had already got into trouble with his executive for an attack on Benn, had cast his union's vote for the electricians' nominee Tom Breakell, not for Clarke as required under the terms of the triple alliance. Weighell argued that he had written to Scargill, by then president of the mineworkers, about the arrangements for supporting each other's candidates — the mineworkers had, as required, cast their votes for the moderate railwayman Russell Tuck — but had not had a satisfactory answer.

His good faith still being in doubt in some eyes, after that explanation, Weighell announced he would resign — confident, his friends told journalists, that his Executive, conscious of his irreplaceable value, would get him to retract. His Executive did not and he found himself pensioned off, with what some of his members doubtless felt was an eminently satisfactory pension by railway standards.

The furore over that did not leave the remaining Bennites on the NEC confident that the victors would exert themselves unduly in papering over the divisions by allowing them to retain some little share of their former positions and influence. Foot stood aside when a proposal by Jim Mortimer, the new party secretary, for the Left to continue to hold some influence was rejected. Benn and Hart were thrown off the Labour Party-TUC Liaison Committee, and the Home Policy and Organization committees reshaped to remove Benn and Heffer from the chairs. Benn was replaced by John Golding and Heffer by Russell Tuck, for whom Scargill had voted under the terms of the alliance with the railwaymen.

Benn was reported to have taken his punishment like a man as the whole headquarters structure was reshaped. Heffer protested such extreme measures would harm the party. Kinnock, now a close associate of Foot, agreed and offered to stand down in favour of one Bennite, but this was refused him.

Perhaps other MPs, not so closely involved, also thought it was too much. When Benn stood for the Shadow Cabinet election later he received more votes than expected and missed election by just one place, finishing ahead of Golding.

The 1982 conference also prepared the ground for a mass purge of the Left in the constituencies where the Left itself had been hard at work purging sitting MPs not to their liking, refusing to reselect them as candidates for the next election. In turn their opponents on the NEC had been trying hard to have the selection of Militants over-ruled but were finding the rule-book troublesome. An adverse report on one Militant, prepared by a group headed by Golding, was thrown out when Golding was found to have been unwise enough, or unfortunate enough, to have himself reported making prejudicial comments in advance. He wanted to be prosecutor, jury, judge and also executioner, complained Heffer.

By roughly three to one the conference decided on action, despite pleas to remember the harm done by previous purges. A right-wing call for firm action against alien groups was accepted, a left-wing motion opposing all witchhunts and expulsions was defeated and a motion for a register of approved organizations was approved. Such a register would lead to some expulsions, the NEC reported. Compared with some proposals it was a call for hamstringing rather than throat-slitting but soon the hamstringers found they might be hamstrung themselves. Golding, who wanted the knife applied nearer the throat by taking a retrospective view to see as unlawful what was hitherto lawful found himself being regarded as a shade too reminiscent of Senator McCarthy, even by some wanting firm action. Then it was discovered that the law of the land might make it more difficult than had been thought to proceed against some Militants, who wanted court rulings on the admissibility of evidence. Foot thought it unreasonable that those with so poor an opinion of capitalist laws should appeal to capitalist courts when it suited them.

Benn was more intent on quoting history to show the futility, in his view, of the whole exercise:

We expelled Stafford Cripps and he came back. We expelled Nye Bevan and he came back . . . What this is really about is an attempt to reverse some very important policies in the party by getting at the people who support them. It won't work because it has never worked before. I would say to local parties 'don't worry, we've been through it all before. It's never worked before and it won't work this time.'

For he had had the satisfaction of seeing his position as

301

the originator of policy confirmed rather than reduced, even with the new NEC in league with the Shadow Cabinet. Even if his ideas for the wholesale nationalization of banks and financial institutions were not accepted the party was committed to strong action on the financial front, supporting his view that it would be impossible to put Labour's industrial strategy into operation without it.

When that industrial strategy was outlined, by Peter Shore, once a Benn associate who had described Benn as the outstanding politician of his generation, but by then closer to Healey, it proved to be much nearer to the theory of the former than to the practice of the latter. Then the party's security services group, with Foot and Shadow Home Secretary Roy Hattersley among its members, produced proposals on control of those services which read as if straight from the Home Policy Committee under Benn.

Perhaps more importantly the 1982 conference voted for unilateral nuclear disarmament even more definitely than before, assuring it a firm commitment in the manifesto. In the fight for that policy may lie Labour's best chance of achieving the other policies its strangely diversified members have in common.

The Militant Tendency episode, like the later history of Benn's fight to make policy decisions binding on the party shows up the party's weakening dichotomy, the clash between principle and expediency. It is a party committed to socialist change of a still capitalist system yet a party committed to the democratic procedures within that system.

As a socialist party, particularly as by far the biggest socialist party in the country, the only one with any prospect of power unless circumstances change radically, it is bound to attract thorough-going socialists. They are bound to press for a commitment to socialism in a way suited to what the Communists call a 'vanguard party', one active in the Marxist class struggle, preparing the way

302

for a time when it can lead older mass parties in a revolutionary situation.

As a party committed to parliamentary democracy and rejecting revolution it must make its appeal to the electorate. The most moderate of its leaders would deplore that most of that electorate cannot be bothered to vote at union meetings, would not dream of attending and voting at a political party meeting. They are very conscious, though, that they will turn up at the booths in a general election.

Benn has accused the Establishment, led by *The Times*, of frightening people off essentially popular Labour policies. Whether the 'capitalist Press' presents the issues impartially, whether the electorate is unduly influenced by it if it does not, are matters which, if not insignificant, are not of over-riding effect on the result.

There is an in-built resistance in most people, if not to change then to too much change. The question for the professional politician with his eye on a seat in Parliament is what is too much. A line has to be drawn beyond which he feels it is inadvisable to go, whatever he personally believes should be the eventual goal. Being an MP, even a hard-working MP, has its attractions. The hard-working local party worker will say he does not care tuppence for the fact that an MP finds attractions or even ambitions in Parliament. So the line is drawn in different positions.

The only parties which can afford to have clear-cut policies are revolutionary parties, even then, perhaps, only at times when revolutions are unlikely. Other parties dependent on votes must blur those policies around that doubtfully acceptable line. Some parties, cynics might say, seem far more blur than line.

Of course there come times when lines can be drawn harder and further out from the 'consensus', that favourite word of middle-road politicians. People are not always unready for change. There have been revolutions, there have even been profound changes by the ballot box. The

Labour victory in 1945 might be quoted as an example, though some historians see it also as a continuation of wartime attitudes and wartime economics — interestingly Benn has likened the actions of a future Labour Government with those of the Churchill wartime coalition.

It is quite possible the elimination of nuclear arms might prove the issue in the 1980's on which people are prepared to take strong electoral action. They might move beyond demonstrations to the point of overturning existing conformist governments and, in so doing, accept profound social changes, as they might have done if Labour had taken a strong line on Europe. Benn, of course, is more identified with the anti-nuclear movement than any other leading politician, not even old pictures of Foot on Aldermaston marches can alter that.

Also, of course, a revolutionary situation can arise within a party as well as within a society. If a moderate Labour party suffered a resounding defeat in an election it would most likely change course to the left, particularly if the reselection process had replaced older, passive MPs by younger, more fervent ones. It would be following the example of the Greater London Council Labour Party which, after a similar reselection, though after a victory, changed its leader and appointed Ken Livingstone, a Benn protégé similarly scorned but equally able in presenting his views with apparent sweet reasonableness.

So it would probably be unwise to say that the anti-Benn successes within the Labour Party in 1982 saw the end of his chances of becoming leader or even prime minister. Another decade as difficult as the seventies for Britain and Labour might turn the party his way and, perhaps, not just the party.

Final Word

'But there is more latitude in eccentrics.
They are always honest and have their own quality of
   madness.
In the final assessment I think they will be the saints.'
                    (Margaret Rutherford on her Cousin Tony)

Index

306

86; enters Parliament 95;
maiden speech 98; censures
Speaker 98–100; ambition
satisfied 98; becomes 'Tony'
134; on changing views on
industry 177, 186 on Europe
201; and open government 171,
240, 265; as a Bogeyman 224,
225; as Dracula 233, 234; on
policy-making through public
discussion 240, 241; on role of
North Sea oil 245, 246, 273,
274; attempts to reform
electricity industry 246–9; and
nuclear energy 255–8; and
nuclear disarmament 261–2,
304; and Home Policy
Committee 226, 262–3, 270,
274, 300; on prime ministerial
patronage 267–70; and
abolition of House of Lords
270, 285, 297–8; on election of
Cabinet 270; deputy-leader
election (1981) 290–2
Benn, Mrs Tony (Caroline De
Camp) 79, 83, 85–95, 290
Benn, Rev. William 1
Benn, William Rutherford 10–15,
70–2; tragedy at Matlock
11–14; theatrical talent 15;
marriage 69; in India 70; death
72
Benn, William Wedgwood
(Viscount Stansgate) 23, 58–64,
66, 105, 107–10, 290; enters
Parliament 59; joins Labour
Party 62, 290; in World War I
60–1; in World War II 63;
becomes a viscount 63, 105;
fights Tony's case in Lords
108–10
Benn, Mrs William Wedgwood
(Viscountess Stansgate) 65–7,
129
Bermondsey 54

Bevan, Andy 278
Bevan Aneurin 108, 278, 292,
301
Bevins, Reginald 142
Black, Sir William 155
Blake, William 58
Blaker, Peter 264
Bland, Hubert 27
Blind Con's Doss'us 36–8
Boeing SST 165, 168
Bottomley, Horatio 54
Boyd, Sir John 286, 287
Boyle, Edward 84, 85
Boyne, H. B. (Sir Harry) 229,
230, 232
Bradlaugh, Charles 111
Brandt, Willi 206, 210
Breakell, Tom 299
Bristol 39, 95, 115
British Aerospace 164
British Airways 173, 174
British Empire 202
British Gas Corporation 241,
254, 259
British Insurance Association 228
British Leyland 151–62, 163, 175
British Motor Corporation
(BMC) 154–5
British National Oil Corporation
243, 244
British Nuclear Fuels 255
British Petroleum (BP) 239
Broadmoor 68, 69, 70, 71
Brown, George (Lord) 112, 117,
165, 206, 226
Bruce of Donnington, Lord 293
BSA 179, 183, 198
Buckton, Ray 236, 237
Burke, Edmund 95, 117
Burns, John 34, 47, 49, 54
Butler, R. A. (Lord) 112, 116,
126

Cabinet Maker, The 19, 20, 21,
23, 24, 25

307

European Technological Community 207
Evans, Edith 74
Export Credit Guarantee Board 191, 193
Ezra, Sir Derek 240, 242

Falkland Islands 168, 297
Farnsworth, Gordon 167
Fast Neutron (Breeder) Reactor 256, 257
Filton 164, 171, 176
Fitzroy, Charles (Baron Southampton) 131
Fletcher, Ray 234
Foot, Dingle 112
Foot, Michael 112, 213, 215, 225, 278, 284, 285, 287, 290, 293, 295, 296, 297, 298
Ford Motor Company 153, 155
Formby, George 179
Fould, Achille 172
fusion 258

Gaitskell, Hugh 83, 101, 112, 281
GEC 151, 156, 196, 215
General and Municipal Workers Union (GMWU) 284, 289, 294
Gielgud, John (Sir) 75
GIRO 140–58
Gladstone, William 10
Glynn, Sir Ralph 98
Golding, John 295, 300, 301
Gollancz, Victor 26, 27
Gorman, Lord 119, 125
Gravel Lane Meeting House 10, 15
Griffiths, Lucy 71
Grigg, John 129
Grimond, Jo 114, 127, 131
Guthrie, Tyrone 74, 75

Hailsham, Lord (Quintin Hogg) 61, 108, 116, 127, 128, 129, 132
Hailwood, Mike 180

Haines, Joe 224, 265
Halifax, Lord 61, 80
Hardware Trade Journal 25–6
Harriman, Sir George 154, 155, 157, 158
Harris, Kenneth 84, 85
Hart, Judith 273, 297, 300
Hastings, Lord 110
Hattersley, Roy 280, 302
Hawkins, Sir Arthur 240, 242, 247
Hayward, Ron 267, 282, 285, 290
Healey, Denis 218, 225, 226, 232, 245, 266, 273, 282, 287, 288, 290, 291, 292, 294, 295, 302
Heath, Edward 91, 167, 170, 183, 184, 198, 201, 205, 209, 211, 212, 214, 217, 220
Heffer, Eric 187, 264, 267, 280, 283, 294, 300
Henry VII 104
Henry VIII 125
Heseltine, Michael 170, 171, 193, 194
Hesketh, Lord 199
Hill, Sir John 255
Hinchingbrooke, Viscount 131
Hitler, Adolf 80
Home, Lord (Sir Alec Douglas Home) 130, 131, 133
Home Policy Committee 225, 226, 263, 264, 265, 270, 272, 274, 295, 298, 300
Honda motorcycle 181, 182
Hoyle, Douglas 299
Huckfield, Leslie 185, 193, 299

Industrial Development Advisory Board 190
Industrial Policy Committee 273
Industrial Reorganisation Corporation 156, 157, 159, 188
Industry Act (1972) 184, 187
Industry Act (1975) 227

310

Sillar, James 234
Simmons, Dawn 69, 75
Simon, Prof. Brian 91
Snow, C. P. (Lord) 138, 149
Social Democratic Party 289, 290, 295
Squibb, C. D. 133
St Clair, Malcolm 115, 119, 126, 129
St George's-in-the-East 50, 53, 56, 59
Stalin, Joseph 97, 245
Steam Generating Heavy Water reactor (SGHW) 256–7
Steel, David 235, 236, 248
Stevas, Norman St John 272
Stokes, Lord 152, 155, 156, 157, 158, 159, 162, 163, 188, 195
Stonehouse, John 166
Surtees, John 180
Sweden 137

Taverne, Dick 112–3
Thatcher, Margaret 91, 147, 197, 198, 235, 275, 282, 297
Times, The 290, 303
Tommaso, Alessandro de 198
Trades Union Congress (TUC) 282, 291
tramways 34, 41–7
Transport and General Workers Union (TGWU) 216, 236, 261, 281, 284, 291
Trenchard, Lord 197
Tribune 83, 96, 292–3
Tribune group 292
Triumph motorcycle 179, 183, 184, 195, 196
Trotskyists 278
Truck Acts 140–1, 149
TT races 179–82
TU 144 168, 169, 170
Tuck, Russell 299, 300
Turner, Edward 183
Tyler, George 242

UK Atomic Energy Authority 255
unilateral nuclear disarmament 261, 286, 291, 294, 302
United Nations (UN) 203
Unwin, Harry 187
Upper Clyde shipyards 211
USDAW 289

Varley, Eric 192, 193, 194, 215, 237, 243, 294
Volpes, John 168

wage snatches 140–1, 148
Wages, Payment of, Act 142
Walker, Peter 231–2, 235
Watkinson, Lord 233
Webb, Sidney and Beatrice 34, 69, 96
Weighell, Sid 299–300
Wells, H. G. 27
Westminster School 79, 87, 88
Whitelaw, William 218
Williams, Shirley 225, 226, 278, 280, 285, 286, 289, 296
Wilson, Andrew 169
Wilson, Harold (Sir) 137, 138, 143, 144, 145, 149, 157, 163, 164, 165, 166, 172, 183, 189, 192, 198, 205, 206, 207, 208, 209, 213, 214, 215, 216, 220, 224, 226, 227, 229, 230, 231, 232, 233, 234, 235, 237, 239, 243, 263, 265, 268, 269, 270, 281
Windscale 255
Winterton, Lord 61
Wolmer, Viscount 113, 122
Woolley, Richard 30
Workers Control, Institute of 186

Yamaha motorcycle 182, 198
Yerkes, Charles Tyson 39–41